Sir Philip Sidney's
An Apology for Poetry
and
Astrophil and Stella

Forthcoming Renaissance titles from College Publishing

Four Shrew Plays
edited by Margaret Maurer and Susan Cerasano
of Colgate University

Sir Philip Sidney's
An Apology for Poetry
and
Astrophil and Stella:
Texts and Contexts

Edited by
Peter C. Herman
San Diego State University

College Publishing
Glen Allen, Virginia

College Publishing books
are printed on acid-free paper

ISBN: 0-9679121-1-3
Library of Congress Card Number: 2001086029

College Publishing
12309 Lynwood Drive, Glen Allen, VA 23059
T (804) 364-8410 • F (804) 364-8408
collegepub@mindspring.com

Acknowledgments

I have benefited tremendously from the patience and generosity of many people. David Lupher helped locate many classical references that I would not have found otherwise. Patrick Cheney read the manuscript at an early stage and his counsel improved everything. Roger Kuin kindly read the introduction and provided invaluable assistance. Members of the Renaissance discussion list, FICINO, regularly contributed helpful bits of information whenever I asked. Paul Voss, Cliff Davis, and Sandra Sherman were always there when I needed them. Stephen Mosberg has been the perfect editor.

My greatest debt, however, is to Anne Lake Prescott, the *sine qua non* of this volume. If this edition has any merit, I gladly pass all praise on to her. The blame is all mine.

Sir Philip Sidney's
An Apology for Poetry
and
Astrophil and Stella:
Texts and Contexts

Introduction

Sidney's Life

It would have surprised and probably disappointed Sir Philip Sidney to learn that his reputation today rests mainly on his literary works. Born to a politically prominent family on November 30, 1554, Sidney was brought up to serve the state, a goal he fully embraced. But Sidney's life—indeed, the life of the Sidney family—is a tale of great expectations and even greater disappointments.

Sidney's father, Sir Henry Sidney (1529-1586) was a gentleman of the privy chamber of Edward VI and received his knighthood in 1550. Although not a member of the aristocracy, Henry was sufficiently promising that he could marry a member of one of the greatest families in the realm, Mary, one of John Dudley, Duke of Northumberland's daughters (d. 1586). Even though Henry participated in helping Lady Jane Grey ascend to the throne (she was deposed and executed ten days later), he rapidly changed his loyalties to the Catholic Mary I, thus retaining his place at court. Under Elizabeth, Henry served twice as the Lord Deputy of Ireland (1565-1571, 1575-1578). Yet despite this strong record, he was never adequately remunerated. Consequently, even though Elizabeth did offer him a barony—the lowest level of peerage—Henry could not accept it because he could not afford the honor (something Elizabeth likely knew).[1] Mary, Sir Philip's mother, also suffered from Elizabeth's ingratitude. In 1562, she helped nurse the queen through an attack of smallpox, and although Elizabeth survived the disease unscathed, Mary Sidney was so deeply scarred that she would not thereafter appear at court without a mask. To make matters worse, Elizabeth

---

[1] Sir Henry complained to Walsingham that "I find there is no hope of relief of her Majesty for my decayed estate in her Highness's service" (March 1st, 1583, quoted in Malcolm W. Wallace, *The Life of Sir Philip Sidney*, 292).

apparently did not take great care for her servant's physical comfort; numerous letters survive in which she asked the Queen for better and warmer accommodations. In sum, despite his family's service to Elizabeth, and despite his mother's Dudley forebears, of which both Henry and his son were inordinately proud,[2] the Sidneys' experience was not one of loyalty justly and amply rewarded. Indeed, it is clear that Elizabeth never entirely trusted Sir Henry and, though happy to take what he offered and while both retained access to the court (many would-be courtiers did not), nonetheless kept both him and his wife at a distance. Unfortunately, this pattern would repeat itself in their son's career.

Like other male children born to a politically prominent station, Philip Sidney was groomed for state service from the start. When he entered grammar school in 1564, the academy at Shrewsbury offered a solid humanist education, which meant that Sidney learned how to read and write by studying in the original Latin or Greek such authors as Cicero, Virgil, Sallust, Cato, and Xenophon (all of whom would figure prominently in the *Apology*). Of course, he also studied the Bible. The point, however, of this curriculum, or as Sidney would write in the *Apology*, the "ending end of all earthly learning," was not knowledge for its own sake but "virtuous action," which meant serving the commonwealth as a statesman or public servant. Fulke Greville, Sidney's exact contemporary (they entered the Shrewsbury school together), a courtier under both Elizabeth and James and later Sidney's biographer, emphasized the practical nature of Sidney's schooling: "his end was not writing, even while he wrote; nor his knowledge molded for tables, or schools; but both his wit, and understanding bent upon his heart, to

---

[2] In the first letter Sir Henry wrote to Philip while he was at the Shrewsbury school, Henry enjoined his son to remember "the noble blood you are descended from by your mother's side" (quoted in Katherine Duncan-Jones, *Sir Philip Sidney: Courtier Poet*, 5). Sidney evidently took his father's advice very much to heart. In 1585, in his *Defense of the Earl of Leicester*, Sidney proclaimed, "I am a Dudley in blood, that Duke's daughter's son, and do acknowledge, though in truth I may justly affirm that I am by my father's

make himself and others, not in words or opinion, but in life, and action, good and great."[3]

To this end, at age 13, Sidney entered Oxford University in 1567-1568, where he stayed for three years and did not earn a degree. He did not have to, and it is important that the year before he went up to Oxford, he enrolled in Gray's Inn. Nominally, the Inns of Court were, in today's terms, law schools, but at the time they probably more closely resembled finishing schools for aristocrats and future courtiers as well as providing training for future lawyers.

In 1568, Sir Henry tried to arrange a marriage for his son with Anne Cecil, the daughter of William Cecil, later Lord Burleigh and one of Elizabeth's closest advisors. Unfortunately, the fate of this arrangement in some ways established the pattern for Sidney's political life. The problem was that despite Henry's continuing good service to Elizabeth, and despite Philip's promise, in terms of both money and class, Anne brought a great deal more to the table than did the Sidneys, and the fact that Sir Henry had to refuse Elizabeth's offer of a barony because she did not also provide means of supporting the title did not help Philip's case. Henry went so far as signing a marriage contract with Cecil, but by 1571 the project had clearly lapsed for a variety of reasons, including lack of interest on both Anne's and Philip's part. Anne Cecil found herself betrothed to Edward de Vere, the seventeenth Earl of Oxford, a wild, possibly psychopathic aristocrat who murdered a servant and, as we will see, would continue to be Sidney's rival. According to another of Anne's suitors, the announcement of the marriage "hath caused weeping, wailing and sorrowful cheer of those that hoped to have

---

side of ancient and always well esteemed and well matched gentry, yet I do acknowledge, I say, that my chiefest honor is to be a Dudley, and truly am glad to have cause to set forth the nobility of that blood whereof I am descended . . . (*Miscellaneous Prose*, 134).

[3] Sir Fulke Greville, *A Dedication to Sir Philip Sidney*, in *The Prose Works of Fulke Greville, Lord Brooke*, 12. See also F. J. Levy, "Philip Sidney Reconsidered," *Sidney in Retrospect: Selections from "English Literary Renaissance"*, 4-5.

had that golden day," and apparently Anne herself was none too happy about her marital fate.[4] Nonetheless, in Cecil's eyes, the Earl's wealth and rank outweighed Sidney's promise and meager purse. Nor was this to be the last time that Sidney would endure the frustration and disappointment of a great opportunity gone sour.

To complete his education, Sidney set out in 1572 for what would later be called the Grand Tour of the continent. His passport stated that he had permission to travel overseas for two years for the purpose of "his attaining to the knowledge of foreign languages,"[5] but the reasons went beyond improving his linguistic skills. The Grand Tour gave Sidney, a future courtier, the opportunity to observe the different political arrangements throughout Europe and to make contacts that would be useful in his later diplomatic life. One also suspects that his relatives give Sidney an opportunity to mature somewhat. In a letter to Sir Francis Walsingham, Sidney's uncle Robert Dudley, Earl of Leicester, described his nephew as "young and raw" and asked Sir Francis—then the English ambassador in Paris— to look after him, because Leicester worried that Sidney "no doubt shall find those countries and the demeanors of the people somewhat strange unto him."[6] Sidney's elders need not have worried, for he took full advantage of Europe's offerings, and he blossomed politically, socially, and intellectually. Over the next three years (one more than Elizabeth originally granted him), Sidney visited an extraordinarily wide area of Europe, including such cities as Strasbourg, Paris, Cracow, Heidelburg, Frankfurt, Vienna, Padua, Genoa, and Florence, and he began lifelong friendships

---

[4] Duncan-Jones, *Sir Philip Sidney*, 52-53.

[5] *Ibid*, 55.

[6] *Ibid*, 56.

[7] Sidney translated part of Mornay's *De la vérité de la religion chrétienne* (*A Work Concerning the Trueness of the Christian Religion*), but rather than leaving the work partly done, he asked the Elizabethan translator, Arthur Golding, to complete the task. Mornay is also credited with writing the anonymous *Vindiciae Contra Tyrannos*, a highly influential

with such important figures as Philippe Duplessis-Mornay, Michel de l'Hôpital, and Hubert Languet.[7]

At the beginning of his tour, however, Sidney witnessed a horrific event that cannot have failed to make an indelible impression upon him. His first destination after leaving England was Paris, where it seemed that the violent conflict between Protestants and Catholics was on the point of being resolved. After three months of negotiation, an Anglo-French committee produced the Treaty of Blois, which mandated that the French not aid Catholic Spain in any attack on England, and Sidney was attached to an embassy to witness the treaty's ratification. Furthermore, Sidney and his party arrived in time for the celebrations over the marriage of Catherine de Medici's daughter, Marguerite de Valois, to the Protestant Henri de Bourbon, now King, as his mother died on June 9, 1572. This marriage, many hoped, would bring the French Wars of Religion to a close (just as at the end of the fifteenth century in England the Tudor Henry VII's marriage to the Yorkist Elizabeth concluded the decades of dynastic strife known as the War of the Roses). August 9 brought the first of Sidney's diplomatic successes, as the French king created him a "gentleman of the bedchamber" and a baron. Sidney may have regretted this favor later in life (in Sonnet 41 of *Astrophil and Stella* he calls France the "sweet enemy"), and Elizabeth certainly did not appreciate the gesture, but it is likely that at the time these honors gave Sidney tremendous satisfaction. Everything looked extremely hopeful. Then, on August 22, someone attempted to assassinate Admiral de Coligny, the most eminent Protestant in Paris, and on August 24, St. Bartholomew's Day,

---

tract arguing the legitimacy of actively resisting tyranny. The work has also been attributed to Philip's friend and mentor, the Protestant humanist Hubert Languet. On l'Hôpital, see the *Apology*, p. 110, n. 217. Much of Sidney's correspondence with his continental friends is reproduced in James M. Osborn, *Young Philip Sidney 1572-1577*. The letters between Sidney and Languet are reproduced in *The Correspondence of Sir Philip Sidney and Hubert Languet*.

the massacre of Protestants began in earnest. Thousands were slaughtered, and it is said that the Seine ran red with blood. Among the murdered were several of Sidney's new friends, including the highly influential logician Peter Ramus. Although Sidney never overtly referred to the St. Bartholomew Massacre, Languet called it a "monstrous massacre of so many innocent men,"[8] and in all likelihood it deepened Sidney's adherence to militant Protestantism. In 1574, he referred to the latter as "our cause."[9]

The rest of Sidney's Grand Tour unfolded in a much happier fashion, in good part because of the admiration, friendship, and guidance of Hubert Languet, who introduced his protégé to many of Europe's leading Protestant thinkers and politicians as well as guided Sidney's intellectual development. The letters exchanged between the two clearly show that Sidney tended as much to his own intellectual pursuits as to understanding the political situation in Europe. In a letter dated December 19, 1573, for example, Sidney asks Languet to send him "Plutarch's works in French" and to tell him whether Languet has read six "interesting" Italian works on such topics as history, emblems, and examples of letters of great men. Sidney's comments to Languet collectively demonstrate Sidney's fluency in Italian and his taste for exemplary literature.[10] In another letter, Sidney declares that he is giving up (with Languet's approval) the study of astronomy, but "about geometry I hardly know what to determine." Although Sidney concedes that "it is of the greatest service in the art of war," he evidently believed he did not have the time or perhaps the skill to master it, preferring instead to continue perfecting his Greek. His aim, as he writes to Languet, is to "learn only so much as shall suffice for the perfect under-

---

[8] Languet to Sidney, April 1, 1574 (*Correspondence*, 43).
[9] Sidney to Languet, June 1574 (*Correspondence*, 75).
[10] *Correspondence*, 9.

standing of Aristotle. For though translations are made almost daily, still I suspect they do not declare the meaning of the author plainly or aptly enough; and besides, I am utterly ashamed to be following the stream, as Cicero says, and not go to the fountainhead."[11] Sidney also found time to have his portrait done by Paolo Veronese, a work now unfortunately lost.

Sidney returned to England in 1575, and although his greatest difficulties at court were still several years off, Sidney must have keenly felt the contrast between his success on the Continent and his family's political fortunes at home. Henry Sidney remained bitter at Elizabeth's refusal to grant him money or affordable honors for his Irish service, and Philip spent most of this year waiting on Elizabeth, participating in court festivities intended to display his talents to his monarch.

In 1577, however, Sidney's apprenticeship seemed finally to have paid off. Elizabeth decided to send Philip to condole the Emperor Rudolph on the death of his father, Maximilian I. But the real purpose of this mission was something much closer to Sidney's heart: to gauge the state of religious opinion and loyalties on the Continent along with exploring the possibility of forming a Protestant League to combat the incursions and imperial ambitions of Catholic Spain. Following his uncle, the Earl of Leicester, Sidney joined the Protestant activists at court urging a more hawkish foreign policy that would materially aid the cause of Continental Protestantism, and especially support William of Orange's revolt against Spain in the Netherlands.[12] Significantly, Leicester provided a letter of introduction to the Count Palatine, Prince John Casimir, a firm Calvinist and one of the prime movers behind the idea of a Protestant League. Sidney admired Casimir, writing to Languet that "all [the German princes] except the Palatine have made up their minds to

---

[11] February 4, 1574 (*Correspondence*, 29).
[12] See *Astrophil and Stella* 30.

neglect their people and ruin themselves,"[13] but unfortunately, as Sidney reported to Walsingham, the prospects of a Protestant League did not appear promising, especially because Rudolph and his court leaned toward Spain. Even so, Sidney continued his diplomacy, but it may have been at precisely this juncture that his political fortunes started to droop.

There is no doubt that Sidney's diplomatic mission was widely considered a great success. A letter to Sidney's father by Edward Waterhouse reported that "Mr. Sidney is returned safe into England, with great good acceptation of his service at Her Majesty's hands; allowed of by all the Lords [of the Privy Council] to have been handled with great judgement and discretion, and hath been honored abroad in all princes' courts with much extraordinary favor." Walsingham also reported to Sidney's father that "There hath not been any gentleman I am sure these many years that hath gone through so honorable a charge with as great commendations as he."[14] Doubtless Sir Henry glowed at his son's achievements. One person, however, remained unconvinced: Elizabeth. Perhaps the first sign that his monarch held him in less esteem than did her councilors was her witholding from Sidney a personal title, despite his family connections and his good service. True, Sidney did attain the office of the Royal Cupbearer, but this position was an inherited honor, not a recognition of merit. The sad fact, as Katherine Duncan-Jones puts it, is that "Elizabeth, while acknowledging Sidney's talent, never did quite trust him."[15] Consequently, Sidney remained without significant employment after his return, a condition that clearly grated on him. In a letter to Languet dated March 1, 1578, Sidney revealed his unhappiness with both his career and the court in terms that would later echo in the *Apology*:

---

[13] Sidney to Languet, May 7, 1574 (*Correspondence*, 59).
[14] Both are letters are quoted by Duncan-Jones, *Sir Philip Sidney*, 133.
[15] Duncan-Jones, *Sir Philip Sidney*, 135.

[M]y mind itself, if it was ever active in anything, is now beginning, by reason of my indolent ease, imperceptibly to lose its strength, and to relax without any reluctance. For to what purpose should our thoughts be directed to various kinds of knowledge, unless room be afforded for putting it into practice, so that public advantage may be the result, which in a corrupt age we cannot hope for?[16]

There are several possible reasons for Elizabeth's keeping Sidney at a distance. First, he may have exceeded the bounds of his mission by pressing too hard for the establishment of a Protestant League, and he may even have appeared to Elizabeth as a loose cannon. Languet, for example, reports that Sidney so wanted to talk with William of Orange, the leader of the Protestant resistance in the Netherlands, that he planned to do so as a private person. Fortunately, Sidney then received a letter from Elizabeth directing him to meet with William of Orange, and so, Languet writes, "I perceived that by this means without any risk to yourself, your wish might be satisfied." Nonetheless, Sidney's plans suggest that he was not above using his diplomatic station to pursue his own agenda rather than restricting himself to his commission. In the same letter, Languet also reveals that Sidney's reputation must have already been at risk: "I had warned you to be careful not to give anyone occasion of speaking ill of you . . . ."[17] Sidney's enthusiasm for a Protestant League, and his concomitant enthusiasm for sending English troops to fight Spain in the Netherlands, clashed with Elizabeth's distaste for war (which stemmed from a complex mixture of parsimony and policy).

Despite their fervent Protestantism, Sidney and his father were very friendly with a number of Catholics, and that too might have contributed to Elizabeth's distrust. Philip's relations

---

[16] *Correspondence*, 143. It should be remembered that the primacy of the public over the private sphere was a conventional sentiment in Sidney's time (in fact, it stretches back to Aristotle and Plato).
[17] Languet to Sidney, June 14, 1577 (*Correspondence*, 106, 107).

with Catholics were so warm that Languet felt he had to warn Sidney that his friends had "begun to suspect you on the score of religion, because at Venice you were so intimate with those who profess a different creed from your own." [18] Languet also wrote to reassure Walsingham of Sidney's reliability. In particular, Sidney was friendly with Edmund Campion, who had taught rhetoric at Oxford when Sidney attended. Campion had left England, eventually to become a Jesuit, and had taken up residence in Prague, where Sidney met him again. After he returned to England in 1580, he was executed in the most brutal fashion for spying and plotting to overthrow the Queen (it is unlikely that he was guilty of either charge). For obvious reasons, Sidney did not include his conversations with Campion in his official correspondence, but there are several accounts (granted, all later, and all by Catholics) attesting to how Sidney promised Campion that he would never "hurt or injure any Catholic" and how Sidney even, amazingly, considered converting![19]

Events would soon further alienate Sidney from his queen, and the immediate cause would be Elizabeth's relationship with the Duke of Alençon, François-Hercule, brother and heir to the French king, Henry III, and a Catholic. The Queen had for several years been conducting a low-level, if highly political, flirtation with the Duke, whom she called her "frog" and others called "Monsieur," for some years, but in 1579 the intensity increased significantly, and the militant Protestants at court, led by Leicester and Walsingham, were seriously alarmed. Doubtless, there were political advantages to the match (which, given Elizabeth's age, was unlikely to produce children), but the antimarriage faction worried deeply over the effect of this alliance on the Protestant cause in England—not to mention the horrific prospect of England having a French king. There was

[18] Languet to Sidney, March 10, 1575 (*Correspondence*, 93).
[19] See Duncan-Jones, *Sir Philip Sidney*, 135, and Roger Howell, *Sir Philip Sidney: The Shepherd Knight*, 38.

also considerable popular opposition, and in response to the Duke's visit to England in August 1579, John Stubbs penned an attack called *The Discovery of a Gaping Gulf, whereinto England is like to be Swallowed by Another French Marriage*. Elizabeth on principle did not take kindly to being told how to conduct herself, she certainly did not like being advised on her proposed marriages, and she especially did not like public opposition to her policies, as Stubbs discovered. According to the contemporary historian William Camden, Elizabeth was "much incensed at [this book's] smart and stinging style," and Camden's account is worth quoting at length because of its importance to Sidney's career and its depiction of the extent and limits of popular resistance to Elizabeth:

> From this time forward she [Elizabeth] began to be a little more incensed against the Puritans, or innovators, from whom she easily believed these kinds of things proceeded. And indeed within a few days after, John Stubbs, of Lincoln's Inn, a fervent hot-headed professor of religion . . ., [and] the author of this book, William Page, who dispersed the copies, and [Hugh] Singleton, the printer, were apprehended. Against whom sentence was given that their right hands should be cut off, according to an act of [King] Philip [of Spain] and [his wife] Mary [Tudor, or Mary I], *Against the Authors and Publishers of Seditious Writings*.[20] Though some lawyers muttered that the sentence was erroneous and void by reason of the false noting of the time wherein the law was made, and that the act was only temporary, and died with Queen Mary .
> . . . Hereupon Stubbs and Page had their right hands cut off with a cleaver, driven through the wrist by the force of a mallet, upon a scaffold in the marketplace in Westminster. The printer was pardoned. I remember (being there present) that

---

[20] Camden's readers would have immediately recognized the irony of this act, promulgated by two Catholic monarchs, being used to punish a radical Protestant screed against Elizabeth marrying a Catholic.

when Stubbs, after his right hand was cut off, put off his hat with his left, and said with a loud voice, "God save the queen," the multitude standing about was deeply silent, either out of an horror at this new and unwonted kind of punishment, or else out of commiseration towards the man, as being of an honest and unblamable repute, or else out of hatred of the marriage, which most men presaged would be the overthrow of religion.[21]

Sidney also would write against the French marriage. In August, Leicester convened a meeting of the antimarriage faction in which both Sidneys participated,[22] and the result was Philip's *Letter to Queen Elizabeth touching her marriage to Monsieur.*

Scholars remain divided as to whether Sidney's rustication was voluntary or enforced. The evidence for Sidney's withdrawing from the court on his own is as follows: First, Fulke Greville asserted in his biographical sketch of Sidney that after the *Letter* he "kept his access to her Majesty as before,"[23] and as we have seen, Sidney was also starting to have his doubts about the probity of the court. Furthermore, in another letter, sent a year before prospects for the Alençon match heated up, Languet writes that he is "especially sorry you say that you are weary of the life to which I have no doubt God has called you, and desire to fly from the light of your court and betake yourself to the privacy of secluded places to escape the tempest of affairs by which statesmen are generally harassed"[24] Clearly, Sidney was thinking seriously about retirement long before he wrote the *Letter.*

---

[21] William Camden, *The History of the Most Renowned and Victorious Princess, Elizabeth*, 270, sig. Nn3v. I have modernized the spelling and the punctuation.

[22] The Spanish ambassador, Bernardino de Mendoza—who, it must be stressed, is far from a reliable witness—reported, "A meeting was held on the same night at the Earl of Pembroke's house, there being present Lord Sidney [sic] and other friends and relatives. They no doubt discussed the matter, and some of them afterwards remarked that Parliament would have something to say as to whether the Queen married or not. The people in general seem to threaten revolution about it" (quoted in Wallace, *The Life of Sir Philip Sidney*, 213).

On the other hand, although Sidney—unlike the unfortunately named John Stubbs—avoided public mutilation, Elizabeth did not take kindly to unsolicited criticism. One also must remember that Greville's purpose was not biographical accuracy but constructing Sidney as a political and moral ideal. Generally speaking, in this genre, exemplarity trumped factual accuracy, and stating that Sidney had gotten himself thrown out of court (if that is indeed what happened) hardly fits with this purpose.[25] Finally, whatever Sidney may have written to Languet in 1578, his dedication to a life of action and service makes an extended voluntary retreat from the court unlikely, though not impossible.

After he left, Sidney told Languet that he had no choice but to write the *Letter*, which conviction Languet uses to excuse Sidney for producing a document that clearly did his career no good:

> I suspected that you had been urged to write by persons who either did not know into what peril they were thrusting you, or did not care for your danger, provided they effected their own object. Since, however, you were ordered to write as you did by those whom you were bound to obey, no fair-judging man can blame you for putting forward freely what you thought good for your country, nor even exaggerating some circumstances in order to convince them of what you judged expedient.[26]

Was Sidney set up to take the fall? Did Leicester and the other grandees protect their position by using Sidney, whose career was already shaky,[27] as their mouthpiece, thereby making

---

[23] Greville, *A Dedication to Sir Philip Sidney*, 38.

[24] October 22, 1578 (*Correspondence*, 155).

[25] In another example, Sidney's first biographer and the family physician, Thomas Moffett, altered the dates when Sidney wrote verse. See below, pp.47-48.

[26] *Correspondence*, 187.

[27] Languet also noted that when he visited England in 1578-1579, he "found a sort of cloud over [Sidney's] fortunes" (September 24, 1580 [*Correspondence*, 185]).

the weakest among them the object of Elizabeth's anger? Or did Sidney, perhaps to salvage his reputation with his mentor, make others responsible for his lack of political tact?

A few days before the Leicester meeting that produced the *Letter*, an incident occurred that further diminished Sidney's already low standing at court. As Greville reports, while Sidney was[28]

> one day at tennis, a peer of this realm, born great, greater by alliance, and superlative in the prince's favor [the Earl of Oxford], came abruptly into the tennis-court, and speaking out of these three paramount authorities he forgot to entreat that which he could not legally command. When, by the encounter of a steady object, finding unrespectiveness in himself (though a great lord) not respected by this princely spirit, he grew to expostulate more roughly. The returns of which style coming still from an understanding heart that knew what was due to itself, and what it ought to others, seemed (through the mists of my lord's passion swollen with the wind of his faction then reigning) to provoke in yielding; whereby the less amazement or confusion of thoughts he stirred up in Sir Philip, the more shadows this great lord's own mind was possessed with, till at least with rage—which is ever ill-disciplined—he commands them to depart the court. To this Sir Philip temperately answers that if his lordship had been pleased to express his desire in milder characters, perchance he might have led out those that he should now find would not be driven out with any scourge of fury. This answer—like a bellows blowing up the sparks of excess already kindled—made my lord scornfully call Sir Philip by the name of puppy.

Matters continued to spiral out of control. Sidney repeated himself even louder; Oxford repeated his insult; Sidney responded that "all the world knows puppies are gotten by dogs and children by men"; Alençon's ambassadors, attracted by the tumult,

---

[28] Greville, *A Dedication to Sir Philip Sidney*, 38-39.
[29] Wallace, *The Life of Sir Philip Sidney*, 214.

observed everything; Sidney stormed out and the next day demanded satisfaction from Oxford. This man, described by an earlier biographer of Sidney as "unhampered by any principles except that of self-advancement,"[29] belonged to the pro-marriage faction and vastly out-distanced Sidney in terms of rank. Thus the Queen ultimately had to step in to prevent the duel, explaining to Sidney "the difference in degree between earls and gentlemen,"[30] which, given Sidney's pride in his Dudley heritage, must have particularly rankled. Nobody comes out very well from this incident, but Sidney had much more to lose than Oxford, and his behavior surely did not enhance his credibility or his career.

Whether Elizabeth finally had enough and ordered Sidney gone, or Sidney decided that he was fed up with the constant political frustration and personal humiliation, or some combination of the two we will never know, but whatever the cause, six months later Sidney embarked on a year-long retreat from the court. Although Sidney had started writing verse in 1578 (the probable date for his pastoral drama, *The Lady of May*), this period marks his full immersion in literary matters: he wrote the first complete version of his prose romance, the *Arcadia*, as well as the letters to his younger brother Robert and to Edward Denny, both of which are invaluable in assessing the complexity of Sidney's attitudes toward fiction. Sidney, along with his friends Edward Dyer and Fulke Greville, also began experimenting with trying to write English verse using Latin quantitative prosody (based on the length of syllables) rather than accentual stress, and Sidney included the results in the *Arcadia*.[31]

---

[30] Greville, *A Dedication to Sir Philip Sidney*, 40.

[31] In his published correspondence with Gabriel Harvey, Edmund Spenser claimed that Dyer and Sidney had formed an "Areopagus" in which they "prescribed certain laws and rules of quantities of English syllables for English verse," and that he was intimate with both of them (see the excerpt from the *Two . . . Letters*, p. 273). Scholars generally agree that Spenser made this claim to boost his own prestige, and that no such formal entity existed.

In 1581 Sidney returned to the court, and he signaled his submission by presenting Elizabeth with a New Year's gift of a jewel-encrusted riding whip.[32] But returning to the court did not mean returning to Elizabeth's favor, and Sidney's position suffered yet another blow when his uncle, the Earl of Leicester, and his uncle's second wife, Walter Devereux's widow Lettice, née Knollys, produced a son, Robert.[33] This event, however happy in the short run (the child would die in 1584), devastated Sidney's chances at advancement because he was no longer the heir to his uncle's estates and title. Given Elizabeth's habit of generally preferring inherited title over talent, Sidney's disinheritance meant that Sidney had lost not only the prospect of a fortune, but also a means of recovering his lost prestige. At a tilt held sometime thereafter, Sidney made his disappointment explicit. According to William Camden, "Sir Philip Sidney, who was a long time heir apparent to the Earl of Leicester, after the said Earl had a son born to him, used at the next tilt-day following ~~SPERAVI~~ [I have hoped] thus dashed through, to show his hope therein was dashed."[34]

The end of 1581 and the beginning of 1582 must have been a miserable time for Sidney. He lost the prospect of the Leicester estates, the Duke of Alençon returned to England to continue his "courtship" of Elizabeth, and Sidney's mentor, Hubert Languet, died at the end of September 1581. Making matters even worse, the Earl made Sidney's disinheritance official in January 1582, when he rewrote his will, and, adding political insult to financial injury, Sidney continued to remain without enough meaningful employment at court.

---

[32] See *AS* 41.

[33] Lettice and her first husband had two daughters, Dorothy and Penelope, and the latter would become the subject of Sidney's Petrarchan attentions in *Astrophil and Stella*. One has to wonder at Sidney's attitudes toward the woman whose progeny had such profound effects on his life.

[34] Quoted in Duncan-Jones, 194.

To be sure, Sidney was not completely shut out of either the court or politics. He secured a seat in the House of Commons in 1581, and Elizabeth included Sidney among the party escorting Alençon to Holland in 1582. Yet even when Elizabeth appeared to grant Sidney favor, the largesse came in ways seemingly designed to rankle. In 1581, she finally consented to his plea for a grant of three thousand pounds, but the money came from the property confiscated from English Catholics. While Sidney accepted the cash—he really had no choice—he remained deeply uneasy about its source: "Truly, I like not their persons and much less their religion, but I think my fortune very hard that my fortune must be built upon other men's punishments."[35] Sidney's uncle, the Earl of Warwick, tried for about two and a half years to have his nephew join him in that office, but Elizabeth would only allow Sidney a subordinate appointment (although he would be appointed joint master with Warwick in 1585). Finally, while Elizabeth granted Sidney a knighthood in 1583, this honor, like his appointment as Royal Cupbearer, was ceremonial, not due to any recognition of worth or service. Count Casimir was to be installed as Knight of the Garter, and he named Sidney as his proxy. To serve in this capacity, one must be at least a knight, and so Philip Sidney became Sir Philip Sidney. At the same time, rumors circulated that he would receive the captaincy of the Isle of Wight, but that opportunity, like many others, disappeared.[36] Essentially, Elizabeth used Sidney as a courtly ornament—helpful in entertaining foreign diplomats, handy with a phrase or a poem, impressive in a joust and charming in witty conversation, but unsuitable for a position of genuine influence.[37] It is likely that Sidney started writing both *An Apology*

---

[35] Quoted in Wallace, *The Life of Sir Philip Sidney*, 272.

[36] Wallace, 288-90.

[37] As Wallace puts it, "In the case of Sidney we have a man of high purpose, of fine gifts of nature, and of scholarly attainments, a man eminently fitted to do worthy work for his country and filled with a burning desire to be allowed to do such work, but continu-

for Poetry and *Astrophil and Stella* during this period of political frustration and relative idleness (more on this below), and he embarked on a revision of the *Arcadia*.[38] Probably the only bright moment during this period was Sidney's marriage in 1583 to Frances Walsingham, the daughter of Elizabeth's secretary of state.

In 1584, it seemed that the Queen's opinion of Sidney's diplomatic utility had finally begun to change.[39] On May 31, the Duke of Alençon, who improbably had taken up the Protestant cause in the Netherlands and had badly mismanaged his campaign against the Spaniards, died of typhoid fever in June, and Elizabeth decided to send Sidney on another mission of condolence. Like the first, this mission had a covert political purpose: to sound out French intentions on the Netherlands, information that became especially important in the wake of William of Orange's assassination. One can only speculate whether Sidney and his queen perceived the irony (or perceived the same irony, since the two may have had very different perspectives on this event) of his being sent to condole Henry III and his mother on the death of a man Sidney had demonized in his widely circulated *Letter to Queen Elizabeth Touching Her Marriage to Monsieur*, but Elizabeth certainly did not make her choice lightly, given the political stakes involved. Unfortunately, like so many other opportunities, this one fizzled as well, for the French king, Henry III, had given up mourning for his brother after only six weeks and had departed, along with his court, to Lyons to enjoy

---

ally checked and thwarted, and forced to recognize the sad fact that his energies were largely dissipated in the performance of tasks merely formal" (*The Life of Sir Philip Sidney*, 276).

[38] To distinguish between the two, scholars refer to the complete version as the *Old Arcadia* and the incomplete revision as the *New Arcadia*. In 1593, Sidney's sister, the Countess of Pembroke, sponsored a conflated version. Separate, modernized editions of all three are available (see "Suggestions for Further Reading" at the back of this volume).

[39] Sidney's personal fortunes also improved in 1584 with the sad death of his uncle's three-year-old son. This misfortune meant that Sidney was once again Leicester's heir.

some hunting. The Queen Mother suggested that Sidney's party should return after the King came back, but Elizabeth, according to the Calendar of State Papers, tartly "answered that she had sent [Sidney] to do the King honor, 'but since he did not like to have him go over, she was for her part well content to stay him, and that for sending of him hereafter, she saw no cause thereof.'"[40]

Henry's seeming indifference to his brother's death and to the English embassy may have stemmed from reasons other than frivolity or a lack of proper fraternal regard, for he had finally decided not to back the Protestant revolt against Spain in the Netherlands. The ascendancy of a pro-Catholic, pro-Spanish policy in France gave new impetus to the creation of a Continental Protestant League and to supporting the Protestant rebels with money and English troops. In addition, the prince of Parma, the Spanish king, Philip II's best general, reconquered many towns in the Netherlands, making Spanish domination of the entire country a very real possibility which seriously alarmed Elizabeth.[41] Elizabeth and the Dutch quickly entered into negotiations which eventually led to her committing English troops and money to the Dutch cause, but not before the negotiations bogged down.

At this point, Sidney, driven to utter distraction by the temporizing of both the English and the Dutch, decided that he would join Sir Francis Drake's fleet—without telling Elizabeth—and sail to the New World. As soon as the Queen found out about Sidney's secret plans (Drake informed her), she sent a messenger who carried, as Greville writes, "in the one hand grace, the other thunder."[42] In the latter, the Queen refused permission for the fleet to leave so long as Sidney remained with them,

[40] Quoted in Duncan-Jones, 258.
[41] Geoffrey Parker, *The Dutch Revolt* (London: Allen Lane, 1977), 208-13.
[42] Greville, *A Dedication to Sir Philip Sidney*, 45.

and in the former, she offered Sidney what he had been aching for all his life: a chance at military glory—in this case, "instant employment," as Greville records it, under Leicester, who was now Governor of Flushing. But the Dutch campaign did not go well because Elizabeth allowed the garrison barely enough money to scrape by (she finally signed the Treaty of Nonsuch, which officially committed her to the defense of the Netherlands, on August 20), and, to add yet more personal tragedy to political frustration, Sidney's father, Sir Henry, died in the winter of 1585, and his mother died in 1586.

On September 23, 1586, Sidney and his uncle participated in an ambush of Spanish troops near Zutphen.[43] It is not clear why exactly Sidney took off his leg armor. According to Greville, Sidney initially donned the appropriate amount of protective armor, "but, meeting the marshal of the camp lightly armed . . ., the unspotted emulation of his heart to venture without any inequality made him cast off his cuisses [leg armor]."[44] Another writer, Sir John Smythe, in his 1590 book on weaponry, asserted that Sidney followed a new Continental fashion of dispensing with heavy armor to increase mobility. Thomas Moffett provides a third possibility—that Sidney hurried to the defense of a colleague and so never had time to put on his armor.[45] Alas, none of these sources actually witnessed the event, and so the truth will never be known. Whatever his reasons, Sidney entered the fray with an unprotected leg and a bullet struck his thigh. Greville reports the following legend:

> [B]eing thirsty with excess of bleeding, he called for drink, which was presently brought him; but as he was putting the bottle to his mouth he saw a poor soldier carried along, who

---

[43] While many recent critics have characterized this event as an unimportant skirmish, Zutphen was the site of a small yet very real and not insignificant battle. The English force—300 foot and 250 horse—went up against 4,500 Spanish soldiers, one third of whom were cavalry (Roger Kuin, *Chamber Music*, 133 n.4).

[44] *Ibid*, 76.

[45] John Buxton, "The Mourning for Sidney," *Renaissance Studies* 3 (1989), 46.

had eaten his last at the same feast, ghastly casting up his eyes at the bottle; which Sir Philip perceiving, took it from his head before he drank, and delivered it to the poor man with these words: "Thy necessity is yet greater than mine."[46]

In all likelihood, this incident never happened (none of the earlier biographies mention it), and it is an example of the kind of mythologizing one often finds in Renaissance biography. What followed, however, is indisputable: the wound developed gangrene, and Sidney died on October 17.

When Sidney's father-in-law, Sir Francis Walsingham, heard the news, he wrote, "her Majesty hath lost a rare servant, and the realm a worthy member."[47] Walsingham then gave his late son-in-law funeral more lavish than anything before bestowed on a non-aristocrat (the cost would ruin him financially) and the degree of public mourning would not be rivaled until, according to Osborn, the death of Sir Winston Churchill.[48] Over 700 mourners crowded St. Paul's on February 16, 1587, and several books of elegies were published in Sidney's honor (including one that included a poem on Sidney by the future king of England, King James VI of Scotland).[49] Walsingham hired Thomas Lant to create a roll engraving of Sidney's funeral procession, an unprecedented honor for a person of Sidney's relatively low rank, and for months it was "accounted a sin" for gentlemen to wear festive or colorful clothing.[50] The grief was also ecumenical. Perhaps recalling Sidney's friendliness with those fol-

---

[46] *Ibid*, 77.

[47] Quoted in Osborn, *Young Philip Sidney*, 516.

[48] Ibid, 516.

[49] See Dominic Baker-Smith, "Great Expectations: Sidney's Death and the Poets," 83-103. On James's elegy for Sidney and its connections to James's scheming to be named Elizabeth's heir, see Peter C. Herman, "'Best of Poets, Best of Kings': King James VI/I and the Scene of Monarchical Verse," in *Royal Subjects: Essays on the Writings of James VI/I*, ed. Daniel Fischlin and Mark Fortier, (forthcoming, Wayne State University Press). The books of verse mourning Sidney are reproduced in *Elegies for Sir Philip Sidney (1587)*, ed. A. J. Colaianne and W. L. Godshalk.

lowing Rome, including Campion, the Catholic composer William Byrd wrote three laments for Sidney.

Yet Elizabeth remained unimpressed. In all likelihood, she contributed nothing to help with the funeral's costs, and no high-ranking members of the clergy or the government attended the proceedings.[51] Furthermore, it seems that the manner of Sidney's demise confirmed her opinion of him as unworthy of higher office. When she recalled Lord Mountjoy from Brittany—who had also gone to war without first asking permission—she is reported to have said: "Serve me so (quoth she) once more and I will lay you fast enough for running; you will never leave it till you are knocked over the head as that inconsiderate [rash, not considering the consequences] fellow Sidney was."[52]

Sidney's record of failure makes this outpouring of grief hard to fully explain. True, by the time of his death Sidney had earned a reputation for patronage (explaining perhaps the number of published elegies), but that does not account for the widespread nature of the grief. One possibility is that Sidney was one of only a handful of notable men from his generation to die in action, a fact which would automatically count tremendously in a culture that in many ways still revered chivalric glory. Another view, frequently reiterated, is that Sidney's death represented the death of an ideal. As John Buxton puts it, "[Sidney] seemed to his contemporaries to exhibit to perfection those qualities which went to make up the ideal courtier of Castiglione's description . . . ."[53] Perhaps, but Sidney's contemporaries would have also known that the Queen consistently denied him favor and rank, which hardly comports with Sidney's exemplifying the ideal

---

[50] J. F. R. Day, "Death Be Very Proud: Sidney, Subversion, and Elizabethan Heraldic Funerals," *Tudor Political Culture*, ed. Dale Hoak, 181.

[51] Sander Bos et al., "Sidney's Funeral Portrayed," 49-50.

[52] Buxton, "The Mourning for Sidney," 47.

[53] Ibid, 47.

courtier (unless one assumes that the ideal courtier is synonymous with the politically frustrated courtier).

Another explanation might be that Sidney's popularity stemmed from his dying a martyr to the cause of militant Protestantism, and he died fighting against the hated national enemy, Spain. The crowds at his funeral and the subsequent development of the Sidney legend thus registers a degree of implicit criticism of the Queen, since Elizabeth embraced this cause belatedly, reluctantly and half-heartedly. The crowd, one might recall, stayed remarkably silent at the state's mutilation of John Stubbs for protesting Elizabeth's potential marriage to the Catholic Duke of Alençon, and this in a time when executions served as public entertainment.

In the years immediately following his untimely death, the Sidney legend flourished, the memory of Sidney's political misfortunes waned, and his reputation as a poet and as a defender of poetry grew apace. To give some examples, George Puttenham included Sidney among the "courtly makers" of Elizabeth's reign in *The Art of English Poesy*; in 1587 the rhetorician, poet and translator Angel Day published a commemorative poem called *Upon the Life and Death of the Most Worthy, and Thrice Renowned Knight, Sir Philip Sidney*, which began "Sugared Sidney, Sidney sweet it was, / That to thy soil did give the greatest fame, / Whose honeydews that from his quill did pass, / With honey sweets, advanced thy glorious name"; in 1595 Edmund Spenser published "Astrophel: A Pastoral Elegy of the Most Noble and Valorous Knight, Sir Philip Sidney"; and in 1598, the same year as the folio edition of Sidney's works, Francis Meres put Sidney at the head of his list of authors who have contributed to the development of English in his *Palladis Tamia*: "[As Greek and Latin authors have made their tongues 'famous and eloquent'] so the English tongue is mightily enriched, and gorgeously invested in rare ornaments and resplendent abiliments [clothes, robes]] by Sir Philip Sidney, Spenser, Daniel, Drayton, Warner, Shakespeare,

Marlowe and Chapman."[54] Let us now turn Sidney's poetic works
to see why they made such an impact.

An Apology for Poetry and Astrophil and Stella

Sidney intended neither the *Apology* nor *Astrophil and Stella*
for a broad reading audience, and although both texts circulated
in manuscript,[55] they were not printed until at least four years
after Sidney's death. In other words, Sidney meant these works,
especially the *Astrophil*, for a relatively small, coterie audience of
friends and family intimately acquainted with his life and po-
litical frustrations.[56]

Astrophil and Stella was first published by Thomas Newman
in 1591 (he put out a corrected version later that year) without
the permission of the Sidney family, and although authors and
their heirs normally had no recourse against the pirating of their
works (copyright law would not develop until the eighteenth
century), Mary Sidney, the Countess of Pembroke, managed to
have the government issue an order for the suppression of this
edition.[57] William Ponsonby included a much better edition of
the *Astrophil* in his authorized 1598 folio of Sidney's works.[58]
The *Apology* enjoyed a similar history. Henry Olney published

---

[54] The citations from Puttenham, Day and Meres (who also refers to Shakespeare circu-
lating his "sugared sonnets" among his friends) are from *Sidney: The Critical Heritage*,
96, 111-112, 146; I have quoted the title page of Spenser's poem from the reproduction
in *The Yale Edition of the Shorter Poems of Edmund Spenser*, ed. William A. Oram et al.
(New Haven: Yale University Press, 1989), 564.

[55] On the manuscript circulation of both works, see Woudhuysen, *Sir Philip Sidney and
the Circulation of Manuscripts*.

[56] Unlike the *Old Arcadia*, *Astrophil and Stella* did not achieve widespread circulation in
manuscript, suggesting that Sidney (and his family after his death) wanted to restrict the
readership of this sequence (Woudhuysen, *Sir Philip Sidney and the Circulation of Manu-
scripts*, 365-66).

[57] Ringler, *The Poems of Sir Philip Sidney*, 543. See also Kuin, *Chamber Music*, 181-86,
and Woudhuysen, *Sir Philip Sidney and the Circulation of Manuscripts*, 367-69.

[58] *The Countess of Pembroke's Arcadia. Written by Sir Philip Sidney Knight. Now the Third
Time Published With Sundry New Additions of the Same Author* (1598).

an unauthorized version in 1595 under the title *An Apology for Poetry*, and although Olney escaped official censure (perhaps because a defense of poetry was less damaging to Sidney's posthumous reputation than his sonnet sequence), Ponsonby issued an authorized edition that same year using the title *The Defense of Poesy*.[59] Ironically, Olney's is actually a much better edition than Ponsonby's authorized text; the printing is cleaner, easier to read (the classical quotations, for example, are set off from the rest of the text), and Olney used higher quality paper.

However they came to public notice, both works constituted major watersheds in the history of English Renaissance literature. *An Apology for Poetry* is not precisely the first major statement of poetics by an Englishman (Richard Willes has that honor, and excerpts from his *Disputation Concerning Poetry* [the original title is *De Re Poetica*] can be found in the "Selected Attacks and Defenses " section of this volume), but Sidney's text is undoubtedly the most important, and it quickly took on the status of a classic. Similarly, the publication of *Astrophil and Stella* exerted enormous influence on English poetic production, as it is often credited with starting the craze for writing sonnets and sonnet sequences that persisted throughout the 1590s.[60]

---

[59] I have chosen to use Olney's title, *An Apology for Poetry*, even though the authorized version uses a different title, because that is how the author of the first reference I have found to Sidney's text refers to it. Sir John Harington, in *A Brief Apology for Poetry* (1591) calls this text "Sir Philip Sidney's *Apology*" (*Elizabethan Critical Essays*, ed. G. Gregory Smith, vol. 2, 196). As Harington likely read Sidney's text in manuscript, and as he would have been among the intended coterie audience, he probably knew the preferred title. Today, both are used interchangeably, the determinate factor being the contemporary edition used.

[60] *Astrophil and Stella* is actually the *second* sonnet sequence written in English. The first, a collection of 21 sonnets that meditate upon the 51st Psalm was written by Anne Lock (or Lok) and appended to her translation of the *Sermons of John Calvin Upon the Song that Ezechias Made After He Had Been Sick* . . . (London, 1560). The modern edition is *The Collected Works of Anne Vaughan Lock*, ed. Susan M. Felch (Tempe, AZ: Medieval and Renaissance Texts and Studies, 1999). Sidney's, however, is the first amatory or Petrarchan sequence. It should be noted that "sonnet" in the 16th and 17th centuries was a looser term than today and that it did not refer exclusively to 14 line poems. For example, not one of John Donne's *Songs and Sonnets* is 14 lines long.

The origin of the *Apology* is widely considered to be Stephen Gosson's dedication of his attack on all forms of fictions, *The School of Abuse* (1579), to Sidney. According to Edmund Spenser, Sidney "scorned" both Gosson and his little screed (see the excerpt from Spenser and Harvey's *Two . . . Letters* in this volume), but more recent critics have noted the close relationships between the two texts. If Sidney scorned Gosson's *School of Abuse*, he nonetheless paid close attention to it.[61] Nor did he communicate his scorn to Gosson, who dedicated another attack on fiction to Sidney the next year.

Sidney's purpose in the *Apology* is to defend poetry against the charges of *mysomousoi*, or poet-haters, as Sidney terms them. Thus, both Sidney and Gosson are participating in a very long tradition that predates Plato, who wrote in the *Republic* that there is "from of old a quarrel between philosophy and poetry." Plato charged that poetry has no place in the ideal republic because it corrupts its consumers by stirring up the irrational part of the soul, and from Plato onward, antipoetic sentiment enjoyed a long and distinguished history in Western thought. The immediate cause for the Elizabethan upsurge in antipoetic sentiment and its close cousin, the antitheatrical prejudice,[62] can be found in the rise of the public theater in the 1570s, a development which led London's civic authorities to commission Gosson to write *The School of Abuse*. Whatever the differences in style, context, and intellectual heft, the charges leveled by Gosson and Plato are virtually identical: Both assert that poets are liars and that their works incite immorality. Implicit in Plato, but very explicit in Gosson and his brethren, are the charges that poetry

---

[61] See Arthur F. Kinney, "Parody and Its Implications in Sydney's Defense of Poesie," *Studies in English Literature* 12 (1972): 1-19.

[62] On the former, see Russell Fraser, *The War Against Poetry* and Peter C. Herman, *Squitterwits and Muse-haters: Sidney, Spenser, Milton, and Renaissance Antipoetic Sentiment*; on the latter, see Jonas Barish, *The Antitheatrical Prejudice*.

erodes masculinity and that one cannot serve the Muses and the commonwealth at the same time. As Justice Overdo, a character in Ben Jonson's *Bartholomew Fair*, exclaims concerning a young thief, "I begin shrewdly to suspect their familiarity; and the young man of a terrible taint, poetry! with which idle disease if he be infected, there's no hope of him in a state-course. *Actum est* of him for a commonwealth's-man if he go to't in rhyme once."

To these charges, Sidney replied with a text that takes the form of an eight-part classical oration:[63]

1. *Exordium* (introduction): the opening anecdote concerning Edward Wotton and the horse-master, John Pietro Pugliano (pp. 56-57)

2. *Narratio* (outline of the subject matter): general facts concerning poetry, (pp. 57-64)

3. *Propositio* (statement of the thesis): the nature of poetry itself, poetry as creation, poetry as imitation (pp. 64-66)

4. *Divisio* (division of the argument into parts for discussion): the three types of poetry, introduction of the Right Poet (pp. 66-69)

5. *Confirmatio* (provides evidence to prove thesis): the competition between poetry, philosophy and history over who best inspires virtuous action, the different kinds of poetry (pp. 70-94).

6. *Refutatio* (consideration and refutation of opposing arguments): charges against poetry, in particular Plato's (pp. 94-108)

7. *Digressio* (digression): the present state of English poetry (pp. 108-24)

8. *Peroratio* (conclusion, pp. 124-26)

---

[63] On Sidney's use of classical oratory, see Myrick, *Sir Philip Sidney as Literary Craftsman*.

Overall, Sidney argues that the charges against poetry are unfounded because, as particularly evidenced in the *confirmatio*, there is no science, or form of knowledge, that inspires the reader to active virtue better than poetry. Historians may have narrative on their side, but they are tied, Sidney writes, to retelling what actually happened, and while philosophers can discuss virtue in the abstract, their works are too obscure, too difficult to understand. Only the poet can combine the virtues of both and come up with a text whose images and conceits will actually get people to *do* virtuous deeds. As Sidney puts it, it is not *gnosis*, or abstract knowledge, that is important, but *praxis*, or practice. Reading poetry is not an act of idleness but a preparation for action:

> Truly I have known men that even with reading *Amadis de Gaul*, which, God knoweth, wanteth much of a perfect poesy, have found their hearts moved to the exercise of courtesy, liberality, and especially courage. Who readeth Aeneas carrying old Anchises on his back that wisheth not it were his fortune to perform so excellent an act? (pp. 84-85)

The poet, Sidney explains, has this ability because of the concatenation of two principles. First, poetry, unlike any other science, is *not* tied to nature. Therefore, as he famously writes, the poet,

> disdaining to be tied to any such subjection, lifted up with the vigor of his own invention, doth grow in effect another nature in making things either better than nature bringeth forth, or quite anew, forms such as never were in nature, as the heroes, demigods, Cyclops, Chimeras, Furies, and such like. So as he goeth hand in hand with nature, not enclosed within the narrow warrant of her gifts, but freely ranging only within the zodiac of his own wit (p. 64).

Having created this "idea," which he also calls a "fore-conceit," the poet then couples it with an image which he delivers "forth in such excellency as he had imagined them." The result, to use Sidney's example, is that the poet not only creates an ideal *image* of virtuous behavior, such as Cyrus, or Aeneas, but the reader transforms the abstract idea into a concrete *act*. Thus the poet "bestows" a Cyrus or an Aeneas "upon the world." In sum, Sidney rebuts the Muse-haters by arguing that poetry incites the reader to moral rather than immoral acts.

To be sure, Sidney's ideas are not original. He draws much of what he has to say in poetry's defense from Italian literary criticism—Julius Caesar Scaliger in particular (see the excerpt in this volume), whose *Poetics* Sidney had read deeply and carefully. Sidney's contribution, therefore, lies in his injecting these ideas into English literary discourse and in his bringing together an extraordinary mosaic of earlier Renaissance thought about the nature and purpose of poetry.

Recent critics have noted that the *Apology* is far from a unified text,[64] and perhaps the best place to illustrate how the *Apology* consistently presents multiple perspectives on important issues is the *propositio*, the thesis. On the one hand, Sidney states about as explicitly as one could want that the poet is *independent* of Nature: "So as he goeth hand in hand with nature, not enclosed within the narrow warrant of her gifts, but freely ranging only within the zodiac of his own wit" (p. 64). Even further, it is precisely this independence from Nature that allows the poet his superiority, since " Her world is brazen [brass], the poets only deliver a golden [one]" (p. 65).

Yet two paragraphs later, Sidney brackets these concepts as a kind of thought-experiment—"But these arguments will by few be understood, and by fewer granted"— and he restarts his argument with a definition of poetry that is the *opposite* of what he has just proposed: "Poesy, therefore, is an art of imitation, for

---

[64] O. B. Hardison Jr. was the first to explore fully this aspect of Sidney's text in "The Two Voices of Sidney's *Apology for Poetry*." See also Margaret W. Ferguson, *Trials of Desire: Renaissance Defenses of Poetry*, and Ronald Levao, *Renaissance Minds and Their Fictions*.

so Aristotle termeth it in this word *mimesis*, that is to say, a representing, counterfeiting, or figuring forth, to speak metaphorically" (p. 66). To re-present, or to figure forth, or to imitate, means that the poet is no longer "freely ranging only within the zodiac of his own wit" but is now *subject* to Nature.

Sidney fills the *Apology* with many such contradictions. He praises mixing genres in one passage ("some have mingled matters heroical and pastoral, but that cometh all to one in this question, for if severed they be good, the conjunction cannot be hurtful" [p. 87]) only to condemn this practice in another ("mongrel tragicomedy" [p. 116]). Sidney credits poetry as the original source of knowledge, "the first light giver to ignorance" (p. 57); later on, he exculpates the poets for their "wrong opinions" of the gods because they "did not induce such opinions, but did imitate those opinions already induced" (p. 106), which implies that some "science" predated Musaeus and Amphion. He finds merit in *The Ballad of Chevy Chase*; yet toward the end he becomes the finicky critic, qualifying his positive review of Edmund Spenser's *The Shepherd's Calendar* with "that same framing of his style to an old rustic language I dare not allow" (p. 113) because it is without precedent.

The inner conflicts of the *Apology* should also be seen in the context of two letters that Sidney wrote, one to Edward Denny, the other to Sidney's younger brother, Robert, in which Sidney treats the relative merits of poetry and its place in the reading of young men of action (excerpts from both letters are included in this volume). On May 22, 1580, Sidney responded to Denny's request for a bibliography to occupy him during his Irish service, and despite his assertion in the *Apology* that "poetry is the companion of the camps" (p. 102), Sidney declines to recommend any poetry at all, restricting himself instead to history and philosophy. On October 15 of the same year, Sidney wrote a letter to his brother in which he gives yet a third assessment of the relationship between poetry and history; this time, it is the *historian* who becomes a poet "for ornament." History, the dominant science, uses poetry, not vice versa. Thus, in the Denny letter, poetry loses by default, and in the Robert letter, poetry remains subordinate to history.

There are many ways of approaching the divisions of the *Apology* and the fact that Sidney writes three texts at roughly the same time in which he gives three different assessments of poetry's worth. As Sidney writes in his letter to Denny, he may be constructing a reading program tailored to Denny himself (and by implication for Robert too) rather than articulating a broad principle. Or the differences among all three may be evidence of Sidney trying out different ideas about literature without necessarily committing himself to one in particular. As for the contradictions within the *Apology*, one might invoke Sidney's partial adherence to Protestant antipoetic tendencies, "the pressure of a forensic rhetorical tradition . . . that encouraged the summoning to court of all possible witnesses, the marshaling of all possible arguments, no matter how they might quarrel or clash in the vestibule afterwards," the tradition of the paradoxical encomium, in which a seemingly mundane or morally reprehensible subject is shown, through very clever reasoning, to be the opposite (for example, Erasmus' *The Praise of Folly*), and/or the urbane wit of the *Apology* itself. [65] The point, however, should not be to emphasize one context to the exclusion of all others or to attempt to resolve differences that are manifestly not resolvable. Better to try to capture the *Apology*'s full complexity through its engagement with multiple, even contradictory discourses, in other words, to see this text as an example of Sidney's—and his culture's—unsettled dialogue over the nature and purpose of poetry.

[65] Anne Lake Prescott, "King David as a 'Right Poet': Sidney and the Psalmist," 133; on Sidney and the antipoetic strain within English Protestant thought, see Herman, *Squitterwits*, and on the tradition of the paradoxical encomium, see Rosalie Colie, *Paradoxia Epidemica: The Renaissance Tradition of Paradox* (Princeton: Princeton University Press, 1966).

Sidney's sonnet sequence, *Astrophil and Stella*, similarly partakes of a variety of intellectual currents. The progenitor of Sidney's sequence is Petrarch's (1304-1374) collection, variously called the *Rime Sparse* ("Scattered Rhymes") and the *Canzoniere* ("Songbook"), a collection of 366 poems in many lengths and verse forms detailing his unfulfilled love for Laura. Petrarch's *Rime Sparse* ranks among the most influential works ever produced, as it gave the West a language for talking about desire that permeated the Renaissance and remains current to this day.

Petrarch's achievement in this sequence is manifold.[66] First, Petrarch created a coherent sequence made up of several little parts. Although the *Rime Sparse* does not have a plot *per se*, the sequence begins with a retrospective poem and then covers the speaker's constant love for Laura over the course of over twenty years (many of the poems contain chronological markers). At sonnet 267, Laura dies (thus creating a bifold structure of poems dealing with Laura alive, *in vita*, and those dealing with Laura dead, *in morte*). Even Laura's death, the relationship does not end, for her spirit returns to lead the lover to penitence and ultimately to heaven.[67] Second, at a time when Latin was the language of all intellectual discourse, Petrarch wrote his poems in Italian, the vernacular. While for Petrarch himself the language of the *Rime Sparse* may have indicated his sense that these poems are lesser achievements than, for example, his Latin epic, *Africa*, which concerns the Roman military hero *Scipio Africanus*, but for later writers seeking, as Spenser later put it, "the king-

---

[66] Petrarch's innovations build on the previous achievements of Provençal poetry and Dante (in particular, the *Vita Nuova*). The sonnet form itself first developed in Sicily. On the history of the sonnet, see Michael R. G. Spiller, *The Development of the Sonnet: An Introduction* (London: Routledge, 1992).

[67] In Petrarch's *The Secretum*, an imaginary dialogue between the author and St. Augustine, Petrarch answers Augustine's charge that his love for Laura is profane, that it has "detached your mind from the love of heavenly things," by asserting that "the love which I feel for her has most certainly led to love God" (*Petrarch's Secret*, trans. William H. Draper [Westport, CT: Hyperion, 1978], 124).

dom of our own language," Petrarch provided an important model for the dignity and possibilities of writing in languages other than Latin.

Perhaps more importantly, Petrarch transformed the love lyric by concentrating on interiority and emphasizing how one effect of the lover's amorous stability is his internal *instability*.[68] In other words, Petrarch not only made interiority the key subject, but also described interiority as inherently unstable, in flux, and divided against itself. To do this, Petrarch invented a language of oxymoron to talk about his inner state. Sonnet 134, for example, begins "Peace I do not find, and I have no wish to make war; and I fear and hope, and burn and am of ice; and I fly above the heavens and lie on the ground; and I grasp nothing and embrace all the world."[69]

Petrarch's sequence also provided a model for using the personal as a vehicle for displaying one's poetic virtuosity. Although many of the poems consist of fourteen lines, divided structurally between a section of eight lines and a section of six (the form of the Petrarchan sonnet), the *Rime Sparse* contains a variety of verse forms and lengths, and the point, as Petrarch makes explicit in 61 (among other places) is his own glory: "Blessed be the many words I have scattered calling the name of my lady, and the signs and the years and the desire; and blessed be all the pages where I gain fame for her, and my thoughts, which are only of her, so that no other has part in them!" Finally, Petrarch provided a model for combining the personal with the political. Not only does he include several explicitly political poems, but he creates a parallel between the lover's internally divided state

---

[68] See Giuseppe Mazzotta, "The *Canzoniere* and the Language of the Self," and Barbara Estrin, *Laura: Uncovering Gender and Genre in Wyatt, Donne, and Marvell*, 41-90.

[69] The standard contemporary translation of Petrarch's sequence is *Petrarch's Lyric Poems: The "Rime Sparse" and Other Lyrics*, trans. Robert M. Durling. The Italian originals are on the facing page. All citations are to this edition.

and Italy's civil wars (see, in particular, 128, "Italia mia"). From the inception of the Petrarchan tradition, in other words, love and politics have been closely intertwined.

Strangely, however, although Petrarchan sequences were written in other languages,[70] and individual poems by Petrarch were translated or imitated in English, in particular by the "courtly makers" of the late Henrician court, Sir Thomas Wyatt (1503-1542) and Henry Howard, the Earl of Surrey (1516-1547), Sir Philip Sidney is the first in England to write a full sequence of love poems that, like Petrarch's, explores a wide variety of verse forms. The introductory poem presents the reader with a metrical innovation, an English sonnet written in twelve-syllable lines (alexandrines), which are more characteristic of French verse, and the first six sonnets use different rhyme schemes and metrical patterns. In addition, Sidney scatters throughout his sequence poems that are also songs (we know from the Denny Letter that Sidney intended at least some of his verse to be set to music), although the final arrangement arrived only in Ponsonby's 1598 folio edition of Sidney's works, so it is unclear whether the order of the sequence reflects Sidney's intentions.

Like the *Rime Sparse*, *Astrophil and Stella* exhibits a certain dramatic coherence. The first 68 sonnets depict Astrophil continually begging Stella for favor and, in several, an unnamed friend rebuking Astrophil for allowing his passions to dominate his life. Starting with *AS* 69, Stella seems to warm to Astrophil's blandishments, but in Song 2, which follows four sonnets later, Astrophil steals a kiss from Stella while she is sleeping (there are intimations here of rape as well: "See the hand which waking guardeth, / Sleeping, grants a free resort. / Now will I invade the fort, / Cowards love with loss rewardeth" [ll. 13-16]), which

---

[70] Most important for Sidney would be the sequences by Pierre de Ronsard, Joachim Du Bellay, and the five other poets of the "Pléiade." This group intended to enrich the French language and literature by imitating the classical and Italian, Petrarchan poetry.

destroys any chance of a happy, if adulterous, relationship between the two. And unlike Petrarch's narrator, who concludes with a paean to the Virgin, Astrophil spends the rest of the sequence sinking even deeper into solipsistic despair. Finally, like Petrarch, Sidney explores the interior consciousness of his narrator. However, a key difference between the two sequences lies in the degree of biographical content, and this may also help explain the radical differences between the endings of the two sequences.

In all likelihood, Sidney wrote the sequence between November 1, 1581, when Penelope Devereux married Lord Rich, and the end of 1582, a period of tremendous political frustration for Sidney, as we have seen. Ironically, Walter Devereux, the Earl of Essex and Penelope's father, had on his death-bed in 1576 expressed a wish that his daughter marry Philip, but nothing came of the proposed match because at the time Sidney was still Leicester's heir and thus was much sought after by various matchmakers. Even more ironically, Leicester then married the Earl's widow, Lettice, and she gave birth to the child who (temporarily) blighted Sidney's prospects for inherited wealth, a title, and an advantageous marriage. The loss of the Leicester estates made Sidney much less marriagable, and on November 1, 1581, Penelope was married off to Lord Robert Rich, a person generally regarded as a fool—but a fool with a title and estates who certainly could provide for his wife's material comfort much better than Sidney could.

Students today are often enjoined to avoid strictly biographical readings and to concentrate on the tale, not the teller. However, there is little doubt that Sidney intended his sequence to be read autobiographically. At several points, most notably *AS* 24 and 37, Sidney viciously puns on Lord Rich's name; in *AS* 30, Sidney refers to "my father," Sir Henry Sidney, and his service in Ireland; and five of the seven books dedicated to Penelope Rich between 1594 and 1606 connect her with Astrophil, suggesting that she happily accepted the identification.[71] Consequently, *Astrophil and Stella* presents the reader with the spectacle of Sidney using verse to record his adulterous passion for Penelope Rich, but as we will see, the biographical reading can also lead us into interpretations of considerably greater complexity.

Arthur F. Marotti, in his seminal article, "'Love is not Love': Elizabethan Sonnet Sequences and the Social Order," describes how the languages of love and politics often became so intertwined in Elizabeth's court as to be virtually indistinguishable from each other. Sir Christopher Hatton, for example, wrote Elizabeth a note that sounds precisely like a lover pining for his mistress: "Madame, I find the greatest lack that ever poor wretch sustained. No death, no hell, no fear of death shall ever win of my consent so far to wrong myself again as to be absent from you one day . . . . to serve you is a heaven, but to lack you is more than hell's torment . . . . Passion overcometh me. I can write no more. Love me; for I love you . . . ."[72] Elizabeth appropriated the position of a Petrarchan mistress in part as a way of controlling the various factions of her court by making a political liability—her sex— a political advantage in that her courtiers adopted the culturally approved subservient stance of a male lover seeking the favor of his lady. At the same time, the language of Petrarchan desire, which, one must always remember, remains the language of *frustrated* desire because the beloved is always aloof and rejecting, quickly took on the added duty of describing frustrated political ambition, the lover's inability to gain his lady's love paralleling the courtier's inability to advance or gain his monarch's approval.

Clearly, Sidney's original audience would have known very well that "love" in this period often overlapped with "politics," and they would have also been perfectly aware that the author

---

[71] Howell, 182.
[72] Quoted in Marotti, 398-99.

of *Astrophil and Stella* was a politically, economically, and so-cially disappointed young man.[73] But what to do with these facts remains unsettled. Whereas Marotti suggests that Astrophil's erotic defeat compromises his claim that the political world is well lost for love, Maureen Quilligan posits that Sidney used his poetry as a means of achieving the mastery that eluded him in reality: Astrophil "turns his Petrarchan abasement into author-ity, manipulating a character, Stella, who allows him to woo, conquer, and be rejected, and, by his manipulation of that re-jection, discursively to control his own recent misfortunes in his career."[74] Anne R. Jones and Peter Stallybrass provide a third perspective, arguing that Astrophil's manipulation of Petrarchan imagery is a strategy of masculine mastery over an unruly woman.[75]

The relationship between *An Apology for Poetry* and *Astrophil and Stella*, Sidney's poetic *gnosis* and his *praxis*, is similarly un-settled. In the *Apology*, Sidney argues for poetry's superiority over history and philosophy on the grounds that it inspires vir-tuous action, and he scornfully denies the charges of the Muse-haters to the contrary. Yet in *Astrophil and Stella*, Sidney's pro-tagonist—whom he goes out of his way to identify with him-self— continuously tries to seduce a married woman and even, conceivably, attempts to rape her. This is hardly the type of po-

---

[73] *Ibid*, 400.

[74] Maureen Quilligan, "Sidney and His Queen," 189. Marotti writes that "The central irony of *Astrophil and Stella* is that the heterocosm of love to which the poet-lover has fled from the viciously competitive world of the court is no compensation for sociopolitical defeat. Instead it is the locale of a painful repetition of the experience in another mode" ("Love is not Love," 405).

[75] Jones and Stallybrass, "The Politics of *Astrophil and Stella*," 55. The work by Marotti, Quilligan, Jones, and Stallybrass is broadly influenced by the New Historicism of the 1980s. While many critics still mine this vein, others have re-emphasized the erotic rather than political aspects of Petrarchism. See, for example, Heather Dubrow, *Echoes of Desire: English Petrarchism and Its Counterdiscourses* (Ithaca: Cornell University Press, 1995) and Roger Kuin, *Chamber Music: Elizabethan Sonnet Sequences and the Pleasure of Criticism*.

etry Sidney's Right Poet would produce. In fact, this verse serves to confirm rather than deny the charges of poetry's enemies.[76]

Yet alongside their differences, both *Astrophil and Stella* and the *Apology* contain similar refractions of Sidney's political life. To be sure, courtiers were supposed to include poetry among their many social graces. The perfect courtier, Baldesare Castiglione writes, should be able to turn out a properly constructed sonnet at the appropriate time, and Sidney demonstrated his aptitude for courtly verse in such compositions as his pastoral drama *The Lady of May*, presented before Elizabeth in 1578 or 1579. But it is one thing to churn out competent verse as a means of entertaining the queen while simultaneously making a plea for advancement, and quite another to devote oneself to writing verse exclusively, because that means one is not also engaging in state service. That was Sidney's dilemma in 1581-1583 when, in the absence of meaningful state employment, he devoted his energies to creating and defending literature.

Consequently, Sidney's defense of poetry is also a *self*-defense. He sees himself as "in these my not old years and idlest times, having slipped into the title of a poet" (p. 57), the cause of this slippage being Elizabeth's refusal to make use of him. One can hear Sidney's frustration with Elizabeth when he asks, at the beginning of the *digressio*, "why England, the mother of excellent minds, should be grown so hard a stepmother to poets" (p. 108)—why, in other words, Elizabeth has grown so hard to Sidney himself. One also finds throughout the *Astrophil* a sense of wasted career opportunities. In *AS* 18, for example, he exclaims:

> . . . my wealth I have most idly spent.
> My youth doth waste, my knowledge brings forth toys,

---

[76] On the other hand, the eclogues Sidney included in the two versions of the *Arcadia* seem much more along the lines of the kind of poetry Sidney praises in the *Apology*.

My wit doth strive those passions to defend
Which for reward spoil it with vain annoys.
I see my course to lose myself doth bend.

When the speaker complains that his wit has done nothing more worthwhile than defend his "passions," the immediate referent is to his love for Stella, but there is also a sense in which Sidney has in mind defending poetry as well. As Sidney complains to Denny, "the unnoble constitution of our time doth keep us from fit employments" (p. 211). Poetry is, in other words, *not* a fit employment—hence (perhaps) its absence from the Denny letter.

Ironically, though poetry represented for Sidney a second choice, an achievement of the left hand, as Milton would say, and though he used verse to reflect and explore the problems caused by his tense relationship with his queen (among other themes), he nonetheless produced a masterpiece that not only perfectly absorbed the continental traditions of poetic practice but also demonstrated that English verse could equal the best Latin and European poetry. Sidney's *Astrophil and Stella* paved the way for the other great Elizabethan sonnet sequences, Edmund Spenser's *Amoretti*, Michael Drayton's *Idea's Mirror*, and Samuel Daniel's *Delia*, as well as for a host of others of much less distinction. Yet even as Sidney's popular reputation as a poet burgeoned, others who knew Sidney, and perhaps had a more personal stake in tending his legend, evinced considerable anxiety about his poetic doings.

In 1594, for example, Sir Thomas Moffett, the Sidney family's physician, wrote a biography of Sidney for the edification of Sir Philip's young nephew. But Moffett, who knew Sidney well, alters the chronology of Sidney's writing. Instead of having his subject write verse during the period of his political languishing, he resituates Sidney's involvement with verse to his adolescence, and he includes poetry among the "clogs upon the mind" Sidney gave up when he "had begun to enter into the deliberations of the commonwealth."[77] The truth, of course, is the opposite, but evidently Moffett believed that writing the *Astrophil* could not be reconciled with his transforming Sidney into a model Protestant hero.

Sir Philip's friend and later biographer, Fulke Greville, went one step further by avoiding all mention of Sidney's poetic works in his combination life of Sidney and introduction to Greville's own works, *A Dedication to Sir Philip Sidney*. Greville does talk about Sidney's "Arcadian Romances," but only because he can turn them into fictional vehicles for political philosophy, warning "sovereign princes" against various crimes that will entail "the ruin of states and princes."[78] While many after Sidney's death praised his verse and considered him a paragon of courtly virtue, that fact needs to be balanced against the clear discomfort others evinced at Sidney's poetic accomplishments.

The Quarrel Over Poetry: Selected Attacks and Defenses

Sidney's *An Apology for Poetry* and *Astrophil and Stella* also intervene in the quarrel over poetry that has its origins in the mists of antiquity and continues unabated to this day. In 1904, G. Gregory Smith, the editor of the still essential collection of Elizabethan writings on and about fiction, *Elizabethan Critical Essays*, began his introduction by noting that "Elizabethan criticism arose in controversy."[79] That is to say, Elizabethan criticism in general and Sir Philip Sidney's *Apology* answered the charges circulating throughout early modern England that poetry is lewd and—as a seventeenth-century Muse-hater memorably put it, "the mushroom conception of idle brains."[80] Eliza-

---

[77] Thomas Moffett, *Nobilis or A View of the Life and Death of a Sidney*, 73-74, 80-81.

[78] Greville, *A Dedication to Sir Philip Sidney*, 8.

[79] G. Gregory Smith, "Introduction," *Elizabethan Critical Essays* vol. 1, xiv.

[80] John Melton, *A Six-Fold Politician* (1609), quoted in Russell Fraser, *The War Against Poetry*, 6.

bethan attacks and defenses of poetry, however, constitute but one chapter in the argument over the utility and morality of verse that for our purposes begins with Plato, although Plato himself says that the quarrel long predates him.

In order to help contextualize the *Apology*'s argument and to gauge properly the nature of poetry's opposition, I have chosen a selection of attacks and defenses of poetry that collectively illustrate the chronological range and cultural centrality of musophobia. This section begins with excerpts from Plato's *Republic* and the *Laws*. In Book 2, Socrates begins his description of the ideal state by noting the importance of education in making sure that the state's inhabitants hold the "correct" ideas. This, Socrates, quickly says, means censorship, and the tales that ought to be censored are those found in Hesiod and Homer. In Book 10, Socrates returns to the matter of poetry (the control of poetry thus bracketing all the other aspects of the ideal state), only now Socrates moves from censoring the poets to banning them altogether. Plato returns to the matter of poetry in the *Laws*. Significantly, in the *Republic* Plato leaves open the possibility of poetry's defense, but in the *Laws* (a text much better known in the Renaissance than today), he forecloses this possibility altogether, suggesting that as time progressed, Plato's attitudes toward poetry hardened.

After Plato, we move to the Italian Renaissance of the fourteenth century and an excerpt from Boccaccio's influential essay on poetics, which constitutes a model for Sidney's *Apology* in that Boccaccio testifies to the existence and power of antipoetic sentiment in his era and provides some of the stock answers to their charges. While Boccaccio dismisses poetry's enemies as mere fools and antipoetic sentiment as intellectually vacuous, one also finds a distrust of fiction in such impeccable sixteenth-century humanists as Juan Luis Vives and Sir Thomas Elyot. The former, in his dialogue *Truth Dressed Up, or of Poetic License: To What Extent Poets May be Permitted to Vary from the*

Truth, tries to rein in precisely the freedom Sidney initially grants the poet's imagination; and the latter, in *The Defense of Good Women*, puts an attack on verse in the mouth of women's *defender*, making it highly unlikely that he intended these sentiments to redound to the speaker's discredit. Attacks on poetry cannot, therefore, be said to emanate exclusively from the fringe element of Renaissance culture.

While the presence of antipoetic sentiment in humanist discourse demonstrates musophobia's intellectual respectability, its appropriation by Protestant theologians made it impossible for Sidney (or any other Elizabethan who thought deeply about poetry) to ignore. The earliest Protestants attacked the Catholic Church adhering to concepts that have no Biblical warrant (such as purgatory), and therefore, according to these early Protestant polemicists, they must emanate from the imagination. In other words, the early Protestants attacked Catholic dogma as essential *fictitious*. William Tyndale,[81] for example, charged that Catholics "gave themselves only unto poetry, and shut up the Scripture."[82] But if Tyndale's primary target in this quote is the Catholic valuation of tradition as at least equal to Scripture, before long before poetry itself became highly suspect. For example, a marginal note to Tyndale's translation of Genesis 47:22 glosses the Pharoah's priests as ivy trees that "creep up little and little to compass the great trees of the world with hypocrisy, and to thrust the roots of idolatrous superstition in to them and to suck out

---

[81] William Tyndale (1494?-1536), among the most important of the earliest English Reformers, and translator of the first English printed Bible. In his theological works, Tyndale emphasized the primacy of Scripture in deciding doctrinal matters. If something cannot be found in the Bible, Tyndale argued, then it has no value, no matter what tradition says. Tyndale and Sir Thomas More engaged in a fierce polemical battle in which More linked Tyndale with Luther as a leader of the Reformation. Tyndale's works remained influential throughout the English Renaissance, and his translation of the Bible served as a foundation for the King James Version.

[82] Quoted in Stephen J. Greenblatt, *Renaissance Self-Fashioning: From More to Shakespeare* (Chicago: Chicago University Press, 1980), 112.

the juice of them with their poetry."[83] The early reformers were so identified with antipoetic sentiment that John Skelton included it among the "odious, orgolious [proud], and fly-blown opinions" refuted in "A Replication Against Certain Young Scholars Abjured of Late" (1528?):

> Why have ye then disdain
> At poets, and complain
> How poets do but feign? [84]

The Protestant aspect of antipoetic sentiment is represented in this volume by two excerpts from Theodore Beza, Jean Calvin's associate and successor. The first is an amusing poem against poetry, "A Sportful Comparison between Poets and Papists," in which Beza continues lightly brings out the parallels between the over-active imagination and Catholicism; the second is from the more serious prefatory letter to the reader for his verse drama, *The Sacrifice of Abraham*, in which Beza explicitly condemns his earlier attempts at erotic verse.

Yet alongside the attacks, the Renaissance also produced a significant body of literature defending and investigating the nature of poetry. In addition to Boccaccio's text, the most significant statement of poetics before Sidney is Julius Caesar Scaliger's influential *Poetics*. He is followed by Richard Willes, the first Englishman to write a treatise on poetry and whose *De Re Poetica* takes its argument almost verbatim from Scaliger, and George Puttenham, whose *Art of English Poesy* also includes a version of Queen Elizabeth's poem, "The Doubt of Future Foes."

This edition attempts to situate Sidney's *Apology* and *Astrophil and Stella* within their various cultural discourses. Clearly, Sidney's *gnosis* and *praxis*, his theory and his practice,

---

[83] *William Tyndale's Five Books of Moses Called the Pentateuch*, ed. J. I. Mombert (Carbondale: Southern Illinois State University Press, 1967), 143.
[84] John Skelton, *The Complete English Poems*, ed. John Scattergood (New Haven and London: Yale University Press, 1983), ll. 351-353.

draw on the traditions of Petrarchism and on the poetics developed in the Italian Renaissance, but they also engage the parallel tradition of Renaissance *anti*poetics. Similarly, while Sidney's works can be read in splendid isolation of history and each other, they also draw on the specific circumstances of Sidney's life for their meaning, and they beg to be seen in dialogue with each other.

Sidney's works, in sum, embody rather than transcend their age. Although many readers from the Renaissance onward have idealized Sidney, holding him up as an exemplar of Protestant chivalry, the balance has been redressed by such literary critics as Arthur Marotti, who view Sidney's works as arising from the conditions of his political life while also engaging and representing the literary and even theological conflicts of Elizabethan England. Just as the *Apology* is no longer exclusively seen as a meditation on the themes of Italian Renaissance literary criticism, but also as a political *apologia*, so is *Astrophil and Stella* seen as drawing on the Petrarchan politics of the Elizabethan court as well as Petrarch's depictions of desire and interiority. These approaches have not reduced the texts, but rather have opened up new vistas of interpretation and previously unsuspected depths.

A Note on the Text and the Annotations

For this edition of *An Apology for Poetry*, I have collated Olney's and Ponsonby's printed versions with the Norwich manuscript, and I have consulted the list of variants in the De Lisle MS. No 1226 in *Miscellaneous Prose of Sir Philip Sidney*, ed. Katherine Duncan-Jones and Jan Van Dorsten (Oxford: Clarendon Press, 1973). Significant variants, or places where Olney, Ponsonby and Norwich disagree,[85] are indicated in the

---

[85] Although Robert Sidney owned the De L'Isle MS. of the *Apology*, it seems to be the least reliable of the four as it contains many readings and variants not shared by the other three texts.

notes. For *Astrophil and Stella*, I have followed the order of the poems and songs established in the 1598 folio edition of Sidney's works. An accent grave marks when the reader should pronounce every syllable (e.g, "dribbèd") and apostrophes show when a syllable has been dropped (e.g., "glist'ring") in order to make the line scan. When in doing so the word is not immediately recognizable, I have given it in a note. When a three-syllable word is normally pronounced with two syllables, I have not made any marks (e.g., "ransacked"). The modernizations and the notes for Sidney's works and the Renaissance texts in "The Quarrel Over Poetry: Selected Attacks and Defenses," unless noted otherwise, are my own. For ease of reference, again unless noted otherwise, all references to Greek and Roman sources are to the Loeb Classical Library. Excerpts from Plato's *Republic* and the *Laws* are from *The Collected Dialogues of Plato*, ed. Edith Hamilton and Huntington Cairns (New York: Pantheon, 1961). Full references to important primary and secondary sources cited in the notes can be found in the "Suggestions for Further Reading" section at the back of this volume.

THE DEFENCE OF Poesie.

By Sir Phillip Sidney, Knight.

LONDON

Printed for *VVilliam Ponsonby.*

1595.

The Defence of Poesie. This item is reproduced by permission of *The Huntington Library, San Marino, California.*

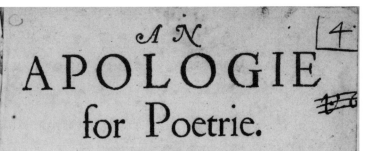

AN
APOLOGIE
for Poetrie.

Written by the right noble, vertu-
ous, and learned, Sir Phillip
Sidney, Knight.

Odi profanum vulgus, et arceo.

AT LONDON,
Printed for *Henry Olney*, and are to be sold at
his shop in Paules Church-yard, at the signe
of the George, neere to Cheap-gate.
Anno, 1595.

An Apology for Poetry. This item is reproduced by permission of *The Huntington Library, San Marino, California.*

An Apology for Poetry

When the right virtuous Edward Wotton[1] and I were at the Emperor's court together, we gave ourselves to learn horsemanship of John Pietro Pugliano, one that with great commendation had the place of an esquire[2] in his stable. And he, according to the fertileness of the Italian wit, did not only afford us the demonstration of his practice, but sought to enrich our minds with the contemplations therein, which he thought most precious. But with none I remember mine ears were at any time more loaden,[3] than when (either angered with slow payment, or moved with our learner-like admiration) he exercised his speech in the praise of his faculty. He said soldiers were the noblest estate of mankind, and horsemen the noblest of soldiers. He said they were the masters of war, and ornaments of peace, speedy goers, and strong abiders, triumphers both in camps and courts. Nay, to so unbelieved a point he proceeded as that no earthly thing bred such wonder to a prince as to be a good horseman. Skill of government was but a *pedanteria*[4] in comparison. Then would he add certain praises by telling what a peerless beast the horse was, the only serviceable courtier without flattery, the beast of most beauty, faithfulness, courage, and such more, that if I had not been a piece of a logician before I came to him, I think he would have persuaded me to have wished myself a horse.[5]

But thus much at least, with his no few words he drove into me, that self-love is better than any gilding to make that seem

---

[1] Edward Wotton (1548-1626) was an English courtier and statesman. Sidney passed the winter of 1574-1575 at the court of Emperor Maximilian II in Vienna. In *AS* 30, Maximilian's rival to the elected Polish crown is called the "right king."

[2] An esquire or equerry is an office in charge of a nobleperson's horses and stables.

[3] Loaded, or laden.

[4] Italian for "pedantry."

[5] The urbane joke is that Philip means "horse-lover" in Greek.

gorgeous wherein ourselves be parties.[6] Wherein, if Pugliano's strong affection and weak arguments will not satisfy you, I will give you a nearer example of myself, who, I know not by what mischance in these my not old years and idlest times, having slipped into the title of a poet, am provoked to say something unto you in the defense of that my unelected vocation, which if I handle with more good will than good reasons, bear with me, since the scholar is to be pardoned that followeth the steps of his master.[7]

And yet I must say, that as I have just cause[8] to make a pitiful defense of poor poetry, which from almost the highest estimation of learning is fallen to be the laughing stock of children, so have I need to bring some more available proofs, since the former is by no man barred of his deserved credit, the silly latter had even the names of philosophers used to the defacing it with great danger of civil war among the Muses. And first, truly, to all them that, professing learning, inveigh against poetry, may be justly objected that they go very near to ungratefulness to seek to deface that which in the noblest nations and languages that are known, hath been the first light-giver to ignorance and first nurse, whose whole milk little and little enabled them to feed afterwards of tougher knowledges. And will they now play the hedge-

---

[6] Ironically, Sidney warns his reader to beware of his defense's rhetoric. On the *Apology* as a self-consuming artifact, see Margaret W. Ferguson, *Trials of Desire: Renaissance Defenses of Poetry* and Ronald Levao, *Renaissance Minds and Their Fictions.*

[7] Most critics and historians think that at the time Sidney wrote the *Apology* and *Astrophil and Stella*, he had probably been banished from the court by Elizabeth on account of his overly blunt disapproval of her possible marriage to the Duke of Alençon, who was not only French, but Catholic as well. Sidney's friend and mentor, Hubert Languet, wrote that Sidney withdrew from the court under "a sort of cloud." But Sidney's close friend and later biographer, Fulke Greville, claimed that Sidney did not suffer any royal disfavor or banishment. For two views of the matter, see Katherine Duncan-Jones (*Sir Philip Sidney: Courtier Poet,* 164), who thinks it likely that Sidney left voluntarily, and Maureen Quilligan ("Sidney and his Queen," *The Historical Renaissance,* 171-96), who argues that Sidney in all likelihood was banished. See also the introduction, pp.18-24.

[8] Ponsonby: "more just cause"; Norwich: "A just cause."

hog, that, being received into the den, drove out his host? Or rather the vipers, that with their birth kill their parents.

Let learned Greece in any of his manifold sciences be able to show me one book before Musaeus, Homer, and Hesiod,[9] all three nothing else but poets. Nay, let any history be brought that can say any writers were there before them, if they were not men of the same skill, as Orpheus, Linus,[10] and some other are named, who, having been the first of that country that made pens deliverers of their knowledge to the posterity, nay, justly challenge to be called their fathers in learning. For not only in time they had this priority (although in itself antiquity be venerable), but went before them, as causes to draw with their charming sweetness the wild untamed wits to an admiration of knowledge.

So as Amphion was said to move stones with his poetry, to build Thebes,[11] and Orpheus to be listened to by beasts, indeed stony and beastly people. So among the Romans were Livius, Andronicus and Ennius,[12] so in the Italian language, the first that made it aspire to be a treasure-house of science,[13] were the

---

[9] Musaeus, a mythical poet, was supposedly a pupil of Orpheus. Plato, in the *Republic*, writing on the deleterious effects poetry has on morality, asserts that both are the offspring of the moon and the Muses (bk. 2, 364e). Homer is the name traditionally given to the "author" of the *Iliad* and the *Odyssey* (in all probability, the works were originally oral compositions, and different versions of them circulated in antiquity). Hesiod (c. 8th century B. C.) wrote the *Theogony*, a poetic treatment of the universe's origins, as well as *Works and Days*. These three poets were commonly regarded as the first pagan theologians.

[10] Orpheus, according to Greek myth and the mythographers of the Renaissance, represented poetry's highest powers. His songs were so powerful that they even convinced Pluto, god of the underworld, to allow Orpheus to bring his beloved wife, Eurydice, back from the dead. His failure, however, to bring back his wife also signaled the limits of poetry's powers. Linus, another legendary poet, was supposed to be Orpheus's teacher.

[11] Amphion, the son of Zeus and Antiope, was credited with inventing music, which was supposed to be so powerful that it could make stones move. The legend is that he raised the walls of Thebes through his melodies.

[12] Livius Andronicus (3rd century B. C.), composed the first Latin tragedy and comedy; Ennius (239-169 B. C.), the most influential of early Latin poets, also known as the father of Roman poetry.

[13] Knowledge.

poets Dante, Bocace, and Petrarch.[14] So in our English, were Gower and Chaucer,[15] after whom, encouraged and delighted with their excellent foregoing, others have followed to beautify our mother tongue, as well in the same kind as others arts. This did so notably show itself that the philosophers of Greece durst not a long time appear to the world, but under the masks of poets. So Thales, Empedocles and Parmenides sang their natural philosophy in verses. [16] So did Pythagoras and Phocylides, their moral counsels.[17] So did Tyrtaeus in war matters, and Solon in matters of policy, [18] or rather, they being poets, did exercise their delightful vein in those points of highest knowledge which before them lay hidden to the world. For that wise Solon was directly a poet, it is manifest, having written in verse the notable fable of the Atlantic Island, which was continued by Plato.[19] And truly even Plato, whosoever well considereth, shall find that in the body of his work, though the inside and strength were phi-

---

[14] Dante Alighieri (1265-1321), author of *La Vita Nuova*, a series of love sonnets to Beatrice separated by prose interludes, and the *Divine Comedy*; Giovanni Boccaccio (1313-1375) is today best known for the *Decameron*, a prose collection of 100 tales, but also the author of many other poems and prose works; Petrarch (Francesco Petrarca, 1304-1374), author of the *Rime Sparse*, an extremely influential sequence of 366 poems frequently, at times slavishly, imitated by later writers. Petrarch's lyrics are marked by their concentration upon the speaker's inner state and the use of paradox and oxymoron (e.g., freezing fire, sweet enemy). Petrarch's verse is an important model for Sidney's *Astrophil and Stella* (see the introduction, pp.40-42). While all three writers also wrote in Latin, Sidney cites them here for their contributions to vernacular literature.

[15] John Gower (1330-1408), author of the Latin *Vox Clamantis*, a satire dealing with the Peasant's Rebellion. His major English poem, *Confessio Amantis*, is a collection of verse stories. Geoffrey Chaucer (1340-1400), best known for the *Canterbury Tales*, was for Sidney's generation the most important English writer.

[16] Thales (c. 6th century, B. C.), wrote such "scientific" versified works as *Nautical Astronomy* and *On First Causes*; Empedocles (c. 5th century B. C.) wrote *On Nature* and *Purifications*, although only fragments of his works survive; Parmenides (also c. 5th century B. C.) founded the Eleatic school of philosophy and is also famous for his participation in Plato's dialogue *Parmenides*.

[17] Pythagoras (c. 5th century B. C.) discovered the intervals of the musical scale and is associated with Orphic poetry; Phocylides (c. 6th century B. C.), a Greek poet whose works survive only in fragments.

[18] Tyrtaeus (c. 7th century B. C.), a poet whose verse (which also survives only in fragments) supposedly so raised the morale of the Spartan forces that they won the Second

losophy, the skin, as it were, and beauty depended most of poetry. For all standeth upon dialogues wherein he feigns many honest burgesses of Athens to speak of such matters that if they had been set on the rack they would never have confessed them. Besides his poetical describing the circumstances of their meetings, as the well ordering of a banquet, the delicacy of a walk, with the interlacing mere tales, as Gyges' ring and others, which who knoweth not to be flowers of poetry, did never walk into Apollo's garden.[20]

And even historiographers, although their lips found of things done, and verity be written in their foreheads, have been glad to borrow both fashion and perchance weight of the poets. So Herodotus entitled his history by the name of the nine Muses, and both he and all the rest that followed him either stale[21] or usurped of poetry their passionate describing of passions, the many particularities of battles which no man could affirm. Or if that be denied me, long orations put in the mouths of great kings and captains which it is certain they never pronounced.

So that truly neither philosopher nor historiographer could at the first have entered into the gates of popular judgments if they had not taken a great passport of poetry, which in all nations at this day where learning flourisheth not is plain to be seen, in all which they have some feeling of poetry.

Messenian War. Compare Scaligers's and Gosson's positive citation of Tyrtaeus as representative of the "right use of ancient poetry" (pp. 243, 271); Solon (c. 600 B. C.), Athenian statesman and legislator who ostensibly wrote a lost epic on Atlantis.

[19] See Plato, *Timaeus*, 20e ff.

[20] Plato recounts this legend in the *Republic*, 360b-c, and it is also found in Herodotus, *The Histories*, 1.8-15 (trans. David Grene). The details of the story differ considerably. In Plato, Gyges is a shepherd who finds a magic ring that renders the bearer invisible after an earthquake. He then seduces the king's wife, murders the king, and possesses his kingdom. In Herodotus, the king makes Gyges view his wife naked. But the queen catches Gyges, and then forces him to kill her husband and take over the kingdom. He does so and rules successfully. For both writers Gyges represents the archetypal tyrant whose crimes go unpunished, so Sidney's example detracts from rather than supports his brief in poetry's favor. The speaker's allusion to the Tale of Gyges thus proves how self-interest leads to "strong affection and weak arguments."

[21] Stole.

In Turkey, besides their law-giving divines, they have no other writers but poets. In our neighbor country, Ireland, where truly, learning goes very bare,[22] yet are their poets held in a devout reverence. Even among the most barbarous and simple Indians where no writing is, yet have they their poets who make and sing songs, which they call "areytos," both of their ancestors' deeds and praises of their gods.[23] A sufficient probability that if ever learning come among them, it must be by having their hard dull wits softened and sharpened with the sweet delights of poetry, for until they find a pleasure in the exercises of the mind, great promises of much knowledge will little persuade them that know not the fruits of knowledge. In Wales, the true remnant of the ancient Britons, as there are good authorities to show the long time they had poets, which they called "bards," so through all the conquests of Romans, Saxons, Danes and Normans, some of whom did seek to ruin all memory of learning from them, yet do their poets even to this day last. So as it is not more notable in soon beginning than in long continuing. But since the authors of most of our sciences[24] were the Romans, and before them the Greeks, let us a little stand upon their authorities, but even so far as to see what names they have given unto this now-scorned skill.

Among the Romans a poet was called *vates*, which is as much as a diviner, a foreseer or prophet, as by his conjoined words *vaticinium* and *vaticinari* is manifest, so heavenly a title did that excellent people bestow upon this heart-ravishing knowledge, and so far were they carried into the admiration thereof, that they thought in the chanceable hitting upon any such verses great foretokens of their following fortunes were placed. Whereupon

---

[22] The English usually viewed the Irish as uncivilized barbarians. Henry Sidney, Sir Philip's father, was the viceroy in Ireland (see *AS* 30, "How Ulster likes of that same golden bit, / Wherewith my father once made it half tame"). Sidney also wrote his letter to Edward Denny on the occasion of his friend's going to Ireland to help subdue it.

[23] This information comes from Peter Martyr's *Decades*, which appeared as part of Richard Eden's *History of the West Indies* (1555).

[24] Branches of knowledge.

grew the word of *sortes Virgilianae*, when by sudden opening Virgil's book they lighted upon some verse of his, whereof the histories of the emperors are full: as of Albinus, the governor of our island, who in his childhood met this verse,

Arma amens capio, nec sat rationis in armis,[25]

and in his age performed it.[26] Which although it were a very vain and godless superstition,[27] as also it was to think spirits were commanded by such verse, whereupon this word, "charms," derived of *carmina*, cometh, so yet serveth it to show the great reverence those wits were held in. And altogether not without ground, since both the oracles of Delphos and Sybilla's prophecies were wholly delivered in verses, for that same exquisite observing of number and measure in the words, and that high flying liberty of conceit proper to the poet did seem to have some divine force in it.[28]

And may not I presume a little farther to show the reasonableness of this word, *vates*, and say that the holy David's Psalms are a divine poem?[29] If I do, I shall not do it without the testimony of great learned men both ancient and modern. But even the name of Psalms will speak for me, which, being interpreted, is nothing but songs, then that it is fully written in meter ,as all

[25] "Madly I seized my arms, although there was little reason in arms" (*Aeneid*, 2.314). The quotation is from Aeneas's description of Troy's fall. Virgil (70-19 B. C.), considered the greatest Roman poet, and author of the *Eclogues*, the *Georgics*, and the *Aeneid*, an epic concerning the founding of Lavinium (parent town of Rome) by Aeneas, a Trojan who, under divine guidance, fled Troy's burning ruins on this epic quest. The importance and influence of the *Aeneid* in the early modern period cannot be overstated.

[26] The reference is ironic. Albinus, encouraged by supposedly prophetic signs, marched on Rome in a vain attempt to become emperor and was killed in 197 A. D.

[27] Sidney's undercutting his argument is characteristic of both the *Apology*'s irony and the problematic place of pagan literature within Christian culture.

[28] Later in the *Apology* Sidney will say "that it is not rhyming and versing that maketh a poet ... but it is that feigning notable images of virtues, vices, or what else, with that delightful teaching, which must be the right describing note to know a poet by" (p. 69). Note also that Sidney says the pagan prophecies *seem* to have divine force in them.

[29] On Sidney and the Psalms, see Anne Lake Prescott, "King David as a 'Right Poet': Sidney and the Psalmist."

learned Hebricians agree, although the rules be not yet fully found. Lastly and principally, his handling his prophecy, which is merely poetical. For what else is the awaking his musical instruments, the often and free changing of persons, his notable *prosopopoeias*,[30] when he maketh you, as it were, see God coming in his majesty, his telling of the beasts' joyfulness, and hills leaping, but a heavenly poesy, wherein almost he showeth himself a passionate lover of the unspeakable and everlasting beauty, to be seen by the eyes of the mind, only cleared by faith? But truly, now having named him, I fear me I seem to profane that holy name, applying it to poetry, which is among us thrown down to so ridiculous an estimation.[31] But they that with quiet judgments will look a little deeper into it shall find the end and working of it such, as being rightly applied, deserveth not to be scourged out of the church of God.

But now let us see how the Greeks have named it, and how they deemed of it. The Greeks called him a "poet," which name hath, as the most excellent, gone through other languages, it cometh of this word, *poiein*, which is, "to make," wherein I know not whether by luck or wisdom, we Englishmen have met with the Greeks in calling him a "maker." Which name, how high and incomparable a title it is, I had rather were known by marking the scope of other sciences than by my partial allegation.

---

[30] In *The Art of English Poesy* (1589), George Puttenham gives this definition: "But if ye will feign any person with such features, qualities and conditions, or if ye will attribute any human quality, as reason or speech, to dumb creatures or other insensible things, and do study, as one may say, to give them a human person, it is ... *prosopopeia*, because it is by way of fiction, and no prettier examples can be given to you thereof, than in the Romant of the rose translated out of French by Chaucer [Jean de Meun and Guillaume de Lorris's *Roman de la Rose*], describing the persons of avarice, envie, old age, and many others, whereby much morality is taught" (3.246).

[31] Compare Sidney's description of poetry's dismal situation to the excerpt from Puttenham's *The Arte of English Poesie* describing how poets have "now become contemptible." See also Edmund Spenser's *October* Eclogue, from *The Shepherd's Calender* (1579), in which Piers complains of the decline of poetry's fortunes, as well as the *Tears of the Muses* (1591).

There is no art delivered to mankind that hath not the works of nature for his principal object,[32] without which they could not consist, and on which they so depend as they become actors and players, as it were, of what nature will have set forth. So doth the Astronomer look upon the stars, and by that he seeth, set down what order nature hath taken therein. So doth the geometrician and arithmetician in their divers sorts of quantities. So doth the musician in times tell you which by nature agree, which not. The natural philosopher standeth upon the natural virtues, vices, or passions of man. And follow nature, saith he therein, and thou shalt not err. The lawyer saith what men have determined. The historian, what men have done. The grammarian speaketh only of the rules of speech, and the rhetorician and logician considering what in nature will soonest prove, and persuade, thereon give artificial rules which still are compassed within the circle of a question, according to the proposed manner. The physician weigheth the nature of a man's body and the nature of things helpful or hurtful unto it. And the metaphysic, though it be in the second and abstract notions, and therefore be counted supernatural, yet doth he indeed build upon the depth of nature.

Only the poet, disdaining to be tied to any such subjection, lifted up with the vigor of his own invention, doth grow in effect another nature in making things either better than nature bringeth forth, or quite anew, forms such as never were in nature, as the heroes, demigods, Cyclops, Chimeras, Furies, and such like. So as he goeth hand in hand with nature, not enclosed within the narrow warrant of her gifts, but freely ranging only within the zodiac of his own wit.[33] Nature never set forth the earth in so rich

[32] Throughout this section, Sidney genders nature as feminine and the "arts" as masculine. The relationship between the two reflects the notion (expressed in such official documents as "The Homily on Marriage" [1573]) that men were inherently superior to women. This theory, however, was frequently challenged in both print and reality. On the importance of gender, see Mary Ellen Lamb, "Apologizing for Pleasure in Sidney's *Apology for Poetry*."

[33] Compare *AS* 1, 3 and 6. Sidney's view of poetic freedom contrasts with the excerpt from Vives, *Truth Dressed Up*.

tapestry as divers poets have done, neither with pleasant rivers, fruitful trees, sweet-smelling flowers, nor whatsoever else may make the too-much-loved earth more lovely. Her world is brazen,[34] the poets only deliver a golden.

But let those things alone and go to man, for whom as the other things are, so it seemeth in him her uttermost cunning, and know whether she have brought forth so true a lover as Theagenes, so constant a friend as Pylades, so valiant a man as Orlando, so right a prince as Xenophon's Cyrus, so excellent a man every way as Virgil's Aeneas.[35] Neither let this be jestingly conceived, because the works of the one be essential, the other in imitation or fiction; for any understanding knoweth the skill of each artificer standeth in that *Idea*, or fore-conceit, of the work, and not in the work itself. [36]And that the poet hath that *Idea* is manifest by delivering them forth in such excellency as he hath imagined them, which delivering forth also is not wholly imaginative, as we are wont to say, by them that build castles in the air, but so far substantially it worketh, not only to make a Cyrus, which had been but a particular excellency, as nature might have done, but to bestow a Cyrus upon the world to make many Cyruses, if they will learn aright why and how that maker made him.

Neither let it be deemed too saucy a comparison to balance the highest point of man's wit with the efficacy of nature, but rather give right honor to the heavenly Maker of that maker,

[34] Brass.

[35] Theagenes is the hero of a Greek prose romance, *Theagenes and Chariclea*, by Heliodorus (c. 4th century, A. D.); Pylades is Orestes' friend, and in Aeschylus' *Oresteia*, he helps Orestes avenge the murder of his father, Agamemnon, by his mother, Clytemnestra; Orlando is the hero of Ariosto's epic romance, *Orlando Furioso*, which Sir John Harington was to translate into English in 1591; Xenophon (c. 5th century B. C.), described the education of Cyrus, who founded the Achaemenid Persian Empire, in his *Cyropaedia*. Both Cyrus and Aeneas, the hero of the *Aeneid*, Virgil's epic on Rome's origins, constituted models of virtuous leaders.

[36] For help with this very tricky concept, see A. Leigh DeNeef, *Spenser and the Motives of Metaphor*, ch. 1.

Erected wit / infected wry

who, having made man to His own likeness, set him beyond and over all the works of that second nature. Which in nothing he showeth so much as in poetry, when with the force of a divine breath he bringeth things forth surpassing her doings, with no small argument to the incredulous of that first accursed fall of Adam, since our erected wit maketh us know what perfection is, and yet our infected will keepeth us from reaching unto it.

But these arguments will by few be understood, and by fewer granted. Thus much, I hope, will be given me: that the Greeks with some probability of reason gave him the name above all names of learning.

Now let us go to a more ordinary opening of him, that the truth may be the more palpable, and so I hope, though we get not so unmatched a praise as the etymology of his names will grant, yet his very description, which no man will deny, shall not justly be barred from a principal commendation.

Poesy, therefore, is an art of imitation, for so Aristotle termeth it in this word *mimesis*, that is to say, a representing, counterfeiting, or figuring forth, to speak metaphorically.[37] A speaking picture, with this end—to teach and delight.[38]

Of this have been three general kinds, the chief both in antiquity and excellency were they that did imitate the inconceivable excellencies of God. Such were David in his Psalms, Solomon

---

[37] This definition of poetry as imitating nature differs significantly from Sidney's first view of poetry as independent of and superior to nature. Although this concept is a Renaissance commonplace, it originates in Aristotle's assertion that poetry originated in imitation and is therefore an essentially imitative art (*Poetics* 1448b-1450a). All three sources give different versions of what is modified by "metaphorically: Ponsonby: "or figuring forth to speak metaphorically. A speaking picture . . ."; Olney: "or figuring forth: to speak metaphorically, a speaking picture . . ."; Norwich: "or figuring forth to speak. Metaphorically, a speaking picture . . . ." I am grateful to Anne Lake Prescott for alerting me to these variants.

[38] Horace (65-8 B. C.), contemporary of Virgil, celebrated Roman poet, author of verse essays (*Satires, Epistles,* and the *Art of Poetry*) and lyric poetry (*Odes* and *Epodes*). The notion that poetry should "teach and delight" is a Renaissance commonplace; it originates in Horace's *Ars Poetica* (*The Art of Poetry*): "He has won every vote who has blended profit with pleasure" (l.343).

in his Song of Songs, in his Ecclesiastes, and Proverbs.[39] Moses and Deborah, in their hymns, and the writer of Job, which beside other, the learned Emanuel Tremelius, and Franciscus Junius,[40] do entitle the poetical part of the Scripture, against these none will speak that hath the Holy Ghost in due holy reverence. In this kind, though in a full-wrong divinity, were Orpheus, Amphion, Homer in his hymns, and many other, both Greeks and Romans. And this poesy must be used by whosoever will follow Saint James's counsel in singing Psalms when they are merry,[41] and I know is used with the fruit of comfort by some when, in sorrowful pangs of their death-bringing sins, they find the consolation of the never-leaving goodness.

The second kind is of them that deal with matters philosophical, either moral, as Tyrtaeus, Phocylides, Cato;[42] or natural, as Lucretius, and Virgil's *Georgics*;[43] or astronomical, as Manilius and Pontanus;[44] or historical, as Lucan.[45] Which, who mislike, the fault is in their judgment quite out of taste, and not in the sweet food of sweetly uttered knowledge.

But because this second sort is wrapped within the fold of the proposed subject, and takes not the course of his own invention, whether they properly be poets or no, let grammarians dispute, and go to the third, indeed Right Poets, of whom chiefly this question ariseth. Betwixt whom and these second is such a kind of difference as betwixt the meaner sort of painters, who

---

[39] Solomon was reputed to be the author of these three books of the Hebrew Bible.

[40] Tremelius and Junius together produced a Latin translation of the Bible that was printed in Frankfurt in 1575.

[41] "Is any among you afflicted? Let him pray. Is any merry? Let him sing psalms" (James 5:13).

[42] Dionysus Cato (4th century, A. D.), author of the *Distichs*, an important source of moral lore often used in education.

[43] Lucretius (c. 99-50 B. C.), author of the scientific poem, *De Rerum Natura* (*On the Nature of Things*); Virgil's *Georgics*, ostensibly about farming, also concern politics.

[44] Manilius (1st century, A. D.) wrote the *Astronomica*; Giovanni Pontano (1426-1503) also wrote an astronomical poem, *Urania*.

[45] Lucan (39-65 A. D.), author of the *Pharsalia*, an unfinished republican epic on the Roman civil wars.

counterfeit only such faces as are set before them, and the more excellent, who, having no law but wit, bestow that in colors upon you which is fittest for the eye to see, as the constant though lamenting look of Lucretia, when she punished in her self another's fault,[46] wherein he painted not Lucretia, whom he never saw, but painteth the outward beauty of such a virtue.

For these third be they which most properly do imitate to teach and delight, and to imitate, borrow nothing of what is, hath been, or shall be, but range only reined with learned discretion into the divine consideration of what may be and should be.[47] These be they that as the first and most noble may justly be termed *vates*, so these are waited on in the excellentest languages and best understanding with the fore-described name of poets. For these indeed do merely make to imitate, and imitate both to delight and teach, and delight to move men to take that goodness in hand which, without delight, they would fly as from a stranger, and teach to make them know that goodness whereunto they are moved. Which being the noblest scope to which ever any learning was directed, yet want there not idle tongues to bark at them. [48]

These be subdivided into sundry more special denominations. The most notable be the heroic, lyric, tragic, comic, satiri-

---

[46] Lucretia, a very beautiful Roman wife, was raped by Tarquin, whose father was king of Rome. She committed suicide, even though her husband held her blameless, and her rape led to the expulsion of the ruling Tarquin dynasty and to the Roman hatred of monarchy (Livy, *Early History of Rome*, 1.57-58). Shakespeare versified this story in *The Rape of Lucrece*. On the political importance of this event for Renaissance thought, see Stephanie H. Jed, *Chaste Thinking: The Rape of Lucretia and the Birth of Humanism*.

[47] The Right Poet charts a middle course between ranging "freely" and imitation, between following nature and being independent of nature.

[48] Stephen Gosson, whose *School of Abuse* Sidney sets out to rebut in the *Apology*, gives a remarkably similar definition of poetry's proper function: "The right use of ancient poetry was to have the notable exploits of worthy captains, the wholesome counsels of good fathers, and virtuous lives of predecessors set down in numbers, and sung to the instrument at solemn feasts, that the sound of the one might draw the hearers from kissing the cup too often, the sense of the other put them in mind of things past, and chalk out the way to do the like" (pp. 270-71).

cal, iambic, elegiac, pastoral, and certain others, some of these being termed according to the matter they deal with, some by the sorts of verse they liked best to write in, for indeed, the greatest part of poets have appareled their poetical inventions in that numbrous kind of writing which is called "verse."[49] Indeed but appareled, being but an ornament and no cause to poetry, since there have been many most excellent poets that never versified, and now swarm many versifiers that need never answer to the name of poets.

For Xenophon, who did imitate so excellently as to give us *effigiem justi imperii,* the portraiture of a just empire, under the name of Cyrus, as Cicero saith of him,[50] made therein an absolute heroical poem. So did Heliodorus, in his sugared invention of that picture of love in Theagenes and Chariclea. And yet both these wrote in prose, which I speak to show that it is not rhyming and versing that maketh a poet—no more than a long gown maketh an advocate, who, though he pleaded in armor, should be an advocate and no soldier—but it is that feigning notable images of virtues, vices, or what else, with that delightful teaching, which must be the right describing note to know a poet by. Although indeed the senate of poets hath chosen verse as their fittest rainment, meaning, as in matter, they passed all in all, so in manner to go beyond them, not speaking table-talk fashion, or like men in a dream, words as they chanceably fall from the mouth, but peising[51] each syllable of each word by just proportion, according to the dignity of the subject.

---

[49] The kind of writing that follows meter.

[50] "Only a really great man, gentle by nature and cultivated to the highest pursuits, can so behave himself in a position of such power that those under his rule desire no other person than him. Such a one was Cyrus, as described by Xenophon, not according to historical truth, but as the pattern of a just ruler; in him the philosopher created a matchless blend of firmness and courtesy" (Cicero, *Epistles to His Brother Quintus,* 1.1.23 ff.; *Cicero's Letters to His Friends,* trans. B. R. Shackleton Bailey.

[51] Weighing.

Now therefore it shall not be amiss first to weigh this latter sort of poetry by his works, and then by his parts, and if in neither of these anatomies he be condemnable, I hope we shall obtain a more favorable sentence. This purifying of wit, this enriching of memory, enabling of judgment, and enlarging of conceit, which commonly we call learning, under what name so ever it come forth, or to what immediate end soever it be directed, the final end is to lead and draw us to as high a perfection as our degenerate souls, made worse by their clayey lodging,[52] can be capable of.[53]

This, according to the inclination of man, bred many formed impressions. For some that thought this felicity principally to be gotten by knowledge, and no knowledge to be so high or heavenly as acquaintance with the stars, gave themselves to astronomy. Others, persuading themselves to be demigods if they knew the causes of things, became natural and supernatural philosophers. Some an admirable delight drew to music, and some the certainty of demonstration to the mathematics. But all, one and other, having this scope: to know, and by knowledge to lift up the mind from the dungeon of the body, to the enjoying his own divine essence. But when by the balance of experience it was found that the astronomer looking to the stars might fall in a ditch, that the inquiring philosopher might be blind in himself, and the mathematician might draw forth a straight line with a crooked hand, then lo, did proof, the over-ruler of opinions, make manifest that all these are but serving sciences, which, as they have each a private end in themselves, so yet are they all directed to the highest end of the Mistress Knowledge, by the Greeks called *architectonike*, which stands, as I think, in the knowledge of a

[52] The physical body; Ponsonby has "clay lodging."
[53] Sidney does not say that poetry's final end is to lead and draw us to perfection. Instead, he qualifies his assertion with a highly Calvinist acknowledgment of the limitations on human possibility imposed on us by the Fall.

man's self, in the ethic and politic consideration, with the end of well-doing, and not of well-knowing only. Even as the saddler's next end is to make a good saddle, but his further end, to serve a nobler faculty, which is horsemanship, so the horseman's to soldiery, and the soldier not only to have the skill, but to perform the practice of a soldier.

So, that the ending end of all earthly learning being virtuous action, those skills that most serve to bring forth that have a most just title to be princes over all the rest. Wherein if we can show the poet's nobleness by setting him before his other competitors, among whom as principal challengers step forth the moral philosophers,[54] whom methinks I see coming towards me with a sullen gravity, as though they could not abide vice by daylight, rudely clothed, for to witness outwardly their contempt of outward things, with books in their hands against glory, whereto they set their names, sophistically speaking subtlety, and angry with any man in whom they see the sole fault of anger.[55] These men, casting largess as they go of definitions, divisions, and distinctions, with a scornful interrogative, do soberly ask whether it be possible to find any path so ready to lead a man to virtue as that which teacheth what virtue is, and teacheth it not only by delivering forth his very being, his causes and effects, but also by making known his enemy, vice, which must be destroyed, and his cumbersome servant, passion, which must be mastered, by showing the generalities that containeth it and the specialities that are derived from it. Lastly, by plain setting down how it extends itself out of the limits of a man's own little world to the government of families and maintaining of public societies.

The historian scarcely gives leisure to the moralist to say so much but that he, loaden with old mouse-eaten records, autho-

---

[54] Ponsonby: "Wherein if we can show that poet is worthy to have it before any other competitors, among whom principally to challenge it, step forth moral philosophers ...."
[55] Sidney's humorously dismissive treatment of moral philosophy in the *Apology* contrasts with its importance in the letter to Edward Denny (see pp. 212-13).

rizing himself for the most part upon other histories, whose greatest authorities are built upon the notable foundation of hearsay, having much ado to accord differing writers and to pick truth out of partiality, better acquainted with 1000 years ago than with the present age, and yet better knowing how this world goes than how his own wit runs, curious for antiquities, and inquisitive of novelties, a wonder to young folks and a tyrant in table talk, denieth in a great chafe that any man for teaching of virtue and virtuous actions is comparable to him.[56] I am *testis temporum, lux veritatis, vita memoriae, magistra vitae, nuncia vetustatis.*[57] The philosopher, saith he, teacheth a disputative virtue, but I do an active. His virtue is excellent in the dangerous academy of Plato, but mine showeth forth her honorable face in the battles of Marathon, Pharsalia, Poitiers, and Agincourt.[58] He teacheth virtue by certain abstract considerations, but I only bid you follow the footing of them that have gone before you. Old-aged experience goeth beyond the fine-witted philosopher, but I give the experience of many ages. Lastly, if he make the songbook, I put the learner's hand to the lute, and if he be the guide, I am the light. Then he would allege you innumerable examples, confirming story by stories, how much the wisest senators and princes have been directed by the credit of history, as Brutus, Alphonsus of Aragon,[59] and who not, if need be? At length, the long line of their disputa-

---

[56] Compare Sidney's treatment of history in the letters to Denny and to Robert Sidney.

[57] The full sentence is "And as history, which bears witness to the passing of the ages, sheds light upon reality, gives life to recollection and guidance to human existence, and brings tidings to ancient days, whose voice, but orator's, can entrust her to immortality?" (Cicero, *De Oratore [On Oration]*, 2.9.36). In Olney and Norwich, this line reads, "I am *Lux vitae, temporum magistra, vita memoriae, nuncia vetustatis*, etc."

[58] Famous battles. The Greeks defeated the Persians at Marathon in 490 B. C.; Julius Caesar defeated Pompey at Pharsalia in 48 B. C. (this battle is the subject of Lucan's *Pharsalia*); Edward, the Black Prince, defeated the French at Poitiers in 1356; and at Agincourt in 1415, Henry V's massively outnumbered troops did the same (commemorated in Shakespeare's *Henry V*).

[59] According to Plutarch (1st century A. D.), Brutus was dedicated to "books and literature," so much so that the night before the Battle of Pharsalia (see above), instead of sleeping, he "was busy until evening in making and writing a compend of Polybius"

tion makes a point in this: that the one giveth the precept, and the other the example.

Now whom shall we find, since the question standeth for the highest form in the school of learning, to be moderator? Truly, as me seemeth, the poet, and if not a moderator, even the man that ought to carry the title from them both, and much more from all other serving sciences.[60] Therefore, compare we the poet with the historian and with the moral philosopher, and if he go beyond them both, no other human skill can match him.[61] For as for the divine, with all reverence it is ever to be excepted, not only for having his scope as far beyond any of these, as eternity exceedeth a moment, but even for passing each of these in themselves. And for the lawyer, though *Jus*[62] be the daughter of Justice, and justice the chief of virtues, yet because he seeks to make men good, rather than *formidine poenae* rather than *virtutis amore*;[63] or, to say righter, doth not endeavor to make them good, but that their evil hurt not others, having no care, so he be a good citizen, how bad a man he be. Therefore as our wickedness maketh him necessary, and necessity maketh him honorable, so is he not in the deepest truth to stand in rank with these, who all endeavor to take naughtiness away and plant goodness even in the secretest cabinet of our souls. And these four are all that any way deal in that consideration of men's manners, which, being the supreme knowledge, they that best breed it, deserve the best commendation.

The philosopher, therefore, and the historian, are they which would win the goal, the one by precept, the other by example. But both, not having both, do both halt. For the philosopher

(*Plutarch's Lives*, "Brutus," 4.3). In the preface to his translation of Plutarch (1559-1565), Jacques Amyot writes that after the doctors had given up hope, Alphonsus "determined with himself to take no more medication, but for his recreation caused the story of Quintus Curtius, concerning the deeds of Alexander the Great, to be read before him," and he immediately recovered ("Amyot to the Reader," *Plutarch's Lives of the Grecians and Romans*, trans. Sir Thomas North [New York: AMS Press, 1967], vol. 1, 17-18). Plutarch was a Greek biographer and essayist who ranked among the most popular

setting down with thorny arguments the bare rule, is so hard of utterance and so misty to be conceived that one that hath no other guide but him shall wade in him till he be old before he shall find sufficient cause to be honest. For his knowledge standeth so upon the abstract and general that happy is that man who may understand him, and more happy that can apply what he doth understand. [64] On the other side, the historian, wanting the precept, is so tied, not to what should be, but to what is, to the particular truth of things, and not to the general reason of things, that his example draweth no necessary consequence, and therefore a less fruitful doctrine.

Now doth the peerless poet perform both, for whatsoever the philosopher saith should be done, he giveth a perfect picture of it in someone by whom he presupposeth it was done, so as he coupleth the general notion with the particular example. A perfect picture, I say, for he yieldeth to the powers of the mind an image of that whereof the philosopher bestoweth but a wordish description which doth never strike, pierce, nor possess the sight of the soul so much as that other doth. For as in outward things to a man that had never seen an elephant, or a rhinoceros, who should tell him most exquisitely all their shape, color, bigness, and particular marks? Or of a gorgeous palace, an *architector*,[65] who declaring the full beauties, might well make the hearer able

---

classical authors. His *Lives* and his collection of moral, ethical, religious, political, and literary essays (collectively known as the *Moralia)* were frequently mined for anecdotes and moral examples.

[60] Sidney assumes, as Scaliger does not, the Right Poet must be a man. See the excerpt from Scaliger's *Poetics* in this volume, p. 243.

[61] Sidney will give the opposite evaluation in the Denny letter.

[62] Latin for "law."

[63] "By fear of punishment" rather than "by love of virtue" (Horace, *Epistles* 1.16.52-53); the full passage is "The good hate vice because they love virtue; you [i.e., the slave] will commit no crime because you dread punishment."

[64] In the Denny letter, Sidney will qualify his praise of Aristotle with that admission that he "is something darke and hath need of a logical examination" (p. 212).

[65] Architect.

to repeat, as it were, by rote all he had heard, yet should never satisfy his inward conceit with being witness to itself of a true lively knowledge. But the same man, as soon as he might see those beasts well painted, or the house well in model, should straightways grow without need of any description to a judicial[66] comprehending of them. So, no doubt, the philosopher, with his learned definitions, be it of virtues or vices, matters of public policy or private government, replenisheth the memory with many infallible grounds of wisdom, which notwithstanding lie dark before the imaginative and judging power if they be not illuminated or figured forth by the speaking picture of poesy.

Tully[67] taketh much pains, and many times not without poetical helps, to make us know the force love of our country hath in us. Let us but hear old Anchises speaking in the middest of Troy's flames, or see Ulysses in the fullness of all Calypso's delights bewail his absence from barren and beggarly Ithaca.[68] Anger, the Stoics said, was a short madness— let but Sophocles bring you Ajax on stage, killing and whipping sheep and oxen, thinking them the army of Greeks with their chieftains Agammenon and Menelaus,[69] and tell me if you have not a more familiar insight into anger than finding in the schoolmen his *genus* and difference. See whether wisdom and temperance in Ulysses and Diomedes,[70] friendship in Nisus and Euralus,[71] even to an ignorant man, carry not an apparent shining. And contrarily, the remorse of conscience in Oedipus, the soon-repenting

---

[66] Judicious (the only example of this meaning given in the OED is this sentence).

[67] Cicero. His full name is Marcus Tullius Cicero.

[68] *Aeneid* 2.634-649f.; *Odyssey* 5.149-159.

[69] Sophocles, *Ajax*, l.1061. Sidney probably does not have firsthand knowledge of the play because the action is reported rather than enacted on the stage.

[70] Ulysses was better known for craftiness or wiliness—even sneakiness—than for wisdom (see, for example, Gosson's portrayal of him as a coward in the *School of Abuse*, as well as the highly equivocal character in Shakespeare's T*roilus and Cressida*). Diomedes, "he of the great war-cry" (*Iliad*, 5.114), was known for his ferocity, not temperance.

[71] Devoted friends who died together attacking an enemy camp (*Aeneid*, 9.433-445.).

pride in Agamemnon, the self-devouring cruelty in his father Atreus, the violence of ambition in the two Theban brothers, the sour-sweetness of revenge in Medea,[72] and to fall lower, the Terentian Gnatho,[73] and our Chaucer's Pandar,[74] so expressed, that we now use their names to signify their trades. And finally, all virtues, vices and passions, so in their own natural seats laid to the view that we seem not to hear of them, but clearly to see through them.

But even in the most excellent determination of goodness, what philosopher's counsel can so readily direct a prince as the feigned Cyrus in Xenophon, or a virtuous man in all fortunes as Aeneas in Virgil, or a whole commonwealth, as the way of Sir Thomas More's *Utopia*.[75] I say the way, because where Sir Thomas More erred, it was the fault of the man and not the poet, for that way of patterning a commonwealth was most absolute though he perchance hath not so absolutely performed it.[76] For the question is, whether the feigned image of poetry[77] or the regular in-

---

[72] All references to characters in Greek tragedy: Sophocles, *Oedipus the King*; Aeschylus, *Agamemnon*; the Theban brothers are Polynices and Eteocles; Euripides, *Medea*. Although Sidney clearly read Greek, it is also possible that his knowledge of these tragedies derives from their Latin versions by Seneca, whose works were translated into English between 1559 and 1567.

[73] A character in *The Eunuch* by the Roman comic playwright Terence. The name signified a parasite.

[74] Chaucer, *Troilus and Criseyde*. Pandar, Troilus's uncle, arranged the assignation between the two, ill-fated lovers. Consequently, his name became synonymous with trafficsking in women's bodies.

[75] Ponsonby, Olney, and the Norwich manuscript spell the title "*Eutopia*," which means "happy place," rather than *Utopia* ("no place"), as the word appears on the cover page of the work's first edition. Sidney includes both prose and poetry among his examples, thus further substantiating his earlier statement that verse, or "numbrous" writing, does not in itself equal poetry.

[76] Sidney's inclusion of More as an example of the excellence of poetry raises a delicate issue because the earliest English Protestants, William Tyndale in particular, attacked More as a "poet, without shame." On the early Protestant appropriation of antipoetic sentiment and its continuation through the 1580s, see Herman, *Squitter-wits and Muse-haters*, 34-43.

[77] Ponsonby has "poetry," but the copyist of the Norwich manuscript first writes "Poett," strikes it out, and then writes "Poesy."

struction of philosophy hath the more force in teaching. Wherein if the philosophers have more rightly showed themselves philosophers than the poets have attained to the high top of their profession, as in truth,

> *mediocribus esse poetis*
> *non Dii , non homines, non concessere columnae,*[78]

it is, I say again, not the fault of the art, but that by few men that art can be accomplished.

Certainly, even our Savior Christ could as well have given the moral commonplaces of uncharitableness and humbleness as the divine narration of Dives and Lazarus,[79] or of disobedience and mercy, as that heavenly discourse of the lost child and the gracious father,[80] but that His through searching wisdom knew the estate of Dives burning in hell, and of Lazarus being in Abraham's bosom, would more constantly, as it were, inhabit both the memory and judgment. Truly, for my self, me seems, I see before mine eyes the lost child's disdainful prodigality turned to envy a swine's dinner, which by the learned divines are thought not historical acts, but instructing parables.

For conclusion, I say the philosopher teacheth, but he teacheth obscurely, so as the learned only can understand him; that is to say, he teacheth them that are already taught. But the poet is the food for the tenderest stomachs, the poet is indeed the right popular philosopher. Whereof Aesop's tales give good proof, whose pretty allegories, stealing under the formal tales of beasts, makes many more beastly than beasts begin to hear the sound of virtue from these dumb speakers.[81]

---

[78] "But that poets be of middling rank, neither men nor gods nor booksellers ever brooked" Horace, *Ars Poetica*, 372-373.
[79] Luke 16:20-31.
[80] The Parable of the Prodigal Son; Luke 15:11-31.
[81] Starting with William Caxton's *Fables of Aesop* (1484), Aesop's fables were frequently reprinted in England both as moral tales and as an introduction to the study of Greek.

But now it may be alleged that if this imagining of matters be so fit for the imagination, then must the historian needs surpass, who brings you images of true matters such as indeed were done, and not such as fantastically or falsely may be suggested to have been done.[82] Truly Aristotle himself, in his discourse of poesy, plainly determineth this question, saying that poetry is *philosophoteron* and *spoudaioteron*, that is to say, it is more philosophical and more studiously serious than history. His reason is because poesy dealeth with *katholou*, that is to say, with the universal consideration, and the history with *kath hekaston*, the particular. Now, saith he, the universal weighs what is fit to be said or done, either in likelihood or necessity, which the poesy considereth in his imposed names, and the particular only marketh whether Alcibiades did or suffered this or that.[83] Thus far Aristotle, which reason of his, as all his, is most full of reason.

For indeed, if the question were whether it were better to have a particular act truly or falsely set down, there is no doubt which is to be chosen, no more than whether you had rather have Vespasian's picture right as he was, or at the painter's pleasure nothing resembling. But if the question be for your own use and learning, whether it be better to have it set down as it should be or as it was, then certainly is more doctrinable the feigned Cyrus in Xenophon than the true Cyrus in Justin,[84] and the feigned Aeneas in Virgil than the right Aeneas in Dares Phrygius.[85] As to

---

[82] As with moral philosophy, Sidney will give history a very different evaluation in the Denny letter.

[83] *Poetics* 1451b. Sidney's citations of the *Poetics* is unusual, since this text was not yet well-known in England.

[84] A 3rd A. D. biography of Cyrus, translated into English in 1564, that is both shorter than Xenophon's and much more critical of its subject. Even though Sidney prefers Xenophon over Justin, he nonetheless recommends the latter to Edward Denny (see the letter, p. 214).

[85] A very influential account of the Trojan War, supposedly authored by a soldier mentioned in the *Iliad* 5.9 and believed by many to be genuine history. The work was actually composed in the 5th century A. D.

a lady that desired to fashion her countenance to the best grace, a painter should more benefit her to portrait a most sweet face, writing Canidia upon it, than to paint Canidia as she was, who, Horace sweareth, she was foul and ill-favored.[86]

If the poet do his part aright, he will show you in Tantalus, Atreus, and such like, nothing that is not to be shunned, in Cyrus, Aeneas, Ulysses, each thing to be followed. Where the historian, bound to tell things as things were, cannot be liberal, without he will be poetical of a perfect pattern, but as in Alexander or Scipio himself, show doings, some to be liked, some to be misliked, and then how will you discern what to follow, but by your own discretion, which you had without reading Quintus Curtius?[87] And whereas, a man may say, though in universal consideration of doctrine, the poet prevaileth, yet that the history,[88] in his saying such a thing was done, doth warrant a man more in that he shall follow. The answer is manifest that if he stand upon that was, as if he should argue because it rained yesterday, therefore it should rain today, then indeed hath it some advantage to a gross conceit. But if he know an example only informs a conjectured likelihood, and so go by reason, the poet doth so far exceed him as he is to frame his example to that which is most reasonable, be it in warlike, politic, or private matters, where the historian in his bare "was" hath many times that which we call fortune to overrule the best wisdom. Many times he must tell events whereof he can yield no cause, or if he do, it must be poetically.[89]

For that a feigned example hath as much force to teach as a true example, for as for to move, it is clear, since the feigned may

[86] Horace, *Epodes*, 5. Ponsonby: ". . . she was full ill-favored"; Norwich: "she was who Horace sweareth was full of ill favored."

[87] Quintus Curtius (2nd-3rd century A. D.), author of a ten volume biography of Alexander. Although Sidney here seems dismissive of Quintus Curtius, in the Denny letter he includes him among the recommended historians.

[88] The historian.

[89] Compare his letter to Robert, in which Sidney will write that "The historian makes himself a discourser for profit, and an orator, yea, a poet, sometimes, for ornament" (p. 217).

be tuned to the highest key of passion, let us take one example wherein an historian and a poet did concur. Herodotus and Justin do both testify that Zopirus, King Darius' faithful servant, seeing his master long resisted by the rebellious Babylonians, feigned himself in extreme disgrace of his king, for verifying of which, he caused his own nose and ears to be cut off, and so flying to the Babylonians was received and for his known valor so far credited that he did find means to deliver them over to Darius. Much like matter doth Livy record of Tarquinnius and his son.[90] Xenophon excellently feigneth such another stratagem performed by Abradates in Cyrus's behalf.[91] Now would I fain know if occasion be presented unto you to serve your prince by such an honest dissimulation, why you do not as well learn it of Xenophon's fiction as of the other's verity, and truly so much the better, as you shall save your nose by the bargain. For Abradates did not counterfeit so far. So then, the best of the historian is subject to the poet, for whatsoever action or faction, whatsoever counsel policy, or war stratagem, the historian is bound to recite, that may the poet, if he list, with his imitation make his own, beautifying it both for further teaching and more delighting, as it please him, having all from Dante his heaven to his hell under the authority of his pen. Which if I be asked what poets have done so, as I might well name some, so yet say I, and say again, I speak of the art and not of the artificer.[92]

Now, to that which commonly is attributed to the praise of history, in respect of the notable learning is got by marking the success, as though therein a man should see virtue exalted and vice punished. Truly, that commendation is peculiar to poetry, and far off from history, for indeed poetry ever sets virtue so out

---

[90] Livy, *Early History of Rome*, 1.3-4. The Tarquins, however, were archetypal tyrants.

[91] *Cyropaedia*, 6.1.39. The anecdote, however, concerns Araspas, not Abradates.

[92] Sidney's refusal to name a Right Poet in a text otherwise filled with examples underscores the Platonic nature of his argument (he is describing the Ideal Poet, not an actual poet), but it also contradicts his later statement that "it is not *gnosis* but *praxis* must be the fruit" (p. 83).

in her best colors, making Fortune her well-waiting handmaid that one must be enamored of her. Well may you see Ulysses in a storm and in other hard plights, but they are but exercises of patience and magnanimity to make them shine the more in the near-following prosperity. And of the contrary part, if evil men come to the stage, they ever go out, as the tragedy writer answered to one that misliked such persons, so manacled as they little animate folks to follow them.[93]

But the historian,[94] being captived to the truth of a foolish world, is many times a terror from well-doing, and an encouragement to unbridled wickedness. For see we not valiant Miltiades rot in his fetters?[95] The just Phocion and the accomplished Socrates put to death like traitors?[96] The cruel Severus live prosperously?[97] The excellent Severus miserably murdered?[98] Sylla and Marius dying in their beds?[99] Pompey and Cicero slain then, when they would have thought exile a happiness?[100] See we not virtuous Cato driven to kill himself,[101] and rebel Caesar[102] so ad-

---

[93] Although the precise reference here is to Euripides' comment that he did not take Ixion from the stage until he was punished by being tied to a wheel, this charge is generally present in antipoetic and antitheatrical tracts. Also, Sidney's assertion that in tragedy evil persons are *always* punished jars against his earlier reference to Medea, who revenged herself on Jason by murdering their children and who, at the play's end, leaves by way of a dragon provided by the gods.

[94] Both Ponsonby and Norwich read "the history . . . ."

[95] Athenian general who, despite his winning the Battle of Marathon, was imprisoned by his own people.

[96] Another Athenian general who was condemned for his political views. Plutarch compared his death to Socrates' in the *Life of Phocion* (38.2).

[97] The emperor Lucius Septimus Severus (193-211 A. D.), who died while invading Britain.

[98] The Roman emperor Alexander Severus (222-235 A. D.), was killed by his own troops.

[99] Caius Marius (138-78 B. C.) and Lucius Sulla (157-86 B. C.), Roman generals who engaged in a long and bloody rivalry.

[100] Pompey (106-48 B. C.), defeated by Caesar at Pharsalia; Cicero (106-43 B. C.), famous Roman rhetorician and republican, killed by order of Mark Antony in 43 B. C.

[101] Cato (95-46 B. C.), a Roman aristocratic who also opposed Julius Caesar at Pharsalia, was eventually driven to suicide.

[102] Julius Caesar, whose defeat of Mark Antony and Pompey signaled the end of Roman republicanism. Shakespeare's *Julius Caesar* exemplifies his ambivalent reputation in Elizabethan England.

vanced that his name, yet after 1600 years, lasteth in the highest honor? And mark but even Caesar's own words of the forenamed Sylla, who, in that only did honestly, to put down his dishonest tyranny, *litteras nescivit*,[103] as if want of learning caused him to do well. He meant it not by poetry, which, not content with earthly plagues, deviseth new punishments in hell for tyrants; nor yet by philosophy, which teacheth *occidendos esse*;[104] but no doubt by skill in history, for that indeed can afford you Cypselus, Periander, Phalaris, Dionysus,[105] and I know not how many more of the same kennel, that speed well enough in their abominable injustice of usurpation.

I conclude therefore that he[106] excelleth history, not only in furnishing the mind with knowledge, but in setting it forward to that which deserves to be called and accounted good, which setting forward and moving to well-doing indeed setteth the laurel crown upon the poets as victorious, not only of the historian, but over the philosopher, howsoever in teaching it may be questionable. For suppose it be granted that which I suppose with great reason may be denied, that the philosopher, in respect of his methodical proceeding, teach more perfectly than poet, yet do I think that no man is so much *philophilosophos*[107] as to compare the philosopher in moving with the poet. And that moving is of a higher degree than teaching, it may by this appear, that it is well nigh the cause and the effect of teaching. For who will be

---

[103] Lucius Sylla (138-78 B. C.), Roman dictator; "He was ignorant of letters" (Suetonius, *Life of Caesar*, ch. 77).

[104] "They are to be killed."

[105] Cypselus and his son, Periander, ruled Corinth in the 7th century B. C. According to Herodotus, Cypselus ruled for 30 years and died "in good fortune," leaving the realm to his son, who quickly became even more brutal than his father (5.92). Phalaris, a tyrant in Sicily, 6th century B. C., is known for roasting his victims in a brass bull; Dionysus (5th century B. C.), ruled Syracuse as a tyrant for 38 years. All are tyrants who remained in power despite their crimes.

[106] The poet.

[107] A lover of philosophy.

taught, if he be not moved with desire to be taught? And what so much good doth that teaching bring forth—I speak still of moral doctrine—as that it moveth one to do that which it doth teach. For, as Aristotle saith, it is not *gnosis* but *praxis*[108] must be the fruit, and how *praxis* can be without being moved to practice, it is no hard matter to consider.

The philospher showeth you the way, he informeth you of the particularities, as well of the tediousness, of the way, as of the pleasant lodging you shall have when your journey is ended, as of the many by-turnings that may divert you from your way. But this is to no man but to him that will read him, and read him with attentive studious painfulness, which constant desire, whosoever hath in him, hath already past half the hardness of the way, and therefore is beholding to the philosopher but for the other half. Nay, truly learned men have learnedly thought that where once reason hath so much overmastered passion as that the mind hath a free desire to do well, the inward light each mind hath in itself is as good as a philosopher's book, since in nature, we know, it is well to do well, and what is well and what is evil, although not in the words of art which philosophers bestow upon us, for out of natural conceit the philosophers drew it. But to be moved to do that which we know, or to be moved with desire to know, *Hoc opus, hic labor est.*[109]

Now therein of all sciences (I speak still of human,[110] and according to the human conceit) is our poet the monarch. For he doth not only show the way, but giveth so sweet a prospect into the way as will entice any man to enter into it. Nay, he doth as if

[108] Theory, practice.

[109] "This is the task, this is the toil" (Virgil, *Aeneid*, 6.129). The Sybil says this line to Aeneas to describe the difficulty of returning from the underworld.

[110] Earlier, Sidney excludes divinity from his discussion because it is obviously superior to even poetry: " For as for the divine, with all reverence it is ever to be excepted, not only for having his scope as far beyond any of these, as eternity exceedeth a moment, but even for passing each of these in themselves" (p. 73).

your journey should lie through a fair vineyard, at the very first, give you a cluster of grapes that, full of that taste, you may long to pass further. He beginneth not with obscure definitions, which must blur the margent[111] with interpretations and load the memory with doubtfulness, but he cometh to you with words set in delightful proportion, either accompanied with or prepared for the well-enchanting skill of music, and with a tale, forsooth, he cometh unto you, with a tale which holdeth children from play and old men from the chimney corner, and pretending no more, doth intend the winning of the mind from wickedness to virtue, even as the child is often brought to take most wholesome things by hiding them in such other as have a pleasant taste, which, if one should begin to tell them the nature of the *aloes* or *rhubarbarum*[112] they should receive, would sooner take their physic at their ears than at their mouth. So is it in men (most of which are childish in the best things 'til they be cradled in their graves), glad they will be to hear the tales of Hercules, Achilles, Cyrus, Aeneas, and, hearing them, must needs hear the right description of wisdom, valor, and justice, which if they had been barely, that is to say, philosophically, set out, they would swear they be brought to school again.

That imitation whereof poetry is hath the most conveniency to nature of all other, insomuch that, as Aristotle saith, those things which in themselves are horrible, as cruel battles, unnatural monsters, are made in poetical imitation delightful. Truly I have known men that even with reading *Amadis de Gaul*, which, God knoweth, wanteth much of a perfect poesy, have found their hearts moved to the exercise of courtesy, liberality, and especially courage.[113] Who readeth Aeneas carrying old Anchises on his back

---

[111] Margin.

[112] Aloe and rhubarb, that is, bitter medicines; rhubarb in particular was known as a purgative. Compare *AS* 14, in which Sidney complains of the effect his friend's "rhubarb words" have on him.

[113] A Spanish chivalric romance translated into French in 1540.

that wisheth not it were his fortune to perform so excellent an
act? Whom doth not those words of Turnus move, the tale of
Turnus having planted his image in the imagination,

> *fugientem haec terra videbit?*
> *Usque adeone mori miserum est?*[114]

Where the philosophers, as they scorn to delight, so must they be
content little to move; saving wrangling whether *virtus* be the
chief or the only good, whether the contemplative or the active
life do excel, which Plato and Boethius well knew and therefore
made mistress Philosophy very often borrow the masking rai-
ment of poesy. [115]   For even those hard-hearted evil men who
think virtue a school name and know no other good but *indulgere
genio*,[116] and therefore despise the austere admonitions of the
philosopher, and feel not the inward reason they stand upon, yet
will be content to be delighted, which is all the good fellow poet
seems to promise, and so steal to see the form of goodness—
which seen, they cannot but love—ere themselves be aware, as if
they took a medicine of cherries.

Infinite proofs of the strange effects of this poetical invention
might be alleged, only two shall serve, which are so often remem-
bered as I think all men shall know them. The one of Menenius
Agrippa, who when the whole people of Rome had resolutely
divided themselves from the Senate, with apparent show of utter
ruin, though he were for that time an excellent orator, came not
among them upon trust of figurative speeches or cunning insinu-

---

[114] "Shall I turn my back, and shall this land see Turnus in flight? / Is it such a terrible
thing to die?" (Virgil, *Aeneid*, 12.645-646).

[115] The masking robes of poetry. Both Plato and Boethius are problematic references for
Sidney; the former, because of his well-known antipathy towards poetry (see the ex-
cerpts in this volume); and the latter because while *The Consolation of Philosophy* alter-
nates between prose and verse, at the beginning Lady Philosophy banishes the Muses of
poetry: "These are the very women who kill the rich and fruitful harvest of Reason with
the barren thorns of passion. They habituate men to their sickness of mind instead of
curing them" (bk. 1; prose 1, ll. 28-35)

[116] "Indulge your desires" (Persius, *Satires*, 5.151).

ations, and much less with far-fet[117] maxims of philosophy, which, especially if they were Platonic, they must have learned geometry before they could well have conceived. But forsooth, he behaveth himself like a homely and familiar poet. He telleth them a tale, that there was a time when all the parts of the body made a mutinous conspiracy against the belly, which they thought devoured the fruits of each other's labor, they concluded they would let so unprofitable a spender starve. In the end, to be short, for the tale is notorious, and as notorious that it was a tale, with punishing the belly they plagued themselves. This applied by him, wrought such effect in the people as I never read that only words brought forth, but then so sudden and so good an alteration, for upon reasonable conditions a perfect reconcilement ensued.[118]

The other is of Nathan the prophet, who, when the holy David had so far forsaken God as to confirm adultery with murder, when he was to do the tenderest office of a friend in laying his own shame before his eyes, sent by God to call again so chosen a servant, how doth he it? But by telling of a man whose beloved lamb was ungratefully taken from his bosom. The application most divinely true, but the discourse itself feigned, which made David (I speak of the second and instrumental cause) as in a glass see his own filthiness, as that heavenly psalm of mercy well testifieth.[119]

By these, therefore, examples and reasons, I think it may be manifest that the poet with that same hand of delight, doth draw

---

[117] Far-fetched.

[118] This parable is often used as a justification for monarchy, but it should be noted that the body rebels against the stomach, not the head, and that peace ensues after both sides accept "reasonable conditions." On Sidney's republican sympathies, see Blair Worden, *The Sound of Virtue: Philip Sidney's "Arcadia" and Elizabethan Politics*.

[119] II Samuel 12:1-14, and the "heavenly psalm of mercy" is Psalm 51. However, Sidney omits that while God forgives David (at least, he will not kill him), nonetheless, "because by this deed thou hast given great occasion to the enemies of the Lord to blaspheme, the child also that is born unto thee shall surely die" (II Samuel 15; King James translation). The story is not one of mercy and forgiveness, but of the father's sin being visited upon the son.

the mind more effectually than any other art doth. And so a con-
clusion not unfitly ensue, that as virtue is the most excellent rest-
ing place for all worldly learning to make his end of, so poetry,
being the most familiar to teach it, and most princely to move
towards it, in the most excellent work is the most excellent work-
man. But I am content not only to decipher him by his works,
although works in commendation and dispraise must ever hold a
high authority, but more narrowly will examine his parts, so that,
as in a man, though altogether may carry a presence full of maj-
esty and beauty, perchance in some one defectious[120] piece we
may find blemish.

Now in his parts, kinds, or species, as you list to term them,
it is to be noted that some poesies have coupled together two or
three kinds, as the tragical and comical, whereupon is risen the
tragicomical; some in the manner have mingled prose and verse,
as Sannazaro[121] and Boethius; some have mingled matters heroical
and pastoral. But that cometh all to one in this question, for if
severed they be good, the conjunction cannot be hurtful.[122] There-
fore, perchance forgetting some, and leaving some as needless to
be remembered, it shall not be amiss, in a word, to cite the special
kinds, to see what faults may be found in the right use of them.

Is it then the pastoral poem which is misliked? For perchance
where the hedge is lowest they will soonest leap over, is the poor
pipe disdained, which, sometimes out of Meliboeus's mouth, can
show the misery of people under hard lords or ravening soldiers?[123]

---

[120] Defective.

[121] Jacapo Sannazzaro (1458-1530), author of the *Arcadia*, a pastoral romance that com-
bines prose with verse eclogues.

[122] Later on in the *Apology*, Sidney will explicitly condemn the mingling of generic cat-
egories, calling tragicomedy, for example, a "mongrel" genre (see p. 116).

[123] Sidney refers to Virgil's eclogues, which, far from depicting an apolitical and idlyllic
world of shepherds and shepherdesses, directly comment on the effects of Caesar's dis-
placement of farmers, among other themes. George Puttenham asserts that pastoral
poetry was invented "not of purpose to counterfeit or represent the rustical manner of
lives and communication, but under the veil of homely persons, and in rude speeches,

And again by Tityrus,[124] what blessedness is derived to them that lie lowest from the goodness of them that sit highest? Sometimes under the pretty tales of wolves and sheep can include the whole considerations of wrong-doing and patience, sometimes show that contentions for trifles can get but a trifling victory, where perchance a man may see that even Alexander and Darius, when they strave[125] who should be cock of this world's dunghill, the benefit they got was that the after-livers may say:

> *Haec memini et victum frustra contendere Thyrsin.*
> *Ex illo Corydon, Corydon est tempore nobis*[126]

Or is it the lamenting elegiac, which in a kind heart would move rather pity than blame, who bewails with the great philosopher Heraclitus the weakness of mankind and the wretchedness of the world, who surely is to be praised either for compassionate accompanying just causes of lamentations or for rightly painting out how weak be the passions of woefulness? Is it the bitter but wholesome iambic,[127] who rubs the galled mind in making shame the trumpet of villainy with bold and open crying out against naughtiness? Or the satiric, who,

> *Omne vafer vitium ridenti tangit amico,*[128]

who sportingly never leaveth till he make a man laugh at folly, and, at length ashamed, to laugh at himself, which he cannot avoid without avoiding the folly? Who, while

---

to insinuate and glance at greater matters and such as perchance had not been safe to have been disclosed in any other sort," and he uses Virgil's eclogues as his example (*The Art of English Poesy*, 1.18).

[124] One of the speakers in Virgil's *Eclogues*, often understood in the Renaissance as a figure for Virgil himself.

[125] Strived.

[126] "This I remember, and how Thyrsis, vanquished, strove in vain. From that day it is Corydon, Corydon with us " (Virgil, *Eclogues*, 7. 69-70).

[127] In the *Poetics*, Aristotle associates iambic verse with satire (1448b). The verse is "wholesome" because it is morally instructive.

[128] "The rascal probes his laughing friend's every fault" (adapted from Persius, *Satires*, 1.116-17).

circum praecordia ludit,[129]

giveth us to feel how many headaches a passionate life bringeth us to? How, when all is done,

Est Ulubris animus si nos non deficit aequus?[130]

No, perchance it is the comic, whom naughty playmakers and stagekeepers have justly made odious.[131] To the argument of abuse,[132] I will after answer, only thus much now is to be said, that the comedy is an imitation of the common errors of our life, which he presenteth in the most ridiculous and scornful sort that may be so as it is impossible that any beholder can be content to be such a one. Now, as in geometry, the oblique must be known as well as the right, and in arithmetic, the odd as well as the even: so in the actions of our life, who seeth not the filthiness of evil, wanteth a great foil to perceive the beauty of virtue. This doth the comedy handle so in our private and domestical matters, as with hearing it, we get, as it were, an experience what is to looked for of a niggardly Demea, of a crafty Davus, of a flattering Gnatho, of a vainglorious Thraso,[133] and not only to know what effects are to be expected, but to know who be such by the signifying badge given them by the comedian. And little reason hath any man to say that men learn the evil by seeing it so set out,[134] since, as I said before, there is no man living but by the force truth hath in nature, no sooner seeth these men their parts but wisheth them in *pistrinum*,[135] although perchance the lack of his own faults lie so hidden behind his back that he seeth not himself to dance the

---

[129] "He plays around the heart" (Persius, *Satires*, 1.117).

[130] "[What you are seeking is here]; it is at Ulubrae, if a calm mind does not fail us" (Horace, *Epistles*, 1.11.30, editor's translation). The original line is "if a calm mind does not fail *you* [*te*]."

[131] Sidney agrees with Gosson and the other attackers of the stage in his evaluation of contemporary drama.

[132] Possibly a direct allusion to Gosson's *The School of Abuse*.

[133] All four are stock characters in the comedies of the Roman playwright Terence.

[134] A key charge against both poetry and the stage.

[135] Prison; literally, the mill in which recalcitrant slaves were punished by hard labor.

same measure, whereto yet nothing can more open his eyes than to find his own actions contemptibly set forth.

So that the right use of comedy will, I think, by nobody be blamed, and much less the high and excellent tragedy that openeth great wounds and showeth forth the ulcers that are covered with tissue, that maketh kings fear to be tyrants, and tyrants manifest their tyrannical humors, that with stirring the affects of admiration and commiseration teacheth the uncertainty of this world, and upon how weak foundations gilden roofs are builded, that maketh us know

> *Qui sceptra saevus duro imperio regit,*
> *Timet timentes, metus in auctorem redit.*[136]

But how much it can move, Plutarch yieldeth a notable testimony of the abominable tyrant Alexander Pheraus, from whose eyes a tragedy well-made and represented drew abundance of tears, who without all pity had murdered infinite numbers, and some of his own blood, so as he that was not ashamed to make matters for tragedies, yet could not resist the sweet violence of a tragedy. And if it wrought no further good in him, it was that he in despite of himself withdrew himself from harkening to that which might mollify his hardened heart.[137] But it is not the tragedy they do mislike, for it were too absurd to cast out so excellent a representation of whatsoever is most worthy to be learned.[138]

---

[136] "Who harshly wields the scepter with tyrannic sway, fears those who fear, terror recoils upon its author's head" (Seneca, *Oedipus*, ll. 705-06).

[137] "Once when he was seeing a tragedian act the *Trojan Women* of Euripides, he left the theater abruptly, and sent a message to the actor bidding him be of good courage and not put forth any less effort because of his departure, for it was not out of contempt for his acting that he had gone away, but because he was ashamed to have citizens see him, who had never taken pity on any man that he had murdered, weeping over the sorrows of Hecuba and Andromache" (Plutarch, *Life of Pelopidas*, 39.5-6). Plutarch, however, does not say that the tyrant changed his ways.

[138] Sidney is being deliberately disingenuous here, for both Plato and Gosson include tragedy in their condemnations of poetry. For Plato, see the excerpt from the *Republic*, bk. 10, pp. 220-23; for Gosson, see the excerpt from *The School of Abuse*, pp. 263-72.

Is it the lyric that most displeaseth, who with his tuned lyre and well-accorded voice, gives praise, the reward of virtue, to virtuous acts? Who giveth moral precepts and natural problems,[139] who sometime raiseth up his voice to the height of the heavens in singing the lauds[140] of the immortal God? Certainly, I must confess mine own barbarousness, I never heard the old song of Percy and Douglas[141] that I found not my heart moved more than with a trumpet, and yet is it sung by some blind crowder[142] with no rougher voice than rude style, which, being so evil appareled in the dust and cobwebs of that uncivil age, what would it work trimmed in the gorgeous eloquence of Pindar?[143] In Hungary, I have seen it the manner at all feasts and other suchlike meetings to have songs of their ancestors' valor, which that right soldier-like nation think one of the chiefest kindlers of brave courage. The incomparable Lacedemonians[144] did not only carry that kind of music ever with them to the field, but even at home, as such songs were made, so were they all content to be singers of them, when the lusty men were to tell what they did, the old men what they had done, and the young what they would do. And where a man may say that Pindar many times praiseth highly victories of small moment, matters rather of sport than virtue, as it may be answered it was the fault of the poet and not of the poetry, so indeed the chief fault was in the time and custom of the Greeks, who set those toys at so high a price, that Philip of Macedon reckoned a horserace won at Olympus among his three fearful

---

[139] These are questions for discussion, a favorite trope of Petrarchan poets. See *AS* 3.

[140] Praises.

[141] The antagonists of *The Ballad of Chevy Chase.*

[142] A crowd is a Celtic stringed instrument, often mentioned in conjunction with a harp.

[143] Pindar (c. 518-438 B. C.), Greek lyric poet who composed odes in the high style, mainly about heroes such as Hercules and athletes. In *AS* 3, Sidney compares his own method of composing poetry with "Pindar's apes," among others.

[144] The Spartans.

felicities.[145] But as the unimitable Pindar often did, so is that kind most capable and most fit to awake the thought from the sleep of idleness to embrace honorable enterprises.

There rests the heroical, whose very name, I think, should daunt all backbiters. For by what conceit can a tongue be directed to speak evil of that which draweth with him no less champions than Achilles, Cyrus, Aeneas, Turnus, Tydeus, and Rinaldo?[146]—who doth not only teach and move to a truth, but teacheth and moveth to the most high and excellent truth; who maketh magnanimity and justice shine through all misty fearfulness and foggy desires; who, if the saying of Plato and Tully be true, that who could see virtue would be wonderfully ravished with the love of her beauty. This man sets her out to make her more lovely in her holiday apparel to the eye of any that will deign not to disdain until they understand. But if anything be already said in the defense of sweet poetry, all concurreth to the maintaining the heroical, which is not only a kind, but the best and most accomplished kind of poetry. For as the image of each action stirreth and instructeth the mind, so the lofty image of such worthies most inflameth the mind with desire to be worthy, and informs with counsel how to be worthy.

Only let Aeneas be worn in the tablet of your memory, how he governeth himself in the ruin of his country, in the preserving his old father and carrying away his religious ceremonies,[147] in obeying God's commandment to leave Dido,[148] though not only all passionate kindness, but even the human consideration of virtuous gratefulness would have craved other of him, how in storms,

---

[145] The father of Alexander the Great. According to Plutarch, Philip received news of his son's birth, a victory in battle, and a winner at the race track in Olympus on the same day (*Life of Alexander*, 3.4-5).

[146] In order, these heroes appear in Homer's *Iliad*, Xenophon's *Cyropaedia*, Virgil's *Aeneid*, Statius' *Thebaid*, and Ariosto's *Orlando Furioso*.

[147] *Aeneid* 2.705-20.

[148] Not the Christian God, but Jupiter (*Aeneid*, 4.23-34); Olney prints "the gods" instead of God.

how in sports, how in war, how in peace, how a fugitive, how
victorious, how besieged, how besieging, how to strangers, how
to allies, how to enemies, how to his own. Lastly, how in his
inward self, and how in his outward government, and I think in
a mind not prejudiced with a prejudicating humor, he will be
found in excellency fruitful. Yea, as even Horace saith,

melius Chrysippo et Crantore.[149]

But truly I imagine it falleth out with these poet-whippers as
with some good women who are often sick, but in faith, they
cannot tell where.[150] So the name of poetry is odious to them,
but neither his cause nor effects, neither the sum that contains
him nor the particularities descending from him, give any fast
handle to their carping dispraise.

Since then poetry is of all human learnings the most ancient,
and of most fatherly antiquity, as from whence other learnings
have taken their beginnings, since it is so universal that no learned
nation doth despise it, nor barbarous nation is without it, since
both Roman and Greek gave such divine names unto it, the one
of prophesying, the other of making, and that indeed that name
of making is fit for him, considering that where all other arts
retain themselves within their subject and receive, as it were, their
being from it. The poet only bringeth his own stuff, and doth
not learn a conceit out of a matter, but maketh matter for a con-
ceit. Since neither his description nor end containing any evil,
the thing described cannot be evil, since his effects be so good as
to teach goodness, and to delight the learners, since therein
(namely in moral doctrine, the chief of all knowledges) he doth
not only far pass the historian, but for instructing is well-nigh
comparable to the philosopher, for moving, leaveth him behind

---

[149] "Better than Chrysippus and Crantor" (*Epistles*, 1.2.4). Chrysippus was an early Greek
Stoic philosopher, Crantor a Platonist. Sidney's point, and Horace's, is that the poet
teaches virtue better than either of these philosophers.

[150] Sidney turns to rebut the charges of the Muse-haters and Stephen Gosson in particu-
lar. On Sidney and Gosson, see Herman, *Squitter-wits and Muse-haters*, 84-93.

him. Since the Holy Scripture, wherein there is no uncleanness, hath whole parts in it poetical, and that even our Savior, Christ, vouchsafed to use the flowers of it, since all his kinds are not only in their united forms, but in their severed dissections, fully commendable, I think (and think I think rightly) the laurel crown appointed for triumphant captains doth worthily of all other learnings honor the poet's triumph.[151]   But because we have ears as well as tongues, and that the lightest reasons that may be will seem to weigh greatly if nothing be put in the counter-balance, let us hear, and, as well as we can, ponder what objections be made against this art, which may be worthy either of yielding or answering.

First, truly I note, not only in these *mysomousoi*,[152] poet-haters, but in all that kind of people who seek a praise by dispraising others, that they do prodigally spend a great many wandering words in quips and scoffs, carping and taunting at each thing, which by stirring the spleen, may stay the brain from a thorough beholding the worthiness of the subject. Those kind of objections, as they are full of a very idle easiness, since there is nothing of so sacred a majesty but that an itching tongue may rub itself upon it, so deserve they no other answer, but, instead of laughing at the jest, to laugh at the jester. We know a playing wit can praise the discretion of an ass, the comfortableness of being in debt, and the jolly commodities of being sick of the plague.[153] So of the contrary side, if we will turn Ovid's verse,

Ut lateat virtus, proximitate malis,[154]

---

[151] Rhetorically powerful and convincing as this passage may be, the reader should keep in mind Pugliano's earlier, equally high-flown praise of horsemanship, as well as Sidney's stated intention to praise poetry just as Pugliano praised horsemanship. As Sidney puts it at the start of the *Apology*, the problem is that "self-love is better than any gilding to make that seem gorgeous wherein ourselves be parties" (pp. 56-57).

[152] Literally, "Muse-haters."

[153] Sidney refers here to the genre of the paradoxical encomium, rhetorical exercises in which the rhetor praises something conventionally thought unworthy of praise. See Rosalie L. Colie, *Paradoxia Epidemica: The Renaissance Tradition of Paradox*.

that good lie hid in nearness of the evil, Agrippa will be as merry in showing the vanity of science as Erasmus was in the commending of folly,[155] neither shall any man or matter escape some touch of these smiling railers. But for Erasmus and Agrippa, they had another foundation than the superficial part would promise. Marry, these other pleasant fault-finders, who will correct the verb before they understand the noun and confute other's knowledge before they confirm their own, I would have them only remember that scoffing cometh not of wisdom, so as the best title in true English they get with their merriments is to be called good fools, for so have our grave forefathers ever termed that humorous kind of jesters.

But that which giveth greatest scope to their scorning humor is rhyming and versing.[156] It is already said (and as I think, truly said), it is not rhyming and versing that maketh poesy. One may be a poet without versing and a versifier without poetry. But yet presuppose it were inseparable, as indeed it seemeth Scaliger judgeth truly,[157] it were an inseparable commendation. For if *oratio*, next to *ratio*, speech next to reason, be the greatest gift bestowed upon mortality, that cannot be praiseless which doth most polish that blessing of speech, which considereth each word

---

[154] Ovid (43 B. C.-18 A. D.), Roman poet, *Ars Amatoria* (*Art of Love*), 2.662. Robinson points out in his edition that Sidney inverts Ovid's original, "*et lateat vitium proximitate boni*" ("And let its proximity to virtue disguise a fault"). In addition to his amatory works, Ovid is best known for the *Metamorphoses*, a collection of stories about transformation.

[155] Cornelius Agrippa (1486-1535) wrote an attack on human reason, *De Incertitudine et Vanitate Scientarum et Artium* (*On the Uncertainty and Vanity of the Sciences and the Arts*; 1530). Desiderius Erasmus, famous humanist and scholar (1466-1536), published the *Encomium Moriae* (*The Praise of Folly*), in 1511; it was translated into English in 1549.

[156] Sidney sets up a straw argument; none of the attacks on poetry condemned rhyming *per se* but concentrated instead on poetry's supposed ability to waste time, corrupt morals and render its consumers effeminate.

[157] The first line of Scaliger's *Poetics* (1561) is "The word poet is not, as popularly supposed, derived from the fact that the poet employs the fictitious, but from the fact that he makes verse." Scaliger's work is one of the first systematic treatments of poetry, and Sidney was deeply influenced by it. See the excerpt in this edition, p. 238.

not only, as a man may say, by his forcible quality, but by his best measured quantity, carrying even in themselves a harmony, without perchance number, measure, order, proportion, be in our time grown odious. But lay aside the just praise it hath by being the only fit speech for music (music, I say, the most divine striker of the senses). Thus much is undoubtedly true, that if reading be foolish without remembering, memory being the only treasurer of knowledge, those words are fittest for memory are likewise most convenient for knowledge. Now, that verse far exceedeth prose in the knitting up of the memory, the reason is manifest, the words, besides their delight, which hath a great affinity to memory, being so set as one cannot be lost but the whole work fails; which accusing itself calleth the remembrance back to itself, and so most strongly confirmeth it. Besides, one word so, as it were, begetting another, as be it in rhyme or measured verse, by the former a man shall have a near guess to the follower. Lastly, even they that have taught the art of memory have showed nothing so apt for it as a certain room divided into many places well and thoroughly known. Now, that hath the verse in effect perfectly, every word having his natural seat, which seat must needs make the word remembered. But what needs more in a thing so known to all men. Who is it that ever was a scholar that doth not carry away some verses of Virgil, Horace, or Cato, which in his youth he learned and even to his old age serve him for hourly lessons?[158] But the fitness it hath for memory is notably provided by all delivery of arts, wherein, for the most part, from grammar to logic, mathematics, physic, and the rest, the rules chiefly necessary to be born away are compiled in verses. So, that verse being in itself sweet and orderly, and being best for memory,

---

[158] The following examples are present only in Ponsonby's edition, which suggests that they are his (or possibly Mary Sidney's) addition: "*Percontatorum fugito, nam garrulus idem est, Dum sibi quisque placet, credula turba sumus* "Avoid a questioner, for he is also a tattler" [Horace, *Epistle*, 1.18.69]; "While each of us pleases himself, we are a credulous crew" (Ovid, *Remedium Amoris* [*Remedy for Love*], 686).

the only handle of knowledge, it must be in jest that any man can speak against it.

Now then go we to the most important imputations laid to the poor poets, for ought I can yet learn, they are these. First, that there being many other more fruitful knowledges, a man might better spend his time in them than in this. Secondly, that it is the mother of lies. Thirdly, that it is the nurse of abuse, infecting us with many pestilent desires with a siren's sweetness, drawing the mind to the serpent's tail of sinful fancies. And herein especially, comedies give the largest field to err, as Chaucer saith.[159] How, both in other nations and in ours, before poets did soften us, we were full of courage, given to martial exercises, the pillars of man-like liberty, and not lulled asleep in shady idleness with poets' pastimes.[160] And lastly and chiefly, they cry out with open mouth, as if they had overshot Robin Hood, that Plato banished them out of his commonwealth.[161] Truly, this is much, if there be much truth in it.

First, to the first. That a man might better spend his time is a reason indeed, but it doth, as they say, but *petere principium*.[162] For if it be, as I affirm,[163] that no learning is so good as that which teacheth and moveth to virtue, and that none can both teach and move thereto so much as poetry, then is the conclusion manifest: that ink and paper cannot be to a more profitable purpose employed. And certainly, though a man should grant their first assumption, it should follow, methinks, very unwillingly that good is not good because better is better. But I still and utterly deny that there is sprung out of earth a more fruitful knowledge.

---

[159] Ponsonby has "ear," from the old and medieval English word for "plow" (*erian*); *Knight's Tale*, l. 28.

[160] See the excerpt from Gosson, pp. 271-72.

[161] See the excepts from Plato's *Republic* and the *Laws*.

[162] Beg the question.

[163] In the next paragraph, however, Sidney will point out that, given the "cloudy knowledge of mankind," those who "[affirm] many things can ... hardly escape from many lies."

To the second, therefore, that they should be the principal liars, I answer paradoxically, but truly (I think truly), that of all writers under the sun, the poet is the least liar. The astronomer with his cousin, the geometrician, can hardly escape when they take upon them to measure the height of the stars. How often think you do the physicians lie when they aver things good for sickness which afterward send Charon a great number of souls drowned upon a potion before they come to his ferry?[164] And no less of the rest, which take upon them to affirm. Now, for the poet, he nothing affirmeth, and therefore never lieth. For, as I take it, to lie is to affirm that to be true which is false. So, as the other artists, and especially the historian, affirming many things, can in the cloudy knowledge of mankind hardly escape from many lies.

But the poet, as I said before, never affirmeth, the poet never maketh any circles about your imagination, to conjure you to believe for true what he writes. He citeth not authorities of other histories, but even for his entry calleth the sweet Muses to inspire into him a good invention. In truth, not laboring to tell you what is, or is not, but what should, or should not be. And therefore though he recount things not true, yet because he telleth them not for true, lieth not. Without we will say that Nathan lied in his speech before-alleged to David, which as a wicked man durst scarce say, so think I none so simple would say, that Aesop lied in the tales of his beasts, for who thinketh that Aesop wrote it for actually true were well worthy to have his name chronicled among the beasts he writeth of. What child is there that coming to a play and seeing "Thebes" written in great letters upon an old door doth believe that it is Thebes? If then a man can arrive at that child's age[165] to know that the poet's persons and doings are but pictures, what should be, and not stories what have been, they will never give the lie to things not affirmatively,

---

[164] According to Greek myth, Charon ferried the souls of the dead across the river Styx in the underworld.

[165] Ponsonby: "to the child's age"; Norwich: "to that child's age."

but allegorically and figuratively written, and therefore, as in history, looking for truth, they may go away full fraught with falsehood. So in poesy, looking but for fiction, they shall use the narration but as an imaginative groundplot of a profitable invention.

But hereto is replied that the poets give names to men they write of, which argueth a conceit of an actual truth, and so, not being true, proveth a falsehood. And doth the lawyer lie, then, when under the names of John of the Stile and John of the Nokes[166] he putteth his case? But that is easily answered: their naming of men is but to make their picture the more lively, and not to build any history. Painting men, they cannot leave men nameless. We see we cannot play at chess but that we must give names to our chessmen, and yet, methinks, he were a very partial champion of truth that would say we lied for giving a piece of wood the reverend title of a bishop. The poet nameth Cyrus or Aeneas no other way than to show what men of their fames, fortunes, and estates should do.

Their third is how much it abuseth men's wit, training it to wanton sinfulness and lustful love. For indeed that is the principal, if not only, abuse I can hear alleged. They say the comedies rather teach than reprehend amorous conceits. They say the lyric is larded with passionate sonnets, the elegiac weeps the want of his mistress, and that even to the heroical, Cupid hath ambitiously climbed. Alas, Love,[167] I would thou couldst as well defend thy self as thou canst offend others. I would those on whom thou does attend could either put thee away or yield good reason why they keep thee. But grant love of beauty to be a beastly fault, although it be very hard, since only man and no beast hath that gift to discern beauty; grant that lovely name of Love to deserve all hateful reproaches, although even some of my masters the

---

[166] Names used in legal fictions; to "put case" means to present a hypothetical case.
[167] The god Love, or Cupid.

philosophers spent a good deal of their lamp oil in setting forth the excellency of it;[168] grant, I say, whatsoever they will have granted, that not only love but lust, but vanity, but, if they list, scurrility, possesseth many leaves of the poets' books, yet, think I, when this is granted, they will find their sentence may with good manners put the last words foremost, and not say that poetry abuseth man's wit, but that man's wit abuseth poetry.

For I will not deny but that man's wit may make poesy, which should be *eikastike*, which some learned have defined [as] figuring forth good things, to be *phantastike*, which doth contrariwise infect the fancy with unworthy objects.[169] As the painter, that should give to the eye either some excellent perspective or some fine picture fit for building or fortification, or containing in it some notable example, as Abraham sacrificing his son Isaac, Judith killing Holofernes, David fighting with Goliath, may leave those, and please an ill-pleased eye with wanton shows of better hidden matters. But what, shall the abuse of a thing make the right use odious? Nay, truly, though I yield that poesy may not only be abused, but that being abused, by the reason of his sweet charm-

---

[168] Such as Plato, in the *Symposium*.

[169] These terms derive from Plato's *Sophist*, and Sidney's use of them is very problematic. Rather than "figuring forth good things," Plato defines art that is *eikastike* as "a copy that conforms to the proportions of the original in all three dimensions and giving moreover the proper color to every part" (235e). Art that is *phantastike* means an image that "seems to be a likeness, but is not really so" (236b), not an image that corrupts the imagination with "unworthy objects." Although Plato initially seems to prefer *eikastic* over *phantastic* imitation, he does so because the former conforms more closely to the original. Both, however, are nonetheless *imitations*, not the thing in itself or its essence. Furthermore, as the Stranger says, thinking about this topic requires that "we descend into that enclosure" (*Laws* 235b), meaning that the contemplation of imitation requires lowering oneself into a kind of animal pen—hardly a ringing endorsement of any kind of *imitatio*. In the *Republic*, Plato condemns imitation because "the mimetic art is far removed from truth" 598b). Therefore, Socrates asks, "And is it not obvious that the nature of the mimetic poet is not related to this better part of the soul and his cunning is not framed to please it, if he is to win favor with the multitude, but is devoted to the fretful and complicated type of character because it is easy to imitate?" The answer, of course, is "Yes, it is obvious" (see the excerpt from the *Republic*, bk. 10).

ing force, it can do more hurt than any other army of words, yet shall it be so far from concluding that the abuse should give reproach to the abused that, contrariwise, it is a good reason that whatsoever being abused doth most harm, being rightly used (and upon the right use each thing conceiveth his title) doth most good.

Do we not see skill of physic, the best rampire[170] to our often-assaulted bodies, being abused, teach poison, the most violent destroyer? Doth not knowledge of the law, whose end is to even and right all things, being abused, grow the crooked fosterer of horrible injuries? Doth not—to go to the highest—God's word abused breed heresy, and His name abused, become blasphemy? Truly, a needle cannot do much hurt, and as truly (with leave of ladies be it spoken), it cannot do much good. With a sword thou mayst kill thy father, and with a sword thou mayst defend thy prince and country. So that, as in their calling poets fathers of lies, they said nothing, so in this their argument of abuse they prove the commendation.

They allege herewith that before poets began to be in price, our nation hath set their heart's delight upon action, and not imagination, rather doings worthy to be written than writing things fit to be done.[171] What that before-time was, I think scarcely Sphinx can tell, since no memory is so ancient that hath the precedence of poetry. And certain it is that in our plainest homeliness, yet never was the Albion nation without poetry. Marry, this argument, though it be leveled against poetry, yet is it indeed a chain-shot against all learning or bookishness, as they commonly term it.[172] Of such mind were certain Goths, of whom it is written that having in the spoil of a famous city taken a fair library, one hangman (belike fit to execute the fruits of their wits) who

[170] Fortification, rampart.
[171] See the excerpt from Gosson's *The School of Abuse*, pp. 270-71.
[172] See the excerpt from Puttenham, *The Art of English Poesy*, 1.8, which also condemns the disrepute of learning in Elizabethan England.

had murdered a great number of bodies would have set fire in it. No, said another, very gravely, take heed what you do, for while they are busy about these toys, we shall with more leisure conquer their countries. This indeed is the ordinary doctrine of ignorance, and many words sometimes I have heard spent in it. But because this reason is generally against all learning, as well as poetry, or rather all learning but poetry, because it were too large a digression to handle it, or at least too superfluous, since it is manifest that all government of action is to be gotten by knowledge, and knowledge best by gathering many knowledges, which is reading, I only, with Horace, to him that is of that opinion,

Jubeo stultum esse libenter,[173]

for as for poetry itself, it is the freest from this objection, for poetry is the companion of camps.[174]

I dare undertake *Orlando Furioso*, or honest king Arthur, will never displease a soldier, but the quiddity of *ens* and *prima materia*[175] will hardly agree with a corselet.[176] And therefore, as I said in the beginning, even Turks and Tartars are delighted with poets.[177] Homer, a Greek, flourished before Greece flourished, and if to a slight conjecture, a conjecture may be opposed, truly it may seem that as by him their learned men took almost their first light of knowledge, so their active men received their first motions of courage. Only Alexander's example may serve, who, by Plutarch, is accounted of such virtue that Fortune was not his guide, but his footstool, whose acts speak for him, though Plutarch did not, indeed, the phoenix of warlike princes. This Alexander left his schoolmaster, living Aristotle, behind him, but took dead

---

[173] "I freely call him a fool," (adapted from Horace, *Satires*, 1.1.63).

[174] When, however, Sidney puts together his recommended reading list for a soldier, his friend Edward Denny, he declines to include poetry.

[175] "The essence of being" and "unformed matter" are both terms from scholastic philosophy.

[176] Armor designed to protect the body.

[177] See above, p. 61, for Sidney's reference to the Turks, although he does not mention "Tartars" anywhere else. Compare, though *AS* 8, in which Sidney invokes the common association of Turks with cruelty.

Homer with him.[178] He put the philosopher Callisthenes to death for his seeming philosophical, indeed mutinous, stubbornness,[179] but the chief thing he was ever heard to wish for was that Homer had been alive.[180] He well found he received more bravery of mind by the pattern of Achilles than by hearing the definition of fortitude. And therefore, if Cato misliked Fulvius for carrying Ennius with him to the field, it may be answered that if Cato misliked it, the noble Fulvius liked it, or else he had not done it.[181] For it was not the excellent Cato Uticensis,[182] whose authority I would much more have reverenced, but it was the former, in truth, a bitter punisher of faults, but else a man that had never well-sacrificed to the Graces. He misliked and cried out against all Greek learning, and yet, being four-score years old, began to learn it, belike fearing that Pluto[183] understood not Latin. Indeed, the Roman laws allowed no person to be carried to the wars but he that was in the soldier's role. And therefore, though Cato misliked his unmustered person,[184] he misliked not his work. And if he had, Scipio Nasica[185] (judged by common consent the best Roman) loved him, both the other Scipio brothers, who had by their virtues no less surnames than of Asia and Africa, so loved him that they caused his body to be buried in their sepulchre.[186]

---

[178] Plutarch, *Life of Alexander*, 8.2; Sidney means that Alexander took Homer's poems with him.

[179] Plutarch, *Life of Alexander*, 85.5; Callisthenes (c. 360-328 B. C.), Greek historian, philosopher, and relative of Aristotle. Alexander threw Callisthenes into prison on suspicion of his plotting to kill him.

[180] Cicero, *Pro Archia Poeta Oratio* (*On Behalf of Archias the Poet*), 10.24.

[181] Cato the Censor (234-149 B. C.) was noted for his stern moralism, and his dislike of the poet Ennius (see n. 12) is proverbial. In *The School of Abuse*, for instance, Stephen Gosson will note that Cato reproached the consul Marcus Fulvius for bringing Ennius "into his province" (see the excerpt, p. 266). See also *AS* 4.

[182] Cato the Censor's great grandson (95-46 B. C.).

[183] God of the underworld.

[184] That is, Ennius.

[185] Roman consul in 191 B. C. See Livy, *Histories*, 29.19.8-9.

[186] The names of these Roman generals indicate where they earned their military victories. The notion that Ennius was buried in their tomb comes from Cicero, *On Behalf of Archias the Poet*, 9.22.

So as Cato's authority being but against his person, and that answered with so far greater than himself, is herein of no validity.

But now indeed my burden is great, now Plato his name is laid upon me, whom, I must confess, of all philosophers I have ever esteemed most worthy of reverence, and with good reason, since of all philosophers he is the most poetical. Yet if he will defile the fountain out of which his flowing streams have proceeded, let us boldly examine with what reasons he did it.[187]

First, truly a man might maliciously object that Plato, being a philosopher, was a natural enemy of poetry,[188] for indeed after the philosophers had picked out of the sweet mysteries of poetry the right discerning true points of knowledge, they forthwith putting it in method and making a school-art of that which the poets did only teach by a divine delightfulness, beginning to spurn at their guides, like ungrateful prentices,[189] were not content to set up shops for themselves, but sought by all means to discredit their masters, which by the force of delight being barred them, the less they could overthrow them, the more they hated them. For indeed, they found for Homer seven cities, and strove who should have him for their citizen,[190] where many cities banished philosophers as not fit members to live among them. For only repeating certain of Euripides' verses, many Athenians had their lives saved of the Syracusans, where the Athenians themselves

---

[187] Compare Sidney's treatment of Plato with Scaliger's. In 14.19 of the *Genealogy of the Gentile Gods*, Boccaccio tries to deflect this charge by stating that Plato did not mean to banish such poets as Homer, Ennius, or Horace from his republic, but only those who "wrote dirty stories and presented them on the stage, and thus prompted lascivious men to crime" (*Boccaccio on Poetry*, 87-94).

[188] Plato refers in the *Republic*, bk. 10, to the "ancient quarrel" between poetry and philosophy (606b). See the excerpt, p. 222.

[189] Apprentices. Sidney's metaphor refers to more than just youth and inexperience, because apprentices during this period were a group known for political volatility.

[190] Ponsonby: "For indeed they found for Homer, seven cities strave who should have him ..."; Olney: "For indeed, the found for Homer, seven cities strove, who should have him ..."; Norwich: "For indeed they found for Homer seven cities; and strave who should have him ...."

thought many philosophers unworthy to live.[191] Certain poets, as Simonides and Pindar,[192] had so prevailed with Hiero the First, that of a tyrant they made him a just king, where Plato could do so little with Dionysus that he himself of a philosopher was made a slave.[193] But who should do thus, I confess, should requite the objections made against poets with like cavillations against philosophers; as likewise one should do that should bid one read *Phaedrus* or *Symposium* in Plato, or the discourse of love in Plutarch, and see whether any poet do authorize abominable filthiness as they do.[194] Again, a man might ask out of what commonwealth Plato did banish them, in sooth, thence where he himself alloweth community of women.[195] So as belike this banishment grew not for effeminate wantonness, since little should poetical sonnets be hurtful when a man might have what woman he listed.[196]

But I honor philosophical instructions, and bless the wits which bred them, so as they be not abused, which is likewise stretched to poetry. Saint Paul himself, who yet for the credit of poets allegeth twice two poets and one of them by the name of a prophet,[197] sets a watchword upon philosophy, indeed, upon the abuse. So doth Plato upon the abuse, not upon po-

---

[191] Plutarch, *Life of Nicias*, ch. 29. In chapter 23, Plutarch describes how the Athenians exiled, imprisoned, or executed philosophers who denied divine agency.

[192] Pindar. Simonides (c. 556-c. 470 B. C.), Greek lyric poet who, like Pindar, often wrote odes honoring winners in the Olympic games.

[193] Hieron I, tyrant of Syracuse (478-467 B. C.), a despot, supported the arts, and he patronized Pindar and Aeschylus. In 476, Simonides reconciled Hieron with his brother— hence Sidney's assertion that the poet transformed the tyrant into a "just king." Dionysus, a subsequent tyrant of Syracuse (405-367 B. C.) supposedly gave Plato to the Spartan ambassador, who sold the philosopher into slavery.

[194] Sidney refers here to Plato's praise of older-male—younger-male love in these dialogues and Plutarch's assertion that "there is only one genuine love, the love of boys," in "The Dialogue on Love," *Moralia*, 751.

[195] That is, the guardians who rule the state will share these women ("none shall cohabit with any privately"), *Republic* bk. 5 (457d).

[196] Desired, wanted.

[197] Acts 17:28. "Who . . . prophet" is omitted in Ponsonby.

etry.[198] Plato found fault that the poets of his time filled the world with wrong opinions of the gods, making light tales of that unspotted essence, and therefore would not have the youth depraved with such opinions. Herein may much be said, let this suffice: the poets did not induce such opinions, but did imitate those opinions already induced. For all the Greek stories can well testify that the very religion of that time stood upon many and many-fashioned gods, not taught so by the poets, but followed according to their nature of imitation.[199] Who list may read in Plutarch the discourses of Isis and Osiris, of the cause why oracles ceased, of the divine providence, and see whether the theology of that nation stood not upon such dreams, which the poets indeed superstitiously observed.[200] And truly, since they had not the light of Christ, did much better in it than the philosophers, who, shaking off superstition, brought in atheism. Plato, therefore, whose authority I had much rather justly construe than unjustly resist, meant not in general of poets, in those words of which Julius Scaliger saith, *Qua authoritate barbari quidam atque hispidi abuti velint ad poets e republica exigendos,*[201] but only meant to drive out those wrong opinions of the Deity, whereof now, without further law, Christianity hath taken away

---

[198] Boccaccio also asserts that Plato banishes only the poets who "seduced various peoples into the practice of such licentious rites that its own disciples had to blush for it" (*Boccaccio on Poetry*, 94). Compare, however, the excerpts from the *Republic*, Bks. 2 and 10, and the *Laws*. In particular, compare Plato's explicit denunciation of Homer and Hesiod and his rejection of allegorical interpretation in the excerpt from the *Republic*, bk. 2.

[199] Compare Sidney's earlier assertion that poets have been the "first light-giver to ignorance and first nurse" of knowledge and his subsequent challenge to the muse-haters: "Let learned Greece in any of his manifold sciences be able to show me one book before Musaeus, Homer, and Hesiod" (p. 58) Compare also Sidney's earlier assertion of the poet's independent imagination (pp. 64-65).

[200] Plutarch, *Moralia*, "Isis and Osiris," 351-384; "The Obsolescence of Oracles," 410-438; "On the Delays of the Divine Vengeance," 548-568. See also Sidney's treatment of Plutarch in the letter to Denny.

[201] "By whose authority some barbarous and crude men seek to expel poets from the republic" (*Poetics*, 1.2). See the excerpt from Scaliger and Boccaccio's similar attempt to confront Plato (see also note 198 and note 187).

all the hurtful belief, perchance, as he thought, nourished by then-esteemed poets. And a man need go no further than to Plato himself to know his meaning, who, in his dialogue called *Ion*, giveth high, and rightly, divine commendation unto poetry.[202] So, as Plato, banishing the abuse, not the thing, not banishing it, but giving due honor to it, shall be our patron, and not our adversary. For indeed, I had much rather, since truly I may do it, show their mistaking of Plato, under whose lion's skin they would make an ass-like braying against poesy, than go about to overthrow his authority, whom, the wiser a man is, the more just cause he shall find to have in admiration, especially since he attributeth unto poesy more than myself do, namely, to be a very inspiring of a divine force, far above man's wit, in the forenamed dialogue is apparent.

Of the other side, who would show the honors have been by the best sort of judgements granted them, a whole sea of examples would present themselves: Alexanders, Caesars, Scipios, all favorers of poets; Laelius, called the Roman Socrates, himself a poet, so as part of *Heautontimorumenos* in Terence was supposed to be made by him.[203] And even the Greek Socrates, whom Apollo confirmed to be the only wise man, is said to have spent part of his old time in putting Aesop's fables in verse.[204] And therefore full evil should it become his scholar Plato to put such words in

---

[202] In the *Ion*, Plato's Socrates outlines a theory of divine inspiration, calling the poet a "light and winged thing, and holy" (534b) because he can compose only when literally inspired by a god. It is, however, precisely this irrationality that makes poetry suspect in the *Republic* (605b).

[203] Laelius Gaius, fl. 2nd century B. C., a Roman soldier, orator and politician. Cicero writes that Laelius and Socrates shared an ability to keep "an unruffled temper, an unchanging mien and the same cast of countenance in every condition of life" (*De Officiis* [*On Duty*], 1.26.90). He also asserted that Terence's plays "were supposed, from the elegance of their diction, to be the work of Laelius" (*Letters to Atticus*, 7.3.10). The title of Terence's play translates as *The Self-Tormentor*.

[204] As part of his defense, Socrates reminds the court that the Delphic Oracle pronounced him the wisest of all men (*Apology*, 20e-21a). In the *Phaedo*, Socrates says that he has moved from practicing philosophy to versifying in order to obey a recurrent dream in which he is exhorted to "practice and cultivate the arts" (60d-61c).

his master's mouth against poets. But what need more? Aristotle
writes the *Art of Poesy*, and why, if it should not be written?[205]
Plutarch teacheth the use to be gathered of them, and how, if
they should not be read?[206] And who reads Plutarch's either his-
tory or philosophy shall find he trimmeth both their garments
with guards of poesy. But I list not to defend poesy with the help
of his underling, historiography.[207] Let it suffice to have showed
that it is a fit soil for praise to dwell upon, and what dispraise
may set upon it is either easily overcome or transformed into just
commendation. So that, since the excellencies of it may be so
easily and so justly confirmed, and the low-creeping objections
so soon trodden down, it not being an art of lies but of true
doctrine, not of effeminateness, but of notable stirring of cour-
age, not of abusing man's wit, but of strengthening man's wit,
not banished, but honored by Plato: let us rather plant more
laurels for to engarland the poet's head (which honor of being
laureate, as besides them only triumphant captains wear, is a suf-
ficient authority to show the price they ought to be had in), than
suffer the ill-savored breath of such wrong speakers once to blow
upon the clear springs of poesy.

* * *[208]

But since I have run so long a carrier in this matter, methinks,
before I give my pen a full stop, it shall be but a little more lost
time to inquire why England, the mother of excellent minds,
should be grown so hard a stepmother to poets, who certainly in

---

[205] The *Poetics*. Compare Sidney's earlier rather disparaging remarks about philosophy
and scholastic Aristoteleanism (see pp. 71, 73-74, 77).

[206] *Moralia, How to Study Poetry*, 14-37.

[207] Sidney gives a very different evaluation of the relationship between historiography
and poetry in both the letter to Denny and to his brother, Robert.

[208] From this point onward, the *Apology* shifts dramatically from defending poetry to
criticizing contemporary poets and dramatists in terms that often directly contradict
Sidney's previous arguments. On this split, see O. B. Hardison, Jr., "The Two Voices of
Sidney's *Apology for Poetry*."

wit ought to pass all others since all only proceeds from their wit, being indeed makers of themselves, not takers of others. How can I but exclaim,

Musa, mihi causas memora quo numine laeso?[209]

Sweet poesy, that hath anciently had kings, emperors, senators, great captains, such as, besides a thousand others, David, Adrian, Sophocles, Germanicus,[210] not only to favor poets, but to be poets; and of our nearer times, can present for her patrons a Robert, King of Sicily; the great King Francis of France, King James of Scotland;[211] such cardinals as Bembus and Bibiena;[212] such famous preachers and teachers as Beza and Melanchthon;[213] so learned philosophers as Fracastorius and Scaliger;[214] so great orators as Pontanus and Muretus;[215] so piercing wits, as George Buchanan;[216] so grave counselors, as besides many, but before all,

[209] "Tell me, Muse, the reasons, by which the god has been offended?" (*Aeneid*, 1.8; editor's trans.).

[210] David, King of Israel, was the reputed author of the Psalms; Adrian (Hadrian), Emperor of Rome (117-138) and art patron; Sophocles, one of the major Greek tragedians, as well as an Athenian general; Germanicus (15 B. C.- A. D.19), Roman general and emperor, conqueror of Germany, and reputed to have written poems.

[211] Robert II of Anjou (1275-1343) patronized Petrarch; Francis I (1494-1547) supported Erasmus and some of France's leading poets, such as Clément Marot; James VI (later James I of England), one of the few monarchs to publish in print (as opposed to circulating in manuscript) books of verse, *Essayes of a Prentice* (1584) and *His Majesties Poetical Exercises* (1591). It is possible, although unlikely, that Sidney had in mind James I (1394-1437), who was reputed to have written *The Kingis Quair* (*The King's Book*) while a prisoner in England.

[212] Pietro Bembo (1470-1547), cardinal and neoplatonist, also a major figure in Book 4 of Baldesare Castiglione's *The Book of the Courtier*; Bernardo Dovizio, Cardinal Bibbiena (1470-1520), author of a comedy, *Calandria*, derived from the Roman playwright Plautus.

[213] Theodore de Bèze, or Beza (1519-1605), Calvin's friend and successor, the author of many religious works (see the excerpts in this volume) and famous for his Latin epigrams; Philip Melanchthon (1497-1560), an associate of Martin Luther and professor of Greek at Wittenberg.

[214] Girolamo Fracastoro (1478-1553), Italian physician and poet, author of *Naugerius*, a work of literary criticism combining neoplatonic and Aristotelean theories; on Scaliger, see the excerpt.

[215] Giovanni Pontano (1426-1503), author of the *Urania*, an astronomical poem; Marc-Antoine Muret (1526-1585), a French humanist who also wrote a Latin tragedy.

[216] George Buchanan (1506-1582), humanist poet, Latin playwright, translator of the Psalms into Latin metrical verse, the future James VI's tutor, republican theo-

that Hospital of France,[217] than whom, I think, that realm never brought forth a more accomplished judgment, more firmly builded upon virtue. I say these, with numbers of others, not only to read other poesies, but to poetise for others reading.

That poesy, thus embraced in all other places, should only find in our time a hard welcome in England, I think the very earth lamenteth it, and therefore decks our soil with fewer laurels than it was accustomed. For heretofore, poets have in England also flourished, and, which is to be noted, even in those times when the trumpet of Mars did sound loudest.[218] And now that an over-faint quietness should seem to strew the house for poets, they are almost in as good reputation as the mountebanks[219] at Venice. Truly, even that, as of the one side it giveth great praise to poesy, which, like Venus (but to better purpose), had rather be troubled in the net with Mars than enjoy the homely quiet of Vulcan,[220] so serves it for a piece of a reason why they are less grateful to idle England, which now can scarce endure the pain of a pen. Upon this necessarily followeth that base men with servile wits undertake it, who think it enough if they can be rewarded of the printer. And so as Epaminondas[221] is said with the honor of his virtue to have made an office by his exercising it, which

rist, historian of Scotland, and among the chief antagonists of Mary, Queen of Scots. On the connections between Sidney and Buchanan, see Blair Worden, *The Sound of Virtue.*

[217] Michel de l'Hôpital (1507-73), Protestant poet, Chancellor of France (1560-68), and an advocate of religious toleration.

[218] That is, when England was at war.

[219] Charlatans, snake-oil salesmen.

[220] Vulcan captured in a net his wife, Venus, in bed with Mars. He then called in the rest of the gods to witness their perfidy, but they laughed at him rather than condemning the adulterous couple (Ovid, *Metamorphoses,* 4.173-189).

[221] Epaminondas, 4th c. B. C., a Theban general. According to Plutarch, he was appointed to a demeaning position "through envy and as an insult." Yet "he did not neglect his duties, but saying that not only does the office distinguish the man, but also the man the office, he advanced the *telemarchy* to a position of great consideration and

before was contemptible, to become highly respected, so these men, no more but setting their names to it, by their own disgracefulness, disgrace the most graceful poesy. For now, as if all the Muses were got with child to bring forth bastard poets, without any commission they do post over the banks of Helicon[222] till they make the readers more weary than post-horses, while, in the mean time, they,

Queis meliore luto finxit praecordia Titan,[223]

are better content to suppress the outflowings of their wit, than, by publishing them, to be accounted knights of the same order.

But I that, before ever I durst aspire unto the dignity, am admitted into the company of the paper-blurrers, do find the very true cause of our wanting estimation is want of desert, taking upon us to be poets in despite of Pallas. Now, wherein we want desert were a thankworthy labor to express, but if I knew, I should have mended myself. But I, as I never desired the title, so have I neglected the means to come by it, only over-mastered by some thoughts, I yielded an inky tribute unto them. Marry, they that delight in poesy itself should seek to know what they do, and how they do, and especially look themselves in an unflattering glass of reason, if they be inclinable unto it. For poesy must not be drawn by the ears, it must be gently led; or rather, it must lead, which was partly the cause that made the ancient learned affirm it was a divine gift and no human skill, since all other knowledges lie ready for any that hath strength of wit. A poet no

---

dignity, though previously it had been nothing but a sort of supervision of the alleys for the removal of dung and the draining of water in the streets" (Plutarch, *Moralia*, "Precepts of Statecraft," 811B-C).

[222] Mountain in Central Greece sacred to the muses.

[223] "Whose soul the Titan [Prometheus] has fashioned with kindlier skill and of a finer clay" (adapted from Juvenal, *Satires*, 14.35).

[224] An attending spirit.

[225] "The orator is made, the poet born."

industry can make, if his own genius[224] be not carried into it. And therefore is it an old proverb, *orator fit, poeta nascitur.*[225]

Yet confess I always that as the fertilest ground must be manured, so must the highest-flying wit have a Daedalus to guide him.[226] That Daedalus, they say, both in this and in other, hath three wings to bear itself up into the air of due commendation: that is, art, imitation, and exercise. But these neither artificial rules, nor imitative patterns, we much cumber[227] ourselves withal. Exercise indeed we do, but that very fore-backwardly, for where we should exercise to know, we exercise as having known, and so is our brain delivered of much matter which never was begotten by knowledge.[228] For there being two principal parts—matter to be expressed by words, and words to express the matter: in neither we use art or imitation rightly. Our matter is *quodlibet*[229] indeed, though wrongly performing Ovid's verse,

Quicquid conabor dicere, versus erit,[230]

never marshalling it into any assured rank, that almost the readers cannot tell where to find themselves.

Chaucer, undoubtedly, did excellently in his *Troilus and Criseyde*, of whom truly I know not whether to marvel more,

---

[226] "Daedalus" means both the figure from mythology and a guide. Because King Minos kept Daedalus and his son, Icarus, from returning home after he built the maze that im.prisoned the minotaur, Daedalus decided to "alter the laws of nature" and constructed wings for the two of them. Despite his father's warnings, Icarus flew too close to the sun and plunged into the sea. His fate was taken as a warning against defying authority and against human presumption (Ovid, *Metamorphoses*, 8.174-211). Sidney's emphasis on rules contrasts with his earlier statements on the freedom of the poet's imagination. See note 228.

[227] Encumber.

[228] Compare Sidney's earlier assertion of the independence of the poet's imagination: "Only the poet, *disdaining to be tied to any such subjection, lifted up with the vigor of his own invention*, doth grow in effect into another nature in making things either better than nature bringeth forth, or quite anew, *forms such as never were in nature*, as the heroes, demigods, Cyclops, Chimeras, Furies, and such like" (my emphasis) and "The poet only bringeth his own stuff, and doth not learn a conceit out of a matter, but maketh matter for a conceit" (pp. 64, 93).

[229] "Whatever," a term from scholastic philosophy.

[230] "Whatever I try to say will turn into verse"; adapted from Ovid, *Tristia*, 4.10.26.

either that he in that misty time could see so clearly or that we in this clear age go so stumblingly after him. Yet had he great wants, fit to be forgiven in so reverent antiquity.[231] I count the *Mirror for Magistrates* meetly furnished of beautiful parts, and in the Earl of Surrey's lyrics many things tasting of a noble birth.[232] The *Shepherd's Calendar* hath much poetry in his eclogues, indeed worthy the reading, if I be not deceived.[233] That same framing of his style to an old rustic language I dare not allow, since neither Theocritus in Greek, Virgil in Latin, nor Sannazzaro in Italian did affect it. Besides these, I do not remember[234] to have seen but few (to speak boldly) printed that have poetical sinews in them. For proof whereof, let but most of the verses be put in prose, and then ask the meaning, and it will be found that one verse did but beget another, without ordering at the first what should be at the last, which becomes a confused mass of words, with a tingling sound of rhyme, barely accompanied with reason.

Our tragedies and comedies, not without cause cried out against, observing rules neither of honest civility nor skillful poetry, excepting *Gorboduc* (again, I say, of those that I have seen), which notwithstanding as it is full of stately speeches and well-

---

[231] Sidney's qualification of his praise of Chaucer would have been very notable, given Chaucer's extraordinarily high reputation during this period. In the preface to his 1532 edition of Chaucer's works, William Thynne marvels how "in his time, when doubtless all good letters were laid asleep throughout the world ... such an excellent poet in our tongue should ... spring and arise." Similarly, Thomas Speght, in the introduction to his 1598 edition of Chaucer's works, states that "Master Ascham ... calleth him *English Homer* [and says] that he valueth his authoritie of as high estimation as ever he did either *Sophocles* or *Euripides* in Greek." Thomas Wilson, in *The Art of Rhetoric* (1560), reported that expressing familiarity with England's "auncient laureate poet" was a sign of social climbing: "The fine Courtier will talk nothing but Chaucer" (162).

[232] *The Mirror for Magistrates* (1559), a collection of verse tragedies about the fall of political figures; Puttenham called Henry Howard, Earl of Surrey (c. 1517-1547), along with Sir Thomas Wyatt, among the "courtly makers" of the Henrician era. Most of his poems were published in *Tottel's Miscellany* (1557).

[233] Although Edmund Spenser dedicated *The Shepherd's Calendar* (1579) to Sidney, the volume nowhere indicates its authorship, so he may not have known who wrote it.

[234] Olney: "Do I not remember"; Norwich: "Do not I remember."

sounding phrases, climbing to the heights of Seneca, his style, and as full of notable morality, which it doth most delightfully teach, and obtain the very end of poesy.[235] Yet in truth, it is very defectious in the circumstances, which grieveth me because it might not remain as an exact model of all tragedies, for it is faulty in both place and time, the two necessary companions of all corporal actions. For where the stage should always represent but one place, and the uttermost time presupposed in it should be, both by Aristotle's precept[236] and common reason, but one day, there is both many days and many places, inartificially[237] imagined.

But if it be so in *Gorboduc*, how much more in all the rest, where you shall have Asia of the one side and Afric[238] of the other, and so many other under-kingdoms that the player, when he cometh in, must ever begin with telling where he is, or else the tale will not be conceived?[239] Now you shall have three ladies walk to gather flowers, and then we must believe the stage to be a garden. By and by we hear news of shipwreck in the same place, and then we are to blame if we accept it not for a rock. Upon the back of that comes out a hideous monster with fire and smoke, and then the miserable beholders are bound to take it for a cave,

---

[235] This play, performed before Elizabeth at the Inns of Court in 1562, was written by Thomas Norton (1532-1584) and Thomas Sackville (1536-1608). Norton also translated Calvin's *Institutes*, and Sackville contributed to the *Mirror for Magistrates*. The play was published first in 1565 under the title *The Tragedy of Gorboduc* and again in 1571, by a different publisher, with a different title, *The Tragedy of Ferrex and Porrex*.

[236] Aristotle, *Poetics*, 5 (1449b).

[237] Unartfully, poorly.

[238] Africa.

[239] Earlier, Sidney rejected such literalism: "What child is there that coming to a play and seeing 'Thebes' written in great letters upon an old door doth believe that is Thebes? If then a man can arrive to the child's age to know that the poet's persons and doings are but pictures, what should be, and not stories what have been, they will never give the lie to things not affirmatively, but allegorically and figuratively, written, and therefore, as in history looking for truth, they may go away full fraught with falsehood. So in poesy, looking but for fiction, they shall use the narration but as an imaginative groundplot of a profitable invention" (pp. 98-99).

while in the meantime two armies fly in, represented with four swords and bucklers, and then what hard heart will not receive it for a pitched field?

Now, of time they are much more liberal, for ordinary it is that two young princes fall in love. After many traverses[240] she is got with child, delivered of a fair boy. He is lost, groweth a man, falleth in love, and is ready to get another child— and all this in two hours space! Which how absurd it is in sense even sense may imagine, and art hath taught, and all ancient examples justified, and at this day the ordinary players in Italy will not err in. Yet will some bring in an example of *Eunuchus* in Terence that containeth matter of two days,[241] yet far short of twenty years. True it is, and so was it to be played in two days, and so fitted to the time it set forth. And though Plautus have in one place done amiss, let us hit with him and not miss with him.

But they will say, how then shall we set forth a story which contains both many places and many times? And do they not know that a tragedy is tied to the laws of poesy, and not of history, not bound to follow the story, but having liberty either to feign a quite new matter, or to frame the history to the most tragical convenience? Again, many things be told which cannot be showed, if they know the difference betwixt reporting and representing. As, for example, I may speak, though I am here, of Peru, and in speech digress from that to the description of Calicut,[242] But in action, I cannot represent it without Pacolet's horse.[243] And so was the manner the ancients took, by some *nuntius*,[244] to recount things done in former time or other place.

---

[240] Travails, troubles.

[241] In fact, Terence's *Eunuch* takes place over a single day..

[242] Calcutta.

[243] Pacolet, an enchanter in the late medieval French romance *Valentine and Orson* (translated into English c. 1550), had a magical horse that took him wherever he wanted to go.

[244] Messenger.

Lastly, if they will represent an history, they must not, as Horace saith, begin *ab ovo*,[245] but they must come to the principal point of that one action which they will represent. By example this will be best expressed. I have a story of young Polydorus, delivered, for safety's sake, with great riches, by his father Priam to Polymnestor, King of Thrace, in the Trojan war time. He, after some years, hearing the overthrow of Priam, for to make the treasure his own, murdereth the child. The body of the child is taken up by Hecuba, she, the same day, findeth a sleight to be revenged most cruelly of the tyrant.[246] Where now would one of our tragedy writers begin, but with the delivery of the child? Then should he sail over into Thrace and so spend I know not how many years, and travel numbers of places. But where doth Euripides? Even with the finding of the body, the rest leaving to be told by the spirit of Polydorus. This need no further to be enlarged, the dullest wit may conceive it.

But besides these gross absurdities, how all their plays be neither right tragedies, nor right comedies, mingling kings and clowns, not because the matter so carrieth it, but thrust in the clown by the head and shoulders to play a part in majestical matters, with neither decency nor discretion, so as neither the admiration and commiseration, nor the right sportfulness, is by their mongrel tragicomedy obtained.[247] I know Apuleius[248] did somewhat so, but that is a thing recounted with space of time, not represented in one moment, and I know the ancients have one or two examples of tragicomedies, as Plautus hath *Amphitrion*. But, if we mark them well, we shall find that they never or very daintily match hornpipes and funerals. So falleth it out that, having

---

[245] Literally, "from the egg," meaning "from the very beginning" (Horace, *Ars Poetica*, 147).

[246] The plot is from Euripides, *Hecuba*.

[247] Compare Sidney's earlier acceptance of mingling genres: "some have mingled matters heroical and pastoral, but that cometh all to one in this question, for if severed they be good, the conjunction cannot be hurtful" (p. 87).

[248] North African Roman satirist (c. 2nd century, A. D.), author of *The Golden Ass*.

indeed no right comedy in that comical part of our tragedy, we have nothing but scurrility, unworthy of any chaste ears,[249] or some extreme show of doltishness, indeed, fit to lift up a loud laughter, and nothing else: where the whole tract of a comedy should be full of delight, as the tragedy should be still maintained in a well-raised admiration.

But our comedians think there is no delight without laughter, which is very wrong, for though laughter may come with delight, yet cometh it not of delight, as though delight should be the cause of laughter. But well may one thing breed both together. Nay, rather in themselves they have, as it were, a kind of contrarity, for delight we scarcely do but in things that have a conveniency to ourselves, or to the general nature. Laughter almost ever cometh of things most disproportioned to our selves and nature. Delight hath a joy in it, either permanent or present. Laughter hath only scornful tickling. For example, we are ravished with delight to see a fair woman and yet are far from being moved to laughter. We laugh at deformed creatures wherein certainly we cannot delight. We delight in good chances, we laugh at mischances. We delight to hear the happiness of our friends or country, at which he were worthy to be laughed at that would laugh. We shall contrarily laugh sometimes to find a matter quite mistaken, and go down the hill against the bias in the mouth of some such men, as for the respect of them, one shall be heartily sorry, he cannot choose but laugh, and so is rather pained than delighted with laughter.

Yet deny I not but that they may go well together, for as in Alexander's picture well set out, we delight without laughter, and in twenty mad antics we laugh without delight. So in Hercules, painted with his great beard and furious countenance in a woman's

---

[249] Sidney's denunciation of contemporary drama parallels rather than rebuts the charges of Gosson et al.

attire, spinning at Omphale's commandment, it breeds both delight and laughter, for the representing of so strange a power in love procures delight, and the scornfulness of the action, stirreth laughter.[250]

But I speak to this purpose: that all the end of the comical part be not upon such scornful matters as stir laughter only, but, mixed with it, that delightful teaching which is the end of poesy. And the great fault even in that point of laughter, and forbidden plainly by Aristotle,[251] is that they stir laughter in sinful things, which are rather execrable than ridiculous, or in miserable, which are rather to be pitied than scorned. For what is it to make folks gape at a wretched beggar and a beggarly clown, or, against law of hospitality, to jest at strangers because they speak not English so well as we do? What do we learn, since it is certain,

> *Nil habet infelix paupertas durius in se,*
> *Quam quod ridiculos homines facit.*[252]

But rather, a busy loving courtier; a heartless, threatening Thraso; a self-wise, seeming schoolmaster; a wry transformed traveler.[253] These, if we saw walk in stage names, which we play naturally, therein were delightful laughter, and teaching delightfulness, as in the other, the tragedies of Buchanan do justly bring forth a divine admiration.[254]

But I have lavished out too many words of this play matter. I do it because, as they are excelling parts of poesy, so is there none so much used in England, and none can be more pitifully abused, which, like an unmannerly daughter showing a bad edu-

---

[250] According to legend, after he completed his twelve labors, Hercules fell in love with Omphale, Queen of Lydia, who commanded him to perform effeminizing tasks. The story exemplified the corrosive effects of love on masculinity and was a popular topic for painters of the Northern European Renaissance.

[251] *Poetics*, 5 (1449a); *Nicomachean Ethics*, 4.8 (1128a).

[252] "Of all the woes of luckless poverty none is harder to endure than this, that it exposes men to ridicule" (Juvenal, *Satires*, 3.152-53).

[253] Olney has this interesting variant: "A awry-transformed traveler."

[254] On Buchanan, see n. 216..

cation, causeth her mother Poesy's honesty to be called into question.

Other sort of poetry, almost have we none, but that lyrical kind of songs and sonnets, which, Lord, if He gave us so good minds, how well it might be employed, and with how heavenly fruits, both private and public, in singing the praises of the immortal beauty, the immortal goodness of that God who giveth us hands to write and wits to conceive, of which we might well want words but never matter; of which we could turn our eyes to nothing but we should ever have new-budding occasions.[255] But truly many of such writings as come under the banner of unresistable love, if I were a mistress, would never persuade me they were in love, so coldly they apply fiery speeches, as men that had rather read lover's writings, and so caught up certain swelling phrases, which hang together like a man that once told me that wind was at northwest by south because he would be sure to name winds enough, than that in truth they feel those passions, which easily, as I think, may be bewrayed by that same forcibleness, or *energia*,[256] as the Greeks call it, of the writer.[257] But let this be a sufficient, though short, note, that we miss the right use of the material point of poesy.

Now, for the outside of it, which is words, or, as I may term it, diction, it is even well worse. So is that honey-flowing matron, Eloquence, appareled, or rather disguised, in a courtesan-like painted affectation. One time, with so far-fet[258] words that many seem monsters but must seem strangers to any poor En-

---

[255] See the prefatory letter to Beza's *Abraham's Sacrifice*, excerpted in this volume.

[256] Aristotle uses this term to describe the force which brings the object represented vividly "before the eyes" (*Rhetoric*, 3.11.1-4 [1411b]). Homer, for example, owes his popularity to the way his metaphors "energize" or make his verse come alive (*enargeian poien*). On this difficult concept, see Kathy Eden, *Poetic and Legal Fiction in the Aristotelean Tradition*, 71-75, 168-169.

[257] Sidney outlines a similar poetics and a similar criticism of the conventionality of current poets in *AS* 1, 3 and 6.

[258] Far-fetched.

glishman; another time, with coursing of a letter, as if they were bound to follow the method of a dictionary; another time, with figures and flowers, extremely winter-starved. But I would this fault were only peculiar to versifiers and had not as large possession among prose-printers, and (which is to be marveled) among many scholars, and (which is to be pitied) among some preachers. Truly I could wish, if at least I might be so bold to wish in a thing beyond the reach of my capacity, the diligent imitators of Tully and Demosthenes,[259] most worthy to be imitated, did not so much keep Nizolian paper books[260] of their figures and phrases as by attentive translation, as it were, devour them whole and make them wholly theirs. For now they cast sugar and spice upon every dish that is served to the table, like those Indians, not content to wear earrings at the fit and natural place of the ears, but they will thrust jewels through their nose and lips, because they will be sure to be fine.

Tully, when he was to drive out Catiline, as it were, with a thunderbolt of eloquence, often useth that figure of repetition, as *Vivit. Vivit? Imo in senatum venit*, etc.[261] Indeed, inflamed with a well-grounded rage, he would have his words, as it were, double out of his mouth, and so do that artificially[262] which we see men in choler[263] do naturally. And we, having the grace of those words, hale them in sometimes to a familiar epistle, when it were too too much choler to be choleric. How well store of *similiter cadences*[264] doth sound with the gravity of the pulpit, I

---

[259] Cicero; Demosthenes (d. 413 B. C.), the most famous orator of ancient Greece.

[260] Phrase books named after Marius Nizolus, compiler of a famous lexicon of phrases from Cicero.

[261] "He lives. He lives? Indeed, he even comes into the senate!" (*In Catilinam* [*Oration Against Catiline*], 1.1.2) Lucius Sergius Catilina plotted to have Cicero assassinated after losing an election to him. Cicero's spies informed him of the plot and he delivered this oration in the Senate with Catiline present. Catiline later tried to take over the government by force, and he was killed in 62.

[262] That is, artfully

[263] Anger.

[264] Similar cadences.

would but invoke Demosthenes' soul to tell, who with a rare daintiness useth them. Truly, they have made thee think of the sophister,[265] that with too much subtlety would prove two eggs three, and though he might be counted a sophister, had none for his labor. So these men, bringing in such a kind of eloquence, well may they obtain an opinion of a seeming fineness, but persuade few, which should be the end of their fineness.[266]

Now, for similitudes, in certain printed discourses,[267] I think all herbarists, all stories of beasts, fowls, and fishes, are rifled up that they come in multitudes to wait upon any of our conceits, which certainly is as absurd a surfeit to the ears as is possible. For the force of a similitude not being to prove anything to a contrary disputer, but only to explain to a willing hearer. When that is done, the rest is a most tedious prattling, rather over-swaying the memory from the purpose whereto they were applied than any whit informing the judgment, already either satisfied, or by similitudes not to be satisfied. For my part, I do not doubt, when Antonius and Crassus,[268] the great forefathers of Cicero in eloquence, the one, as Cicero testifieth of them,[269] pretended not to know art, the other not to set by it, because with a plain sensibleness they might win credit of popular[270] ears, which credit is the

---

[265] Someone who uses fallacious reasoning and puts clever reasoning and brilliant rhetoric above the truth. The sophist, Protageras (who is also the subject of one of Plato's dialogues), is reputed to have been the first person to write a treatise on argumentation, and was notorious for his claim to "make the weaker argument the stronger." Socrates, by way of contrast, was interested only in discovering the truth.

[266] The passage from "How well store ..." to the end of the paragraph is found only in Ponsonby.

[267] Critics generally assume that Sidney is referring to John Lyly's *Euphues, the Anatomy of Wit* (1578), whose immensely popular style consisted of long series of balanced antitheses and metaphors drawn from the animal kingdom. Sidney's dislike of Lyly was perhaps compounded by the fact that his patron was the Earl of Oxford, who, in an incident over who had preference over a tennis court, quarreled with and humiliated Sidney before a courtly audience.

[268] Marcus Antonius (143-87 B. C.) and Lucius Licinius Crassus (c. 95 B. C.) were important Roman statesmen and orators.

[269] *De Oratore* (*On Oratory*), 2.1.1.

nearest step to persuasion, which persuasion is the chief mark of oratory. I do not doubt, I say, but that they used these knacks very sparingly, which who doth generally use, any man may see doth dance to his own music, and so be noted by the audience more careful to speak curiously than to speak truly. Undoubtedly (at least to my opinion undoubtedly), I have found in divers smally-learned courtiers a more sound style than in some professors of learning, of which I can guess no other cause but that the courtier, following that which by practice he findeth fittest to nature, therein, though he know it not, doth according to art, though not by art, where the other using art show art and not to hide art,[271] as in these cases he should do, flieth from nature, and indeed abuseth art.

But what? methinks I deserve to be pounded for straying from poetry to oratory, but both have such an affinity in this wordish consideration that I think this digression will make my meaning receive the fuller understanding, which is not to take upon me to teach poets how they should do, but only, finding my self sick among the rest,[272] to show some one or two spots of the common infection grown among the most part of writers, that acknowledging our selves somewhat awry, we may bend to the right use both of matter and manner. Whereto our language giveth us great occasion, being indeed capable of any excellent

---

[270] The ears of the populace, the plebians (not the elite).

[271] This theory of artfully hiding art bears considerable resemblance to Baldesare Castiglione's notion of *sprezzatura*, the art of concealing "all art" and making "whatever is done or said appear to be without effort and almost without any thought about it" (*The Book of the Courtier*, trans. Charles Singleton, bk. 1, p. 43).

[272] One could ascribe this passage to Sidney's urbane irony along with the modesty topos, but his self-condemnation finds echoes in both his refusal to recommend poetry to Edward Denny and (according to Edward Moffett, physician to the Sidney family and Sidney's first biographer) his fervently expressed wish as he lay dying to have his poetic and fictive works burned. Moffett's account, however, needs to be read with a grain of salt, although it indicates that an idealizing biography of Sidney required him to retract his fictional works.

exercising of it. I know some will say it is a mingled language. And why not so much the better, taking the best of both the other? Another will say it wanteth grammar. Nay, truly it hath that praise that it wants not grammar, for grammar it might have, but it needs it not, being so easy in itself and so void of those cumbersome differences of cases, genders, moods, and tenses which, I think, was a piece of the Tower of Babylon's curse, that a man should be put to school to learn his mother tongue.[273] But for the uttering sweetly and properly the conceits of the mind, which is the end of speech, that hath it equally with any other tongue in the world, and is particularly happy in compositions of two or three words together, near the Greek, far beyond the Latin, which is one of the greatest beauties can be in a language.

Now, of versifying, there are two sorts, the one ancient, the other modern. The ancient marked the quantity of each syllable, and according to that framed his verse; the modern, observing only number, with some regard of the accent, the chief life of it standeth in that like sounding of the words, which we call rhyme.[274] Whether of these be the more excellent would bear many speeches, the ancient, no doubt, more fit for music, both words and time observing quantity, and more fit lively to express divers passions by the low or lofty sound of the well-weighed syllable. The latter, likewise, with his rhyme striketh a certain music to the ear, and, in fine, since it doth delight, though by another way, it obtains the same purpose, there being in either sweetness and wanting in neither majesty. Truly, the English, before any vulgar[275] language I know, is fit for both sorts. For, for the ancient, the Italian is so full of vowels that it must be ever be

[273] Genesis 11:1-9 tells how Nimrod presumed to attempt building a tower "with its top in the heavens" (the Tower of Babel) and how God punished him through the proliferation of languages. As a result, nobody working on the tower could understand anybody else.
[274] Compare Sidney's earlier separation of rhyming and poetry: "One may be a poet without versing and a versifier without poetry" (p. 95).
[275] Vernacular, not Latin or Greek.

cumbered with elisions; the Dutch, so of the other side, with consonants, that they cannot yield the sweet sliding fit for a verse; the French in his whole language hath not one word that hath his accent in the last syllable saving two, called *antepenultima*; and little more hath the Spanish, and therefore very gracelessly may they use dactyls.[276] The English is subject to none of these defects.

Now, for the rhyme, though we do not observe quantity, yet we observe the accent very precisely, which other languages either cannot do or will not do absolutely. That *caesura*, or breathing place, in the midst of the verse, neither Italian nor Spanish have, the French and we never almost fail of. Lastly, even the very rhyme itself, the Italian cannot put it in the last syllable, by the French named the masculine rhyme, but still in the next to the last, which the French call the female, or the next before that, which the Italian term *sdrucciola*.[277] The example of the former is *buono*, *suono*; of the *sdrucciola* is *femina*, *semina*. The French, of the other side, hath both male as *bon*, *son*; and the female, as *plaise*, *taise*. But the *sdrucciola* he hath not, where the English hath all three, as *due*, *true*; *father*, *rather*; *motion*, *potion*,[278] with much more which might be said, but that already I find the triflings of this discourse is much too enlarged.

So, that since the ever-praiseworthy poesy is full of virtue-breeding-delightfulness, and void of no gift that ought to be in the noble name of learning; since the blames laid against it are either false or feeble; since the cause why it is not esteemed in England is the fault of poet-apes, not poets; since, lastly, our tongue is most fit to honor poesy, and to be honored by poesy, I conjure you[279] all that have had the evil luck to read this ink-wasting toy

---

[276]A dactyl has one accented syllable followed by two unaccented syllables.

[277] Slippery.

[278] Both "motion" and "potion" should be pronounced with three syllables.

[279] Compare Sidney's earlier use of this verb: "the poet never maketh any circles about your imagination, to conjure you to believe for true what he writeth" (p. 98).

of mine,[280] even in the name of the nine Muses, no more to scorn the sacred mysteries of poesy, no more to laugh at the name of poets, as though they were next inheritors to fools; no more to jest at the reverent title of a rhymer,[281] but to believe with Aristotle that they were the ancient treasurers of the Grecian's divinity;[282] to believe with Bembus that they were first bringers in of all civility;[283] to believe with Scaliger that no philosopher's precepts can sooner make you an honest man than the reading of Virgil;[284] to believe with Clauserus, the translator of Cornutus,[285] that it pleased the heavenly Deity by Hesiod and Homer, under the veil of fables, to give us all knowledge, logic, rhetoric, philosophy, natural and moral, and *quid non*?[286] to believe with me that there are many mysteries contained in poetry, which of purpose were written darkly, lest by profane wits it should be abused;[287] to believe with Landino that they are so beloved of the gods that whatsoever they write proceeds of a divine fury.[288] Lastly, to believe themselves when they tell you they will make you immortal by their verses. Thus doing, your name shall flourish in the printer's shops; thus doing, you shall be kin to many a poetical preface;[289] thus doing,

---

[280] In *AS* 18, Sidney writes, " My youth doth waste, my knowledge brings forth toys."

[281] Earlier in the *Apology*, Sidney explicitly divorces poetry from rhyme: " One may be a poet without versing and a versifier without poetry" (p. 95).

[282] Theology. Significantly, given Sidney's earlier criticism of historians for relying on secondary rather than primary sources, this statement derives from Boccaccio (*De Genealogia Deorum Gentilium*, 14.8), who credits Aristotle. Aristotle himself makes no such statement.

[283] See n. 212.

[284] *Poetics*, 3.19.

[285] Cornutus was a Stoic philosopher of the first century, A. D.; Conrad Clauserus, a German humanist, brought out a translation of Cornutus in 1543.

[286] What not.

[287] In *AS* 28, Sidney explicitly condemns allegorical interpretation.

[288] An inspired frenzy. Cristoforo Landino (1424-1504). In addition to writing commentaries on Horace and Virgil, Landino also brought out an important edition of Dante's *Divine Comedy*. Sidney "conjures" the reader, however, to believe something he rejects earlier in the *Apology*: "[Plato] attributeth unto poesy more than myself do, namely, to be a very inspiring of a divine force, far above man's wit ..." (p. 107).

[289] Compare Sidney's earlier condemnation of the proliferation of poets in the shops: "For now, as if all the muses were got with child to bring forth bastard poets, without

you shall dwell upon superlatives; thus doing, though you be *libertino patre natus*,[290] you shall suddenly grow *Herculea proles*,[291]

Si quid mea carmina possunt;[292]

thus doing, you should shall be placed with Dante's Beatrice, or Virgil's Anchises.[293]

But if (fie of such a but) you be born so near the dull-making cataract of Nilus that you cannot hear the planet-like music of poetry;[294] if you have so earth-creeping a mind that it cannot lift itself up to look to the sky of poetry, or rather, by a certain rustical disdain, will become such a mome[295] as to be a Momus[296] of poetry, then though I will not wish unto you the ass's ears of Midas, nor to be driven by a poet's verses as Bubonax was,[297] to hang himself; nor to be rhymed to death, as is said to be done in Ireland. Yet thus much curse I must send you in the behalf of all poets—that while you live, you live in love, and never get favor for lacking skill of a sonnet; and when you die, your memory die for want of an epitaph.

---

any commission they do pass over the banks of Helicon till they make the readers more weary than post-horses ...."

[290] "A freedman's [a former slave's] son" (Horace, *Satires*, 1.6.6).

[291] Descendant of Hercules.

[292] "If my songs can do anything" (Virgil, *Aeneid*, 9.446).

[293] Beatrice, the inspiration of Dante's love poems in the *Vita Nuova*, meets Dante in the *Paradiso*; Aeneas carries his father through the burning ruins of Troy and meets him again in the underworld (*Aeneid*, bk. 6).

[294] According to Cicero, just as the roar of the Nile causes people to go deaf, so are our ears deafened to the music of the spheres (*Somnium Scipionis [Dream of Scipio]*, 5.10-18).

[295] A fool.

[296] God of mockery, a mean-spirited carper or critic.

[297] Bubonax is Sidney's conflation of the names Bupalus and Hipponax, whose story Pliny tells in the *Natural History*: Bupalus, a sculptor, offended the poet Hipponax by making an ugly statue of him. In revenge, Hipponax wrote such a bitter satire that Bupalus killed himself (36.12).

℘ SIR P. S. HIS
ASTROPHEL AND
STELLA.

Wherein the excellence of fweete
Poefie is concluded.

At London,
Printed for Thomas Newman.
Anno Domini. 1591.

Astrophil and Stella. This item is reproduced by permission of *The
Huntington Library, San Marino, California.*

Astrophil and Stella

1.[1]

Loving in truth, and fain in verse my love to show,
That she, dear she,[2] might take some pleasure of my pain.
Pleasure might cause her read, reading might make her know,
Knowledge might pity win, and pity grace obtain.[3]
I sought fit words to paint the blackest face of woe,
Studying inventions fine, her wits to entertain.
Oft turning others' leaves to see if thence would flow
Some fresh and fruitful showers upon my sun-burned brain.
But words came halting forth, wanting invention's stay,
Invention, Nature's child, fled step-dame Study's blows,
And others' feet still seemed but strangers in my way.
Thus great with child to speak, and helpless in my throes,[4]
Biting my truant pen, beating myself for spite,
"Fool," said my Muse to me, "look in thy heart and write."

---

[1] *AS* 1, 3, 6, and 15 seem to introduce a new poetics, one based on originality rather than imitation, that accords with the section of the *Apology* asserting the poet's freedom to range "only within the zodiac of his own wit" (p. 64). However, just as Sidney returns in the *Apology* to imitation as the basis for poetic creation (p. 66), the assertion of originality is also a common trope. Ringler, for example, cites Du Bellay's *Regrets* 4: "I do not want to turn over the pages of Greek models" (*The Poems of Sir Philip Sidney*, 459; my translation).

[2] This phrase is "That the dear she" in the manuscript tradition and in the unauthorized 1591 edition. It was amended to "That she, dear she" in the 1598 folio edition of Sidney's works, which was authorized by Sidney's sister, the Countess of Pembroke.

[3] Compare Stephen Gosson's description of how poetry leads lockstep to sin and death in the excerpt from *The School of Abuse* in this edition, p. 270.

[4] On male poets using feminine birth metaphors to describe the creative act, see Katherine E. Mauss, "A Womb of His Own: Male Renaissance Poets in the Female Body," *Sexuality and Gender in Early Modern Europe*, ed. James G. Turner. Compare *AS* 50. For a similar use of consequences, see *AS* 44.

[5] A bad shot, ineffectual.

[6] Cupid.

2.

Not at first sight, nor with a dribbèd[5] shot,
Love[6] gave the wound which while I breathe will bleed.
But known worth did in mine of time proceed,
'Til by degrees it had full conquest got.
I saw and liked, I liked but lovèd not,
I loved, but straight did not what Love decreed.
At length to Love's decrees, I—forced—agreed,
Yet with repining at so partial lot.
Now even that footstep of lost liberty
Is gone, and now like slave-born Muscovite
I call it praise to suffer tyranny.
And now employ the remnant of my wit
To make myself believe that all is well,
While with a feeling skill I paint my hell.

3.

Let dainty wits cry on the sisters nine[7]
That bravely masked their fancies may be told.
Or Pindar's apes flaunt they in phrases fine,
Enameling with their pied flowers their thoughts of gold.
Or else let them in statelier glory shine,
Ennobling new-found tropes with problems old,
Or with strange similes enrich each line,
Of herbs or beasts which Ind or Afric hold.[8]
For me, in sooth, no Muse but one I know.
Phrases and problems from my reach do grow,
And strange things cost too dear for my poor sprites.[9]
How then? Even thus—in Stella's face I read
What love and beauty be, then all my deed
But copying is what in her Nature writes.[10]

---

[7] The Muses.
[8] India or Africa.
[9] Spirits.
[10] See also *AS* 6 and 55 for a similar treatment of the Muses.

4.

Virtue, alas, now let me take some rest,
Thou sett'st a 'bate[11] between my will and wit.
If vain love have my simple soul oppressed,
Leave what thou likest not, deal not thou with it.
Thy scepter use in some old Cato's breast,[12]
Churches or schools are for thy seat more fit.
I do confess, pardon a fault confessed,
My mouth too tender is for thy hard bit.
But if that needs thou wilt usurping be
The little reason that is left in me,
And still the effect of thy persuasions prove,
I swear, my heart such one show to thee,
That shrines in flesh so true a deity
That Virtue, thou thy self, shalt be in love.

5.

It is most true that eyes are formed to serve
The inward light, and that the heavenly part
Ought to be king, from whose rules who do swerve,
Rebels to Nature, strive for their own smart.
It is most true what we call Cupid's dart
An image is which for ourselves we carve
And, fools, adore in temple of our heart
'Til that good god make church and churchman starve.
True that true beauty virtue is indeed
Whereof this beauty can be but a shade
Which elements with mortal mixture breed.
True that on earth we are but pilgrims made,
And should in soul up to our country move.[13]
True, and yet true that I must Stella love.

---

[11] Debate
[12] Roman moralist and lawmaker. In the *Apology*, Sidney calls him "a bitter punisher of faults" and an enemy of Greek culture (p. 103), which was though to be soft, effeminate, and corrupt.
[13] Heaven.

6.

Some lovers speak when they their Muses entertain
Of hopes begot by fear, of wot not what desires, [14]
Of force of heavenly beams infusing hellish pain,
Of living deaths, dear wounds, fair storms and freezing fires.[15]
Someone his song in Jove and Jove's strange tales attires,
'Broidered with bulls and swans, powdered with golden rain.[16]
Another humbler wit to shepherd's pipes retires,
Yet hiding royal blood full oft in rural vein.
To some a sweetest plaint a sweetest style affords,
While tears pour out his ink, and sighs breath out his words.
His paper, pale Despair and pain his pen doth move.
I can speak what I feel, and feel as much as they,
But think that all the map of my state I display
When trembling voice brings forth that I do Stella love.

7.

When Nature made her chief work, Stella's eyes,
In color black, why wrapped she beams so bright?
Would she in beamy black, like painter wise,
Frame daintiest luster mixed of shades and light?
Or did she else that sober hue devise,
In object best to knit and strength our sight,
Lest if no veil those brave gleams did disguise,
They sun-like should more dazzle than delight?
Or would she her miraculous power show
That whereas black seems beauty's contrary,
She e'en in black doth make all beauties flow?
Both so, and thus, she, minding Love, should be
Placed ever there, gave him this mourning weed
To honor all their deaths who for her bleed.

---

[14] That is, "of who knows not what desires."
[15] These oxymorons are commonplaces of Petrarchan verse.
[16] Embroidered. The bull, the swan, and rain are Jove's disguises.

8.

Love, born in Greece, of late fled from his native place,
Forced by a tedious proof that Turkish hardened heart
Is no fit mark to pierce with his fine pointed dart,
And, pleased with our soft peace, stayed here his flying race.
But finding these north climes do coldly him embrace,
Not used to frozen clips,[17] he strave[18] to find some part
Where with most ease and warmth he might employ his art.
At length he perched himself in Stella's joyful face,
Whose fair skin, beamy eyes, like morning sun on snow,
Deceived the quaking boy, who thought from so pure light
Effects of lively heat must needs in nature grow.
But she, most fair, most cold, made him thence take his flight
To my close heart where, while some firebrands he did lay,
He burned unwares[19] his wings, and cannot fly away.

9.

Queen Virtue's court, which some call Stella's face,
Prepared by Nature's chiefest furniture,
Hath his front built of alabaster pure;
Gold is the covering of that stately place.
The door by which sometimes comes forth her Grace
Red porphyr is, which lock of pearl makes sure,
Whose porches rich, which name of cheeks endure,
Marble mixed red and white do interlace.
The windows now through which this heavenly guest
Looks o'er the world and can find nothing such
Which dare claim from those lights the name of best,
Of touch they are that without touch doth touch,
Which Cupid's self from Beauty's mine did draw,
Of touch they are, and poor I am their straw.

[17] Hugs, embraces.
[18] Strived, tried.
[19] Unwary.

10.

Reason, in faith thou art well served that still
Would'st brabbling[20] be with sense and love in me.
I rather wished thee climb the Muses' hill
Or reach the fruit of Nature's choicest tree,
Or seek heaven's course, or heaven's inside to see.[21]
Why should'st thou toil our thorny soil to till?
Leave Sense, and those which Sense's objects be.
Deal thou with powers of thoughts, leave love to Will.
But thou would'st needs fight both with Love and Sense
With sword of wit, giving wounds of dispraise
'Til downright blows did foil thy cunning fence.
For soon as they strake[22] thee with Stella's rays,
Reason, thou kneelest and offer'st straight to prove
By reason good, good reason her to love.

11.

In truth, O Love, with what a boyish kind
Thou dost proceed in thy most serious ways,
That when the heaven to thee his best displays,
Yet of that best thou leav'st the best behind.
For like a child that some fair book doth find,
With gilded leaves or colored velum plays,
Or at the most on some fine picture stays,
But never heeds the fruit of writer's mind.
So when thou saw'st in Nature's cabinet
Stella, though straight lookst babies in her eyes,
In her cheeks' pit thou did'st thy pitfold[23] set,
And in her breast bo-peep or couching lies,
Playing and shining in each outward part,
But, fool, seek'st not to get into her heart.

---

[20] Arguing, remonstrating.
[21] Study the movements of the stars, but also, to seek transgressive, forbidden knowledge, which includes the writing of poetry.
[22] Struck.
[23] A birdtrap.

12.

Cupid, because thou shin'st in Stella's eyes,
That from her locks, thy day-nets,[24] none 'scapes free,
That those lips swell, so full of thee they be
That her sweet breath makes oft thy flames to rise,
That in her breast thy pap well-sugared lies,
That her grace gracious makes thy wrongs, that she
What words so ere she speaks persuades for thee,
That her clear voice lifts thy fame to the skies.
Thou count'st Stella thine, like those whose powers
Having got up a breach by fighting well,
Cry "Victory, this fair day all is ours."
O no, her heart is such a citadel,[25]
So fortified with wit, stored with disdain,
That to win it is all the skill and pain.

13.

Phoebus was judge between Jove, Mars, and Love,
Of those three gods whose arms the fairest were.
Jove's golden shield did eagle sables bear,
Whose talons held young Ganymede[26] above.
But in vert field[27] Mars bare a golden spear
Which through a bleeding heart his point did shove.
Each had his crest: Mars carried Venus' glove,[28]
Jove on his helm the thunderbolt did rear.
Cupid then smiles, for on his crest there lies

[24] A net for catching larks.

[25] The conceit of woman as fortress and lover as besieger is a commonplace of medieval and early modern poetry.

[26] A boy so beautiful that Jove fell in love with him and, transforming himself into an eagle, carried him to the heavens to be his cup-bearer (Ovid, *Metamorphoses*, 10.155-61); also the commonest epithet for the passive partner in a homosexual relationship. Compare *AS* 70.

[27] A green background.

[28] Vulcan revealed the adultery between his wife, Venus, and Mars by catching the lovers in a net. (Ovid, *Metamorphoses*, 4.173-89). See the *Apology*, n. 220.

[29] Red roses over a silver background. The arms of the Devereux family are three red disks in a silver field.

Stella's fair hair, her face he makes his shield,
Where roses gules are born in silver field.[29]
Phoebus drew wide the curtains of the skies
To blaze[30] these last, and swore devoutly then,
The first, thus matched, were scarcely gentlemen.[31]

14.

Alas, have I not pain enough, my friend,
Upon whose breast a fiercer grip doth tire
Than did on him who first stale[32] down the fire,
While Love on me doth all his quiver spend,
But with your rhubarb words[33] you must contend
To grieve me worse in saying that desire
Doth plunge my well-formed soul even in the mire
Of sinful thoughts, which do in ruin end?
If that be sin, which doth the manners[34] frame,
Well stayed with truth in word and faith of deed,
Ready of wit and fearing naught[35] but shame.
If that be sin, which in fixed hearts doth breed
A loathing of all loose unchastity,
Then love is sin, and let me sinful be.[36]

---

[30] To declare, but also to create a "blazon," a heraldic description of individual parts.

[31] They scarcely deserved a coat of arms. Love's assertion that Stella elevates him above Jove and Mars, that in comparison they are "scarcely gentlemen," suggests an imaginative inversion of Sidney's actual position in the social hierarchy of Elizabethan court and culture.

[32] Stole. The reference is to Prometheus, who, for stealing fire from the gods and giving it to humankind, was condemned to be bound to a rock and having his liver perpetually eaten by an eagle.

[33] Caustic, if medicinal, words. See also the *Apology*, p. 84, and n. 112.

[34] Morality.

[35] Nothing.

[36] Compare Sidney's argument in the *Apology* that poetry teaches virtue (especially his equivocal defense of love poetry on pp. 99-101) and the arguments of poetry's antagonists that it encourages vice.

15.

You that do search for every purling spring
Which from the ribs of old Parnassus flows,
And every flower, not sweet perhaps, which grows
Near thereabout, into your poesy wring,
You that do dictionary's method bring
Into your rhymes, running in rattling rows.
You that poor Petrarch's long-deceased woes[37]
With newborn sighs and denisend[38] wit do sing,
You take wrong ways, those far-fet[39] helps be such
As do bewray[40] a want of inward touch,
And sure at length stolen goods do come to light.[41]
But if, both for your love and skill, your name
You seek to nurse at fullest breasts of Fame,
Stella behold, and then 'gin to endite.[42]

16.

In nature apt to like when I did see
Beauties which were of many carets fine,
My boiling sprites[43] did thither soon incline
And, Love, I thought that I was full of thee.
But finding not those restless flames in me,
Which others said did make their souls to pine,
I thought those babes of some pin's hurt did whine,
By my love judging what love's pain might be.
But while I thus with this young lion played,
Mine eyes—shall I say cursed or blessed?—beheld
Stella. Now she is named, need more be said?
In her sight I a lesson new have spelled,

---

[37] On Petrarch, see the *Apology*, p. 59, and n. 14, and the introduction, pp. 40-42.
[38] Naturalized.
[39] Far-fetched.
[40] Betray.
[41] The images and lines plagiarized from other poets.
[42] Begin to write. Compare Sidney's critique of imitation in *AS* 1, 3, 6, and 15
[43] Spirits.

I now have learned love right, and learned even so
As who by being poisoned doth poison know.

17.
His mother[44] dear Cupid offended late
Because that Mars, grown slacker in her love,
With pricking shot he did not throughly move,[45]
To keep the pace of their first loving state.
The boy refused for fear of Mars's hate,
Who threatened stripes if he his wrath did prove.
But she in chafe[46] him from her lap did shove,
Brake bow, brake shafts, while Cupid weeping sate,[47]
'Til that his grandame Nature, pitying it,
Of Stella's brows made him two better bows,
And in her eyes of arrows infinite.
O how for joy he leaps, O how he crows,
And straight therewith, like wags new got to play,
Falls to shrewd turns, and I was in his way.

18.
With what sharp checks I in myself am shent[48]
When into Reason's audit I do go,
And by just counts myself a bankrout[49] know
Of all those goods which Heaven to me hath lent.
Unable quite to pay even Nature's rent
Which unto it by birthright I do owe.
And which is worse, no good excuse can show
But that my wealth I have most idly spent.
My youth doth waste, my knowledge brings forth toys,[50]

[44] Venus.
[45] Meaning, the shot did not move through him.
[46] Anger.
[47] Sat.
[48] Shamed.
[49] Bankrupt.
[50] Such as love poetry. Also, Sidney calls the *Apology* "this ink-wasting toy of mine" (pp. 124-25).

My wit doth strive those passions to defend
Which for reward spoil it with vain annoys. [51]
I see my course to lose myself doth bend.
I see, and yet no greater sorrow take
Than that I lose no more for Stella's sake.

19.
On Cupid's bow how are my heartstrings bent
That see my wrack[52] and yet embrace the same?
When most I glory, then I feel most shame.
I willing run, yet while I run repent.
My best wits still their own disgrace invent.[53]
My very ink turns straight to Stella's name
And yet my words, as them my pen doth frame,
Avise[54] themselves that they are vainly spent.
For though she passes all things, yet what is all
That unto me, who fare like him that both
Looks to the skies and in a ditch doth fall?
O let me prop my mind, yet in his growth,
And not in nature, for best fruits unfit.
"Scholar," saith Love, "bend hitherward your wit."

20.
Fly, fly, my friends, I have my death wound, fly.
See there that boy, that murth'ring[55] boy, I say,
Who, like a thief hid in dark bush, doth lie
'Til bloody bullet get him wrongful prey.
So, tyrant, he no fitter place could spy,

---

[51] Although today "annoy" means a slight irritation, during this period the term also connoted a great disaster. For example, Shakespeare's Titus Andronicus refers to his daughter's rape as the "root of thy annoy" (*Titus Andronicus* 4. 1. 49; Riverside edition). Significantly, *annoy* is the last word of this sequence (see *AS* 108).

[52] Wreck.

[53] Sidney uses his love poetry as evidence of his moral decline.

[54] Advise, warn.

[55] Murdering.

Nor so fair level[56] in so secret stay,
As that sweet black which veils the heav'nly eye.
There himself with his shot he close doth lay.
Poor passenger, pass now thereby I did,
And stayed, pleased with the prospect of the place,
While that black hue from me the bad guest hid.
But straight I saw motions of lightning's grace
And then descried the glist'ring of his dart;
But ere I could fly thence, it pierced my heart.

21.

Your words, my friend (right healthful caustics) blame
My young mind marred, whom Love doth windlass[57] so
That mine own writings,[58] like bad servants, show
My wits quick in vain thoughts, in virtue lame:
That Plato I read for naught[59] but if he tame
Such coltish gyres; that to my birth I owe
Nobler desires, lest else that friendly foe,
Great expectation, wear a train of shame.
For since mad March great promise made of me,
If now the May of my years much decline,
What can be hoped my harvest time will be?[60]
Sure you say well, your wisdom's golden mine
Dig deep with learning's spade. Now tell me this:
Hath this world ought so fair as Stella is?

22.

In highest way of heaven the sun did ride,
Progressing then from fair twins' golden place,[61]

---

[56] Aim.
[57] Ambush.
[58] That is, the poems of this sequence.
[59] Nothing.
[60] At the time Sidney wrote this sequence, he was known, as Arthur F. Marotti puts it, "as a politically, economically, and socially disappointed young man" ("Love is not Love," 400). For more details on the course of Sidney's political career and his disappointments, see the introduction, pp. 15-32.
[61] The sun moves from Gemini to Cancer, when it is at its hottest.

Having no scarf of clouds before his face,
But shining forth of heat in his chief pride,
When some fair ladies, by hard promise tied,
On horseback met him in his furious race;
Yet each prepared, with fan's well-shading grace,
From that foe's wounds their tender skins to hide.
Stella alone with face unarmèd marched,
Either to do like him, which open shone,
Or careless of the wealth because her own.
Yet were the hid and meaner beauties parched,
Her daintiest bare went free. The cause was this:
The sun, which others burned, did her but kiss.

23.

The curious wits, seeing dull pensiveness
Bewray[62] itself in my long-settled eyes
Whence those same fumes of melancholy rise,
With idle pains and missing aim do guess.
Some, that know how my spring I did address,
Deem that my Muse some fruit of knowledge plies.[63]
Others, because the prince my service tries,
Think that I think state errors to redress.
But harder judges judge ambition's rage,
Scourge of itself, still climbing slipp'ry place,
Holds my young brain captiv'd in golden cage.
O fools, or over-wise, alas, the race
Of all my thoughts hath neither stop nor start
But only Stella's eyes and Stella's heart.[64]

---

[62] Betray, show.

[63] Works busily at, leading to Astrophil's self-absorption. The "fruit of knowledge" is meant to signify a work other than lyric poetry.

[64] The Muse-haters often accused poetry of rendering its practitioners unfit for state service. In his carnivalesque comedy, *Bartholomew Fair*, Ben Jonson mocks this common charge by putting it in the mouth of Justice Overdo, who suspects a young pickpocket "of a terrible taint, poetry! With which idle disease if he be infected, there's no hope of him in a state-course. *Actum est* of him for a commonwealth's-man if he go to't in rhyme once." See also Sonnet 27.

24.

Rich fools there be whose base and filthy heart
Lies hatching still the goods wherein they flow,
And damning their own selves to Tantal's[65] smart,
Wealth breeding want, more bless'd, more wretched grow.
Yet to those fools heaven such wit doth impart
As what their hands do hold, their heads do know,
And knowing, love, and loving, lay apart
As sacred things, far from all danger's show.
But that rich fool,[66] who by blind fortune's lot
The richest gem of love and life enjoys,
And can with foul abuse such beauties blot,
Let him, deprived of sweet but unfelt joys,
Exiled for aye[67] from those high treasures, which
He knows not, grow in only folly rich.

25.

The wisest scholar,[68] of the wight most wise
By Phoebus's doom,[69] with sugared sentence says
That virtue, if it once met with our eyes,
Strange flames of love it in our souls would raise.[70]
But for that man with pain this truth descries,
While he each thing in sense's balance weighs,
And so nor will nor can behold those skies
Which inward sun to heroic mind displays.
Virtue of late, with virtuous care to steer
Love of herself, takes Stella's shape that she
To mortal eyes might sweetly shine in her.
It is most true, for since I her did see,

---

[65] Tantalus.
[66] Penelope Devereux's husband was Lord Robert Rich.
[67] Forever.
[68] Plato.
[69] Verdict, judgment. In his *Apology*, Socrates asserts that a friend of his asked the Delphic oracle who was the wisest man, and Apollo (Phoebus) answered Socrates (21a).
[70] Plato, *Phaedrus*, 250d-251c.

Virtue's great beauty in that face I prove
And find th'effect, for I do burn in love.

26.

Though dusty wits dare scorn astrology,
And fools can think those lamps of purest light
Whose numbers, ways, greatness, eternity
Promising wonders, wonder to invite,
To have for no cause birthright in the sky,
But for to spangle the black weeds of night,
Or for some brawl,[71] which in that chamber high
They should still dance to please a gazer's sight.
For me, I do nature unidle know,
And know great causes great effects procure,
And know those bodies high reign on the low.
And if these rules did fail, proof makes me sure
Who oft fore-judge my after-following race
By only those two stars in Stella's face.[72]

27.[73]

Because I oft in dark abstracted guise
Seem most alone in greatest company,
With dearth of words or answers quite awry
To them that would make speech of speech arise.
They deem, and of their doom the rumor flies
That poison foul of bubbling pride doth lie
So in my swelling breast that only I
Fawn on myself, and others to despise.
Yet pride, I think, doth not my soul possess,
Which looks too oft in his unflatt'ring glass.[74]

---

[71] A type of dance.
[72] The "stars" are Stella's eyes.
[73] As in *AS* 23, the replacement of politics with illicit love as the center of the speaker's universe undermines the speaker's credibility and substantiates the charge that poetry makes one unfit for politics. See note 63.
[74] Mirror.

But one worse fault, ambition, I confess,
That makes me oft my best friends overpass
Unseen, unheard, while Thought to highest place
Bends all his powers, even unto Stella's grace.

28.
You that with allegory's curious frame
Of others' children[75] changelings use to make,
With me those pains for God's sake do not take,
I list not dig so deep for brazen fame.[76]
When I say "Stella," I do mean the same
Princess of beauty for whose only sake
The reins of Love I love, though never slake,[77]
And joy therein though nations count it shame.
I beg no subject to use eloquence,
Nor in hid ways to guide philosophy.
Look at my hands for no such quintessence.
But know that I, in pure simplicity,
Breath out the flames which burn within my heart,
Love only reading unto me this art.[78]

29.
Like some weak lords neighbored by mighty kings,
To keep themselves and their chief cities free
Do easily yield, that all their coasts may be
Ready to store their camps of needful things,
So Stella's heart, finding what pow'r Love brings,
To keep itself in life and liberty
Doth willing grant that in the frontiers he
Use all to help his other conquerings,
And thus her heart escapes. But thus her eyes

---

[75] Others' poetry. Sidney objects to the practice of interpreting poetry allegorically (in which the literal meaning of words signifies another meaning) so that the text means something completely different from the author's intention.

[76] I do not desire ["list"] eternal fame.

[77] The reins of Love never slacken.

[78] *AS* 1,3, 6, and 15 also deal with poetics.

Serve him with shot, her lips his heralds are,
Her breasts his tents, legs his triumphal car,
Her flesh his food, her skin his armor brave,
And I, but for because my prospect lies
Upon that coast, am giv'n up for a slave.

30.

Whether the Turkish new-moon minded be
To fill his horns this year on Christian coast;[79]
How Poles' right king means, without leave of host,
To warm with ill-made fire[80] cold Moscovy;[81]
If French can yet three parts in one agree;[82]
What now the Dutch in their full diets boast;[83]
How Holland hearts, now so good towns be lost,
Trust in the shade of pleasing Orange tree;[84]
How Ulster likes of that same golden bit

[79] The moon and horns refer to the Turkish / Isalmic crescent. The Islamic Turkish empire posed a continuing military threat to Europe. All the references in this sonnet are to matters that were not only of importance to England, but also of particular importance to Sidney himself.

[80] Cannon shot.

[81] Stephen Bathory, elected king in 1576, invaded Russia (Moscovy) in 1580. The other claimant to the throne was the Emperor Maximilian II, also the employer of John Pietro Pugliano (see the *Apology*, n. 1). Sidney concerned himself greatly with Polish political affairs. The letters to Hubert Languet are filled with comments on them, and in a 1574 diplomatic report to uncle, the Earl of Leicester, Sidney observed that "The Polacks heartily repent their so far-fetched election, being now in such case as neither they have the king, nor anything the king with so many oaths had promised, besides, that there is lately stirred up a very dangerous sedition for the same cause [i.e., religious conflict between Catholics and Protestants] that hath bred such lamentable ruins in France and Flanders" (*Correspondence*, n. 1).

[82] The Catholics, the Protestant Hugenots, and the moderate Politiques, who competed for power until well after the accession of Henry IV in 1589.

[83] The diet (parliament) of the Holy Roman Empire, held in 1582. "Dutch," in this case, meant German.

[84] Five Dutch towns were conquered by Spain in 1581-1582, and William of Orange (1533-1584) led the Protestant-based resistance against Spanish rule in the Netherlands. William met Sidney in 1572, and said afterward that he "conceived a great opinion of him." Sidney would ultimately lose his life in this struggle.

[85] Henry Sidney was governor of Ireland three times, his final term ending in 1578.

Wherewith my father once made it half tame;[85]
If in the Scottish court be welt'ring yet;[86]
These questions busy wits to me do frame.
I, cumbered with good manners, answer do
But know not how, for still I think of you.

31.
With how sad steps, O moon, thou climb'st the skies,
How silently, and with how wan a face.
What, may it be that even in heav'nly place
That busy archer[87] his sharp arrows tries?
Sure, if that long-with-love-acquainted eyes
Can judge of love, thou feel'st a lover's case.
I read it in thy looks, thy languished grace,
To me, that feel the like, thy state descries.
Then e'en of fellowship, O moon, tell me,
Is constant love deemed there but want of wit?
Are beauties there as proud as here they be?
Do they above love to be loved, and yet
Those lovers scorn whom that Love doth possess?
Do they call virtue there, ungratefulness?[88]

[86] "Weltering" means violent movement up and down. Sidney was intimately acquainted with the extremely unstable political situation in Scotland because he was deeply involved with Walsingham's negotiations over the amount of Elizabeth's pension for James. In addition, Sidney's activities on James's behalf formed part of his larger project of promoting Protestant activism: a large grant would not only help the Scots Protestants retain political influence, but also help counteract the continental Catholic powers who were also negotiating with James Stuart. James would write an elegy for Sidney that appeared in *Academiae Cantabrigiensis Lachrymae Tumulo Noblilissimi Equitis, D. Philippi Sidneii Sacratae (1587)*, rpt. in *Elegies for Sir Philip Sidney (1587)*, ed. A. J. Colaianne and W. L. Godshalk. On Sidney and James, see Herman, "'Best of Poets, Best of Kings.'"
[87] Cupid.
[88] Katherine Duncan-Jones points out that the "inversion of the order of subject and object makes it hard to determine whether this means 'Do ladies in heaven call their lovers' virtue 'ungratefulness' . . . or 'Do ladies in heaven call their *own* ungratefulness virtue'?" (362). Compare Sidney's use of "virtue" throughout the sequence, but especially in *AS* 4 and 9, and compare also his use of "ungrateful" in Song 5.

32.[89]

Morpheus, the lively son of deadly sleep,[90]
Witness of life to them that living die,
A prophet oft, and oft an history,[91]
A poet eke[92], as humors fly or creep,[93]
Since thou in me so sure a power dost keep
That never I with closed-up sense do lie
But by thy work my Stella I descry,
Teaching blind eyes both how to smile and weep.
Vouchsafe of all acquaintance this to tell,
Whence hast thou ivory, rubies, pearl and gold,
To show her skin, lips, teeth and head so well?
"Fool," answers he, "no Indes[94] such treasures hold,
But from thy heart, while my sire charmeth thee,
Sweet Stella's image I do steal to me."

33.[95]

I might (unhappy word), O me, I might,
And then would not, or could not, see my bliss

---

[89] *AS* 32, 38, and 39 constitute a mini-sequence on sleep. Compare *AS* 98 and 99, which deal with sleep from a different perspective.

[90] Morpheus, the god who brings dreams, is the son of the god of sleep, Somnus. To maintain the meter, it should be pronounced as a two-syllable word ("Mor-fus").

[91] Presumably not an historian, but a storyteller.

[92] Also (an archaic form).

[93] Sidney's culture was deeply ambivalent about the possibility of modern prophecy. On the one hand, some of the more radical Protestants, especially in the 17th century, were given to calling themselves prophets and claiming divine guidance, if not inspiration. On the other hand, the later 16th century witnessed a proliferation of anti-prophecy tracts, such as Henry Howard's *A Defensative against the poyson of supposed Prophesies* (1583). So, the conflation of poetry and prophecy may not work to increase either poetry's or Astrophil's authority.

[94] India, but probably the lands in the Eastern trade routes generally, which generated tremendous wealth during this period. See also *AS* 92.

[95] Sidney's earlier editors agree that this somewhat obscure poem concerns Astrophil/Sidney's regret that he did not marry Stella/Penelope Devereux earlier, when he had the chance, presumably because he was not yet in love with her (see *AS* 2).

'Til now. Wrapped in a most infernal night,
I find how heav'nly day, wretch, I did miss.
Heart, rend thyself, thou dost thyself but right.
No lovely Paris made thy Helen his,[96]
No force, no fraud, robbed thee of thy delight,
Nor Fortune of thy fortune author is.
But to myself myself did give the blow,
While too much wit, forsooth, so troubled me,
That I respects for both our sakes must show,
And yet could not by rising morn foresee
How fair a day was near. O punished eyes,
That I had been more foolish, or more wise!

34.
Come, let me write. "And to what end?" To ease
A burdened heart. "How can words ease, which are
The glasses of thy daily vexing care?"
Oft cruel fights well-pictured forth do please.[97]
"Art not ashamed to publish[98] thy disease?"
Nay, that may breed my fame, it is so rare.
"But will not wise men think thy words fond ware?"[99]
Then be they close, [100]and so none shall displease.
"What idler thing, than speak and not be heard?"
What harder thing than smart and not to speak?
Peace, foolish wit, with wit my wit is marred.
Thus write I while I doubt to write,[101] and wreak
My harms on ink's poor loss. Perhaps some find
Stella's great pow'rs that so confuse my mind.

---

[96] Paris abducted Helen from the Greeks, thereby starting the Trojan War.
[97] In the *Apology*, Sidney writes, "as Aristotle saith, those things which in themselves are horrible, as cruel battles, unnatural monsters, are made in poetical imitation delightful" (p. 84).
[98] To make public, but not print in book form, as the word presently means.
[99] Foolish stuff, mere toys.
[100] Secret.
[101] Doubting the purpose of writing, but also "hesitate" or "fear."

35.

What may words say, or what may words not say,
Where truth itself must speak like flattery?
Within what bounds can one his liking stay
Where Nature doth with infinite agree?[102]
What Nestor's[103] counsel can my flames allay,
Since Reason's self doth blow the coal in me?
And ah, what hope that Hope should once see day
Where Cupid is sworn page to Chastity?
Honor is honored that thou dost possess
Him as thy slave, and now long-needy Fame
Doth even grow rich, naming my Stella's name.
Wit learns in thee perfection to express:
Not thou by praise, but praise in thee is raised.
It is a praise to praise when thou art praised.

36.

Stella, whence doth this new assault arise,
A conquered, yelden,[104] ransacked heart to win?
Whereto long since, through my long-battered eyes,
Whole armies of thy beauties entered in.
And there long since, Love, thy lieutenant, lies,
My forces razed, thy banners raised within.
Of conquest, do not these effects suffice,
But wilt new war upon thine own begin?
With so sweet voice, and by sweet Nature so,
In sweetest strength, so sweetly skilled withal,
In all sweet stratagems sweet Art can show,
That not my soul, which at thy foot did fall,
Long since forced by thy beams, but stone nor tree
By Sense's privilege, can 'scape[105] from thee.

---

[102] According to Ringler, "Stella, though a product of finite nature, is goddess-like and therefore infinite" (472).
[103] The aged counselor in Homer's *Iliad*.
[104] Yielded.
[105] Escape.

37. [106]

My mouth doth water, and my breast doth swell,
My tongue doth itch, my thoughts in labor be.
Listen then, Lordings, with good ear to me,
For of my life I must a riddle tell:
Towards Aurora's court[107] a nymph doth dwell,
Rich in all beauties which man's eye can see,
Beauties so far from reach of words that we
Abase her praise, saying she doth excel:
Rich in the treasure of deserved renown,
Rich in the riches of a royal heart,
Rich in those gifts which give th'eternal crown,
Who though most rich in these and every part,
Which make the patents[108] of true worldly bliss,
Hath no misfortune, but that Rich she is.

38.

This night, while sleep begins with heavy wings
To hatch[109] mine eyes, and that unbitted[110] thought
Doth fall to stray, and my chief powers are brought
To leave the scepter of all subject things.
The first that straight my fancy's error[111] brings
Unto my mind is Stella's image,[112] wrought
By Love's own self, but with so curious draught[113]
That she, methinks, not only shines but sings.

---

[106] The constant punning on "rich" plays on the last name of Stella/Penelope Devereux's husband. This sonnet was omitted from Newman's unauthorized edition, the earliest printed text, but restored in the authorized folio edition.

[107] The east. Lord Rich's family seat was in the eastern county of Essex.

[108] Ringler glosses this phrase as "comprise the grants" (473).

[109] To shade with very fine lines, in this case, to darken.

[110] Free, without a "bit."

[111] The wandering of the imagination, or fancy, as this faculty is sometimes called in Renaissance psychological manuals, freed ("unbitted") from the constraints of reason by sleep.

[112] For a similar emphasis on the self-reflexiveness of Astrophil's passion, see *AS* 5.

[113] So well drawn.

I start, look, hark, but what in closed-up sense
Was held, in opened sense it flies away,
Leaving me nought[114] but wailing eloquence.
I, seeing better sights in sight's decay,
Called it anew, and wooèd sleep again,
But him, her host, that unkind guest had slain.

39.

Come Sleep, O Sleep, the certain knot of peace,
The baiting place of wit, the balm of woe,
The poor man's wealth, the prisoner's release,
Th'indifferent judge 'tween the high and low.
With shield of proof shield me from out the press
Of those fierce darts Despair at me doth throw.
O make in me those civil wars to cease;
I will good tribute pay, if thou do so.
Take thou of me smooth pillows, sweetest bed,
A chamber deaf to noise and blind to light,
A rosy garland, and a weary head.
And if these things, as being thine by right,
Move not thy heavy grace, thou shalt in me,
Livelier than elsewhere, Stella's image see.

40.

As good to write as for to lie and groan.[115]
O Stella dear, how much thy pow'r hath wrought,
That hast my mind, none of the basest, brought
My still-kept course, while others sleep, to moan.
Alas, if from the height of Virtue's throne
Thou canst vouchsafe the influence of a thought

---

[114] Nothing.

[115] The Muse-haters commonly charged that poetry is "vain, idle, unsavory, and unprofitable," as the Puritan Divine, Richard Rogers put it *The Practice of Christianity* (1618; quoted in Russell Fraser, *The War Against Poetry*, 8).

Upon a wretch that long thy grace hath sought,
Weigh then how I by thee am overthrown.
And then think thus: although thy beauty be
Made manifest by such a victory,
Yet noblest conquerors do wrecks avoid.
Since then thou hast so far subduèd me
That in my heart I offer still to thee,
O do not let thy temple be destroyed.

41.

Having this day my horse, my hand, my lance
Guided so well that I obtained the prize,
Both by the judgment of the English eyes
And of some sent from that sweet enemy, France.[116]
Horsemen my skill in horsemanship advance,
Townfolks my strength; a daintier judge applies
His praise to sleight, which from good use doth rise.[117]
Some lucky wits impute it but to chance.
Others, because of both sides I do take
My blood from them who did excel in this,[118]
Think Nature me a man of arms did make.
How far they shoot awry! The true cause is this:
Stella looked on, and from her heavenly face
Sent forth the beams which made so fair my race.[119]

---

[116] The poem's scene is a joust attended by French diplomats. Sidney calls France the "sweet enemy" because it was England's traditional enemy. Also, Sidney vociferously opposed the Elizabeth's proposed marriage with the Duke of Alençon, the French king's brother (see the introduction, pp. 18-22). Impressing the French visitors as well as Stella would have seemed like double vindication. In a nice example of form matching content, this line is an alexandrine (twelve syllables), a rhythm much more common in French poetry.

[117] That is, a more discerning judge praises Astrophil/Sidney's physical dexterity, which arises from much practice.

[118] Sidney's father, grandfather, and uncles were all frequent and successful participants in tournaments.

[119] See, however, *AS* 53 for the opposite results of Stella's intervention.

42.

O eyes, which do the spheres of beauty move,
Whose beams be joys, whose joys all virtues be,
Who, while they make Love conquer, conquer Love,
The schools where Venus hath learned chastity.
O eyes, where humble looks most glorious prove,
Only-loved tyrants, just in cruelty,[120]
Do not, O do not from poor me remove,
Keep still my zenith, ever shine on me.
For though I never see them but straight'ways[121]
My life forgets to nourish languished sprites.
Yet still on me, O eyes, dart down your rays,
And if from majesty of sacred lights,
Oppressing mortal sense, my death proceed,
Wracks triumphs be, which Love (high set) doth breed.[122]

43.

Fair eyes, sweet lips, dear heart, that foolish I
Could hope by Cupid's help on you to prey,
Since to himself he doth your gifts apply
As his main force, choice sport, and easeful stay.
For when he will see who dare him gainsay,[123]
Then with those eyes he looks. Lo, by and by,
Each soul doth at Love's feet his weapons lay,
Glad if for her he give them leave to die.
When he will play, then in her lips he is,
Where blushing red, that Love's self them doth love,
With either lip he doth the other kiss.
But when he will for quiet's sake remove
From all the world, her heart is then his room,
Where he well knows no man to him can come.

---

[120] Oxymorons: the only tyrant Astrophil loves, who is cruel but just (or just but cruel).
[121] Immediately.
[122] My death, this "wrack" (wreck) will be a triumph for Love, who caused it.
[123] That is, dare Love by denying him.

44.

My words I know do well set forth my mind.
My mind bemoans his sense of inward smart;
Such smart may pity claim of any heart,
Her heart, sweet heart, is of no tiger's kind.
And yet she hears, yet I no pity find,
But more I cry, less grace she doth impart.[124]
Alas, what cause is there so overthwart[125]
That Nobleness itself makes thus unkind?
I much do guess, yet find no truth save this:
That when the breath of my complaints doth touch
Those dainty doors unto the court of bliss,
The heav'nly nature of that place is such
That once come there, the sobs of mine annoys[126]
Are metamorphos'd straight to tunes of joys.

45.

Stella oft sees the very face of woe
Painted in my beclouded stormy face,
But cannot skill to pity my disgrace,
Not though thereof the cause herself she know.
Yet hearing late a fable which did show
Of lovers never known a grievous case,
Pity thereof gate[127] in her breast such place
That, from that sea derived, tears' spring did flow.
Alas, if fancy, drawn by imagined things,
'Though false, yet with free scope more grace doth breed
Than servant's wrack, where new doubts honor brings,
Then think, my dear, that you in me do read
Of lover's ruin some sad tragedy:[128]
I am not I; pity the tale of me.

---

[124] Compare *AS* 1.
[125] Perverse.
[126] See n. 51.
[127] Got.
[128] In *AS* 51, Astrophil compares his relationship with Stella to a comedy.

46.

I cursed thee oft, I pity now thy case,
Blind-hitting boy,[129] since she that thee and me
Rules with a beck,[130] so tyrannizeth[131] thee
That thou must want or food, or dwelling place,[132]
For she protests to banish thee her face.
Her face? O Love, a rogue[133] thou then shouldst be,
If Love learn not alone to love and see
Without desire to feed of further grace.
Alas, poor wag, that now a scholar art
To such a school-mistress, whose lessons new
Thou needs must miss and so thou needs must smart.
Yet, dear, let me this pardon get of you,
So long, though he from book much to desire,
'Til without fuel you can make hot fire.

47.

What, have I thus betrayed my liberty?
Can those black beams such burning marks[134] engrave
In my free side? Or am I born a slave
Whose neck becomes such yoke of tyranny?
Or want I sense to feel my misery?
Or sprite,[135] disdain of such disdain to have?
Who, for long faith, though daily help I crave,
May get no alms but scorn of beggary?
Virtue, awake, Beauty but beauty is,
I may, I must, I can, I will, I do
Leave following that which it is gain to miss.

[129] Cupid.
[130] A nod.
[131] Tyrannizes.
[132] Either food or a dwelling place.
[133] *Rogue* in this period signified a homeless, masterless man, a vagabond; a group Elizabethan authorities considered especially threatening to social order.
[134] Brands indicating slavery.
[135] Spirit.

Let her go. Soft, but here she comes. "Go to,
Unkind, I love you not." O me, that eye
Doth make my heart give to my tongue the lie.

48.
Soul's joy, bend not those morning stars from me
Where Virtue is made strong by Beauty's might.
Where Love is chasteness, Pain doth learn delight,
And Humbleness grows one with Majesty.
Whatever may ensue, O let me be
Copartner of the riches of that sight,
Let not mine eyes be hell-driv'n from that light.
O look, O shine, O let me die and see,
For though I oft myself of them bemoan,
That through my heart their beamy darts be gone,[136]
Whose cureless wounds even now most freshly bleed.
Yet since my death-wound is already got,
Dear killer, spare not thy sweet, cruel shot:
A kind of grace it is to slay with speed.

49.[137]
I on my horse, and Love on me doth try
Our horsemanships, while by strange work I prove
A horseman to my horse, a horse to Love.
And now man's wrongs in me, poor beast, descry.[138]
The reins wherewith my rider doth me tie
Are Humbled Thoughts, which bit of Rev'rence move,
Curbed in with Fear but with gilt boss[139] above
Of Hope, which makes it seem fair to the eye.

---

[136] The "darts" sent by Stella's eyes.
[137] The relationship between the passions and reason has often been compared to that between a horse and its rider. The fact that Love, not reason, "rides" Astrophil/Sidney further demonstrates the negative consequences of his infatuation with Stella. See also Song 5.
[138] Perceive.
[139] A gold knob on the bit.

The wand is Will; thou, Fancy, saddle art,
Girt fast by Memory, [140] and while I spur
My horse, he spurs with sharp desire my heart.
He sits me fast, however I do stir,
And now hath made me to his hand so right
That in the manage[141] myself takes delight.

50.
Stella, the fullness of my thoughts of thee
Cannot be stayed within my panting breast,
But they do swell and struggle forth of me
'Til that in words thy figure be expressed.[142]
And yet as soon as they so formèd be
According to my lord Love's own behest,
With sad eyes I their weak proportion see
To portrait that which in this world is best.
So that I cannot choose but write my mind,
And cannot choose but put out what I write,
While those poor babes their death in birth do find.[143]
And now my pen these lines had dashèd quite
But that they stopped his fury from the same
Because their forefront bare sweet Stella's name.

51.
Pardon mine ears, both I and they do pray,
So may your tongue[144] still fluently proceed
To them that do such entertainment need,
So may you still have somewhat new to say.
On silly me do not the burden lay

---

[140] The imagination ("Fancy") is the saddle, strapped tightly ("girt") by memory. On Renaissance faculty psychology, see n. 259.

[141] The control of the horse.

[142] That is, the poems making up this sequence. Compare *AS* 1.

[143] See *AS* 1, n. 2.

[144] Compare Sidney's address to the "friend" in *AS* 14 and 21.

Of all the grave conceits your brain doth breed;
But find some Hercules to bear, instead
Of Atlas tired, your wisdom's heav'nly sway.
For me, while you discourse of courtly tides,
Of cunning'st fishers in most troubled streams,[145]
Of straying ways when valiant Error guides.
Meanwhile, my heart confers with Stella's beams,
And is even irked that so sweet comedy[146]
By such unsuited speech should hindered be.

52.
A strife is grown between Virtue and Love,
While each pretends that Stella must be his.
Her eyes, her lips, her all, saith Love, do this,
Since they do wear his badge, most firmly prove.
But Virtue thus that title doth disprove
That Stella, O dear name, that Stella is,
That virtuous soul, sure heir of heav'nly bliss.
Not this fair outside, which our hearts doth move.
And therefore, though her beauty and her grace
Be Love's indeed, in Stella's self he may
By no pretence claim any manner place.
Well, Love, since this demure[147] our suit doth stay,
Let Virtue have that Stella's self. Yet thus:
That Virtue but that body grant to us.[148]

53.
In martial sports I had my cunning tried,
And yet to break more staves[149] did me address

---

[145] Courtiers seeking the monarch's favor.
[146] Comedy in this period is defined more by its happy ending than by laughter. In *AS*
145 Sidney compares his tale to a tragedy.
[147] Objection.
[148] The explicit sexuality of these lines undermines Astrophil/Sidney's pretense to virtue.
[149] The shaft of a lance.

While, with the people's shouts, I must confess,
Youth, luck, and praise even filled my veins with pride.
When Cupid, having me, his slave, descried
In Mars's livery, prancing in the press,[150]
"What now, sir fool," said he, "I would no less,
Look here, I say." I looked, and Stella spied,
Who hard by made a window send forth light.
My heart then quaked, then dazzled were mine eyes,
One hand forgot to rule, the other to fight.
Nor trumpets' sound I heard, nor friendly cries.
My foe came on, and beat the air for me,
'Til that her blush taught me my shame to see.[151]

54.

Because I breathe not love to everyone,
Nor do not use set colors for to wear,[152]
Nor nourish special locks of vowed hair,
Nor give each speech a full point[153] of a groan,
The courtly nymphs, acquainted with the moan
Of them who in their lips Love's standard bear,
"What, he?" say they of me, "now I dare swear,"
He cannot love. No, no, let him alone."
And think so still, so Stella know my mind,
Profess indeed I do not Cupid's art.
But you, fair maids, at length this true shall find,
That his right badge is but worn in the heart.
Dumb swans, not chatt'ring pies,[154] do lovers prove:
They love indeed who quake to say they love.[155]

---

[150] The crowd.
[151] Stella has the opposite effect in *AS* 41.
[152] Wear the beloved's colors in order to advertise the lover's passion.
[153] Punctuating the end of a speech with a groan rather than a period.
[154] Magpies.
[155] Compare *AS* 104.

55.

Muses, I oft invoked your holy aid,
With choicest flowers my speech to engarland so
That it, despised in true but naked show,
Might win some grace in your sweet skill arrayed.
And oft whole troops of saddest words I stayed,
Striving abroad a-foraging to go,
Until by your inspiring I might know
How their black banner might be best displayed.
But now I mean no more your help to try,
Nor other sug'ring of my speech to prove
But on her name incessantly to cry.
For let me but name her whom I do love,
So sweet sounds straight mine ear and heart do hit
That I well find no eloquence like it.[156]

56.

Fie, school of Patience, fie, your lesson is
Far far too long to learn it without book.
What, a whole week without one piece of look,
And think I should not your large precepts miss?
When I might read those letters fair of bliss,
Which in her face teach virtue, I could brook
Somewhat thy leaden counsels, which I took
As of a friend that meant not much amiss.
But now that I, alas, do want[157] her sight,
What, dost thou think that I can ever take
In thy cold stuff a phlegmatic[158] delight?
No, Patience, if thou wilt[159] my good, then make
Her come, and hear with patience my desire,
And then with patience bid me bear my fire.

---

[156] Sidney also treats this theme in *AS* 3 and 6.
[157] Meaning both "lack" and "desire."
[158] The cold, moist humor, resulting in a slow, stolid temperament.
[159] Would desire.

57.

Woe, having made with many fights his own
Each sense of mine, each gift, each power of mind,
Grown now his slaves, he forced them out to find
The thorough'st words,[160] fit for Woe's self to groan,
Hoping that when they might find Stella alone,
Before she could prepare to be unkind,
Her soul, armed but with such a dainty rind,[161]
Should soon be pierced with sharpness of the moan.
She heard my plaints, and did not only hear,
But them, so sweet is she, most sweetly sing,[162]
With that fair breast making woe's darkness clear.
A pretty case! I hoped her to bring
To feel my griefs, and she with face and voice
So sweets my pains that my pains me rejoice.

58.

Doubt there hath been, when with his golden chain
The Orator so far men's hearts doth bind
That no pace else their guided steps can find
But as he them more short or slack doth rein,
Whether with words this sovereignty he gain,
Clothed with fine tropes, with strongest reasons lined,
Or else pronouncing grace, wherewith his mind
Prints his own lively form in rudest brain.[163]
Now judge by this: in piercing phrases late,
The anatomy of all my woes I wrate,[164]

---

[160] Words that pierce, go through.
[161] Delicate skin.
[162] Stella sings the poems Astrophil/Sidney brings her. At the end of Sidney's letter to Edward Denny, he enjoins his friend to "remember with your good voice to sing my songs ..." (p. 215). See also *AS* 59 and 70.
[163] Sidney refers to the controversy over whether the efficacy of rhetoric originates in the words themselves or in their delivery.
[164] Wrote.
[165] Despite, pronounced "maw-gray."

Stella's sweet breath the same to me did read.
O voice, O face, maugre[165] my speech's might,
Which wooed woe, most ravishing delight
Even those sad words even in sad me did breed.

59.[166]

Dear, why make you more of a dog than me?
If he do love, I burn, I burn in love;
If he wait well, I never thence would move;
If he be fair, yet but a dog can be;
Little he is, so little worth is he;
He barks, my songs thine own voice oft doth prove;[167]
Bidden, perhaps he fetcheth thee a glove,
But I unbid fetch even my soul to thee.
Yet while I languish, him that bosom clips,[168]
That lap doth lap, nay, lets, in spite of spite,
This sour-breathed mate taste of those sugared lips.
Alas, if you grant only such delight
To witless things, then Love, I hope, since wit
Becomes a clog, will soon ease me of it.

60.

When my good angel guides me to the place
Where all my good I do in Stella see,
That heaven of joys throws only down on me
Thundered disdains and lightnings of disgrace.
But when the rugged'st step of Fortune's race
Makes me fall from her sight, then sweetly she
With words, wherein the Muses' treasures be,
Shows love and pity to my absent case.
Now I, wit-beaten long by hardest Fate,
So dull am that I cannot look into
The ground of this fierce love and lovely hate.

[166] In *AS* 83, Astrophil/Sidney expresses his jealousy toward Stella's pet bird.
[167] Compare *AS* 57.
[168] Hugs.

Then some good body tell me how I do,
Whose presence absence, absence presence is:
Blissed[169] in my curse, and cursed in my bliss.

61.

Oft with true sighs, oft with uncalled tears,
Now with slow words, now with dumb eloquence,
I Stella's eyes assail, invade her ears,
But this at last is her sweet-breathed defense,
That who indeed in-felt affection bears,
So captives to his saint both soul and sense,
That wholly hers, all selfness[170] he forbears,
Thence his desires he learns, his life's course thence.
Now, since her chaste mind hates this love in me,
With chastened mind I straight must show that she
Shall quickly me from what she hates remove.
O Doctor[171] Cupid, thou for me reply,
Driven else to grant, by angel's sophistry,
That I love not without I leave to love.

62.

Late tired with woe, even ready for to pine
With rage of Love, I called my love unkind.
She in whose eyes Love, though unfelt, doth shine,
Sweet said that I true love in her should find.
I joyed, but straight thus watered was my wine,
That love she did, but loved a love not blind,
Which would not let me, whom she loved, decline
From nobler course, fit for my birth and mind.
And therefore by her love's authority,

---

[169] Some manuscripts have "blest," but in order to maintain the balance of the chiasmus, I prefer "blissed."
[170] Self-centeredness, egocentricism.
[171] A learned man, someone with an advanced degree, especially a professor of logic and/ or grammar.

Willed me these tempests of vain love to fly,
And anchor fast myself on Virtue's shore.
Alas, if this the only metal be
Of love, new-coined to help my beggary,
Dear, love me not, that you may love me more.[172]

63.
O grammar rules, O now your virtues[173] show,
So children still read you with awful eyes,[174]
As my young dove may in your precepts wise
Her grant to me, by her own virtue, know.
For late with heart most high, with eyes most low,
I craved the thing which ever she denies.
She, lightning Love, displaying Venus's skies,
Lest once should not be heard, twice said, "No, no."
Sing then, my Muse, now Io Paean sing,[175]
Heavens, envy not at my high triumphing,
But Grammar's force with sweet success confirm,
For Grammar says (O this dear Stella weigh),
For Grammar says (to Grammar, who says nay)
That in one speech two negatives affirm.[176]

Song 1
Doubt you to whom my Muse these notes intendeth,
Which now my breast o'recharged to music lendeth?
To you, to you all song of praise is due,
Only in you my song begins and endeth.[177]

---

[172] This sonnet plays with the distinction between spiritual and carnal love.
[173] Powers.
[174] Eyes filled with awe.
[175] An exclamation of joy taken from the section in Ovid's *The Art of Love* wherein the would-be lover's mistress finally acquiesces.
[176] This rule, however, applies only to Latin, not to English.
[177] One needs to balance the traditional exaggerations of amatory rhetoric with a realization of how this statement might appear blasphemous to stricter minds.

Who hath the eyes which marry state with pleasure,
Who keeps the key of Nature's chiefest treasure?
To you, to you, all song of praise is due,
Only for you the heaven forgate[178] all measure.

Who hath the lips, where wit in fairness reigneth,
Who womankind at once both 'decks[179] and staineth?[180]   10
To you, to you, all song of praise is due,
Only by you Cupid his crown maintaineth.

Who hath the feet, whose step all sweetness planteth,
Who else for whom Fame worthy trumpets wanteth?[181]
To you, to you, all song of praise is due,
Only to you her scepter Venus granteth.

Who hath the breast, whose milk doth passions nourish,
Whose grace is such, that when it chides doth cherish?
To you, to you, all song of praise is due,
Only through you the tree of life doth flourish.[182]   20

Who hath the hand which without stroke subdueth,
Who long-dead beauty with increase reneweth?[183]
To you, to you, all song of praise is due,
Only at you all envy hopeless rueth.

Who hath the hair, which, loosest, fastest tieth,
Who makes a man live, then glad when he dieth?

---

[178] Forgot.
[179] Bedecks, adorns.
[180] "Staineth" means that Stella throws other women into the shade by her superior beauty; she eclipses them (the OED states that this meaning was very common in the 16th century, although obsolete today, and uses an example from the *Arcadia*).
[181] Meaning, Fame lacks ("wanteth") trumpets sufficiently worthy of Stella's beauty.
[182] See note 177.
[183] Presumably, such "long dead" beauties as Helen of Troy, Cleopatra, and Laura (see *AS* 15).

To you, to you, all song of praise is due,
Only of you the flatterer never lieth.

Who hath the voice, which soul from senses sunders,
Whose force but yours the bolts of beauty thunders?   30
To you, to you, all song of praise is due.
Only with you not miracles are wonders.

Doubt you to whom my Muse these notes intendeth,
Which now my breast o'ercharged to music lendeth?
To you, to you, all song of praise is due,
Only in you my song begins and endeth.

Countess of Pembroke's *Arcadia*. This item is reproduced by permission of *The Huntington Library, San Marino, California.*

---

[184] In the Letter to Denny, Sidney places Aristotle's *Ethics* ahead of even Cicero's *Offices*, and according to Blair Worden, the statesman Sidney admired most was Julius Caesar (*The Sound of Virtue*, 318).

64.

No more, my dear, no more these counsels try,
O give my passions leave to run their race.
Let Fortune lay on me her worst disgrace;
Let folk o'ercharged with brain against me cry;
Let clouds bedim my face, break in mine eye;
Let me no steps but of lost labor trace;
Let all the earth with scorn recount my case,
But do not will me from my love to fly.
I do not envy Aristotle's wit,
Nor do aspire to Caesar's bleeding fame,[184]
Nor ought do care though some above me sit,
Nor hope nor wish another course to frame,
But that which once may win thy cruel heart.
Thou art my wit, and thou my virtue art.

65.

Love, by sure proof I may call thee unkind,
That giv'st no better ear to my just cries.
Thou whom to me such my good turns should bind,
As I may well recount, but none can prize.
For when, nak'd boy, thou could'st no harbor find
In this old world, grown now so too too wise,
I lodged thee in my heart, and, being blind
By Nature born, I gave to thee mine eyes.
Mine eyes, my light, my heart, my life, alas,
If so great services may scornèd be,
Yet let this thought thy tig'rish[185] courage pass,
That I, perhaps, am somewhat kin to thee,
Since in thine arms, if learned Fame truth hath spread,
Thou bear'st the arrow, I the arrow head.[186]

---

[185] Tigerish.
[186] The Sidney coat of arms has a pheon, or arrow-head, at its center (see the detail on p. 165 taken from the title page of the 1590 *Arcadia*; the arrow head is in the top left box), although the phallic resonances are probably intended as well. See *AS* 71, l. 14, and *AS* 72, l. 8.

66.

And do I see some cause a hope to feed,
Or doth the tedious burd'n of long woe
In weakened minds quick apprehending breed
Of every image which may comfort show?
I cannot brag of word, much less of deed,
Fortune wheels still with me in one sort slow,[187]
My wealth no more, and no whit less my need,
Desire still on the stilts[188] of fear doth go.
And yet amid all fears a hope there is,
Stol'n to my heart, since last fair night, nay, day,
Stella's eyes sent to me the beams of bliss,
Looking on me while I looked other way.
But when mine eyes back to their heav'n did move,
They fled with blush,[189] which guilty seemed of love.

67.

Hope, art thou true, or dost thou flatter me?
Doth Stella now begin with piteous eye
The ruins of her conquest to espy?
Will she take time before all wracked be?[190]
Her eyes' speech is translated thus by thee:
But fail'st thou not in phrase so heav'nly high?
Look on again, the fair text better try:
What blushing notes dost thou in margin see?
What sighs stol'n out, or killed before full born?
Hast thou found such and such-like arguments?
Or art thou else to comfort me foresworn?
Well, how so thou interpret the contents,
I am resolved thy error to maintain
Rather than by more truth to get more pain.

---

[187] I.e., Fortune's wheel still moves for me ("wheels still with me") very slowly.

[188] Crutches.

[189] Stella's eyes fled.

[190] Ringler points out that "time" here means "opportunity" (479), and so the line means, Will Stella seize this opportunity before all is ruined ("wracked")?

68.

Stella, the only planet of my light,
Light of my life, and life of my desire,
Chief good whereto my hope doth only aspire,
World of my wealth, and heav'n of my delight.
Why dost thou spend the treasures of thy sprite
With voice more fit to wed Amphion's lyre,[191]
Seeking to quench in me the noble fire,
Fed by thy worth, and kindled by thy sight?
And all in vain, for while thy breath most sweet,
With choicest words, thy words with reasons rare,
Thy reasons firmly set on Virtue's feet,
Labor to kill in me this killing care,
O think I then, what paradise of joy
It is, so fair a virtue to enjoy.

69.

O joy too high for my low style[192] to show,
O bliss fit for a nobler state than me,
Envy, put out thine eyes, lest thou do see
What oceans of delight in me do flow.
My friend, that oft saw through all masks my woe,
Come, come, and let me pour myself on thee.
Gone is the winter of my misery,
My spring appears, O see what here doth grow.
For Stella hath with words where faith doth shine
Of her high heart given me the monarchy.
I, I, O I may say that she is mine.
And though she give but thus condition'ly[193]

---

[191] On Amphion, see the *Apology*, note 11.
[192] "Style" means both the manner of writing and a writing instrument.
[193] In order to maintain the rhythm, this word should be pronounced with three, not four, syllables.

This realm of bliss, while virtuous course I take,
No kings be crowned but they some covenants make.[194]

70.

My Muse may well grudge at my heav'nly joy,
If still I force her in sad rhymes to creep.
She oft hath drunk my tears, now hopes to enjoy
Nectar of mirth, since I Jove's cup do keep.[195]
Sonnets be not bound 'prentice[196] to annoy,[197]
Trebles sing high as well as basses deep,
Grief but Love's winter livery is, the boy
Hath cheeks to smile as well as eyes to weep.
Come then, my Muse, show thou height of delight
In well-raised notes, my pen the best it may
Shall paint out joy, though but in black and white.
Cease, eager Muse, peace, pen, for my sake stay;
I give you here my hand for truth of this,
Wise silence is best music unto bliss.[198]

71.

Who will in fairest book of Nature know
How Virtue may best lodged in beauty be,
Let him but learn of love to read in thee,
Stella, those fair lines which true goodness show.

---

[194] Many in Sidney's political circles believed that monarchs are bound by earthly covenants, and any monarch who breaks these covenants can and should be deposed. According to Worden (*The Sound of Virtue*), there is considerable evidence in the *Old Arcadia* that Sidney at least partly sympathized with this position. The speaker's abuse of this doctrine, by joking about it in the service of an adulterous seduction, would have further eroded his credibility.

[195] Jove was so taken by Ganymede's beauty that he transported him to the heavens to be his cup-bearer (Ovid, *Metamorphoses*, 10. 155-161). On the homoerotic resonances of Ganymede, see *AS* 13, n. 26.

[196] An apprentice bound to serve his master for a certain period of time. Sidney drops the first syllable to maintain the meter.

[197] See n. 51.

[198] Compare Song 10, ll. 1—12.

There shall he find all vices' overthrow,
Not by rude force, but sweetest sovereignty
Of reason, from whose light those night-birds fly,
That inward sun in thine eyes shineth so.
And not content to be Perfection's heir,
Thyself dost strive all minds that way to move
Who mark in thee what is in thee most fair.
So while thy beauty draws the heart to love,
As fast thy virtue bends that love to good.
"But ah," Desire still cries, "Give me some food."[199]

72.
Desire, though thou my old companion art,
And oft so clings to my pure love that I
One from the other scarcely can descry,
While each doth blow the fire of my heart.
Now from thy fellowship I needs must part.
Venus is taught with Dian's[200] wings to fly,
I must no more in thy sweet passions lie.
Virtue's gold now must head my Cupid's dart.
Service and honor, wonder with delight,
Fear to offend, will worthy to appear,
Care shining in mine eyes, faith in my sprite,
These things are left me by my only dear.
But thou, Desire, because thou would'st have all,
Now banish'd art, but yet, alas, how shall?

Song 2.
Have I caught my heav'nly jewel
Teaching sleep most fair to be?
Now will I teach her that she,
When she wakes, is too too cruel.

---

[199] Compare *AS* 65, l. 14.
[200] Diana, the chaste goddess of the hunt.

Since sweet Sleep her eyes hath charmed,
The two only darts of Love,
Now will I with that boy prove
Some play while he is disarmed.

Her tongue waking still refuseth,
Giving frankly niggard "no."   10
Now will I attempt to know[201]
What "no" her tongue sleeping useth.

See the hand which waking guardeth,
Sleeping grants a free resort.
Now will I invade the fort;
Cowards love with loss rewardeth.[202]

But, O fool, think of the danger,
Of her just and high disdain.
Now will I alas refrain,
Love fears nothing else but anger.   20

Yet those lips so sweetly swelling
Do invite a stealing kiss.
Now will I but venture this,
Who will read must first learn spelling.

O sweet kiss, but ah, she is waking,
Louring[203] beauty chastens me.
Now will I away hence flee.
Fool, more fool, for no more taking.

---

[201] Sidney's punning on "no" also includes sexual knowledge.

[202] The intimation of rape in these stanzas resonates with Astrophil's inability to banish sexual desire in the previous sonnets.

[203] Glaring, scowling.

73.

Love still a boy, and oft a wanton is,
Schooled only by his mother's tender eye.
What wonder then if he his lesson miss
When for so soft a rod dear play he try?
And yet, my star,[204] because a sugared kiss
In sport[205] I sucked while she asleep did lie,
Doth lour, nay, chide, nay, threat for only this.
Sweet, it was saucy Love, not humble I.
But no 'scuse[206] serves. She makes her wrath appear
In Beauty's throne. See now who dares come near
Those scarlet judges,[207] threat'ning bloody pain?
O heav'nly fool, thy most kiss-worthy face
Anger invests with such a lovely grace
That Anger's self I needs must kiss again.

74.

I never drank of Aganippe well,[208]
Nor ever did in shade of Tempe sit,[209]
And Muses scorn with vulgar brains to dwell.
Poor layman I, for sacred rites unfit.
Some do I hear of poets' fury[210] tell,
But, God wot,[211] wot not what they mean by it.
And this, I swear by blackest brook of hell,
I am no pick-purse of another's wit.[212]
How falls it then that with so smooth an ease

---

[204] Stella.
[205] Compare Song 2, stanza 4.
[206] Excuse.
[207] Her lips. Important judges also wore scarlet robes.
[208] A spring on Mt. Helicon sacred to the Muses. Its waters supposedly imparted poetic inspiration.
[209] Where Apollo chased Daphne, resulting in her transformation into the laurel tree (Ovid, *Metamorphoses*, 1.452-567).
[210] Inspiration, not anger.
[211] God knows.
[212] Compare *AS* 1, 3, 6, and 15.

My thoughts I speak, and what I speak doth flow
In verse, and that my verse best wits doth please?
Guess we the cause: "What, is it thus?" Fie, no.
"Or so?" Much less. "How then?" Sure thus it is:
My lips are sweet, inspired with Stella's kiss.

75.
Of all the kings that ever here did reign,
Edward named fourth as first in praise I name,
Not for his fair outside, nor well-lined brain,
Although less gifts imp feathers oft on Fame.[213]
Nor that he could young-wise, wise-valiant frame
His sire's revenge, joined with a kingdom's gain,
And gained by Mars,[214] could yet mad Mars so tame
That balance weighed what sword did late obtain.
Nor that he made the fleur-de-luce[215] so 'fraid,
Though strongly hedged of bloody lion's paws,
That witty Louis to him a tribute paid. [216]
Nor this, nor that, nor any such small cause,
But only for this worthy knight durst prove:
To lose his crown rather than fail his love.[217]

---

[213] To "imp" means to engraft feathers on a falcon's wing to improve its flight (Ringler, 481). The line means that lesser gifts than Edward's well-lined brain" have been rewarded by Fame.

[214] The Yorkist Edward IV won the throne in 1461 after his father died fighting the Lancastrians in the War of the Roses.

[215] Fleur de lis; a symbol for France.

[216] In 1474 Edward invaded France, but Louis XI's offer of a huge sum of money persuaded Edward to withdraw.

[217] Rather than agreeing to the diplomatic marriage with a French princess, Edward married Elizabeth Grey in 1461. This led to a rebellion in 1470 and Edward's brief exile (he regained the throne in 1471). Although 16th-century chroniclers agree that the later years of his reign were prosperous and calm, they also condemned him for allowing his sexual self-indulgence with both Elizabeth Grey and his mistress, Jane Shore, to cloud his political judgment and endanger the commonwealth. See Thomas More's *History of King Richard III* and *The Mirror for Magistrates*. Astrophil's praising Edward for preferring his personal desires over public responsibilities only demonstrates the degree to which his own political judgment has eroded. In Song 10, ll. 31-34, Astrophil dreams of using his "princely power" to indulge his "greedy lickerous [lecherous] senses."

76.

She comes, and straight therewith her shining twins[218] do move
Their rays to me, who in her tedious absence lay
Benighted in cold woe, but now appears my day,
The only light of joy, the only warmth of love.
She comes with light and warmth, which like Aurora[219] prove
Of gentle force, so that mine eyes dare gladly play
With such a rosy morn, whose beams most freshly gay
Scorched not, but only do dark chilling sprites remove.
But lo, while I do speak, it groweth noon with me,
Her flamey glistering lights[220] increase with time and place.
My heart cries, "Ah, it burns!" Mine eyes now dazzled be.
No wind, no shade can cool. What help then in my case,
But with short breath, long looks, stayed feet and walking head,[221]
Pray that my sun go down with meeker beams to bed.

77.

Those looks, whose beams be joy, whose motion is delight;
That face, whose lecture shows what perfect beauty is;
That presence, which doth give dark hearts a living light;
That grace, which Venus weeps that herself doth miss;
That hand, which without touch holds more than Atlas might;
Those lips, which make death's-pay a mean price for a kiss;
That skin, whose pass-praise hue scorns this poor term of white;
Those words, which do sublime the quintessence[222] of bliss;
That voice, which makes the soul plant himself in the ears;
That conversation sweet, where such high comforts be,
As constered[223] in true speech, the name of heav'n it bears,

---

[218] Her eyes.
[219] The dawn.
[220] Stella's eyes, which seem as though they are on fire.
[221] His thoughts "walk" (are agitated) while he remains stationary ("stayed").
[222] According to the OED, "to sublime" means to "subject a substance to the action of heat in a vessel so as to convert it into vapor," or in this case, the "quintessence," or the most essential element, of bliss. The phrase is often used in medieval and Renaissance metallurgy and alchemy texts.
[223] Construed, interpreted.

Makes me in my best thoughts and quietest judgment see,
That in no more but these I might be fully blessed,
Yet ah, my maiden Muse doth blush to tell the rest.[224]

78.
O how the pleasant airs of true love be
Infected by those vapors which arise
From out that noisome gulf which gaping lies
Between the jaws of hellish Jealousy,
A monster,[225] other's harm, self-misery,
Beauty's plague, Virtue's scourge, succor of lies,
Who his own joy to his own hurt applies,
And only cherish doth with injury,
Who, since he hath by Nature's special grace,
So piercing paws, as spoil when they embrace,
So nimble feet, as stir still though on thorns,
So many eyes aye seeking their own woe,
So many ample ears, as never good news know,
Is it not evil that such a devil wants horns?[226]

79.
Sweet kiss, thy sweets I fain would sweetly indite,[227]
Which even of sweetness sweetest sweet'ner art.
Pleasing'st consort,[228] where each sense holds a part,
Which, coupling doves, guides Venus's chariot right,
Best charge and bravest retreat in Cupid's fight,
A double key, which opens to the heart,
Most rich, when most his riches it impart,
Nest of young joys, schoolmaster of delight,
Teaching the mean, at once to take and give,

---

[224] Compare the endings of *AS* 71 and 72.
[225] Jealousy.
[226] Horns are a sign of cuckoldry. Sidney/Astrophil probably means to cast Stella/Penelope Devereux's husband, Lord Rich, as the devil, but the fact that the devil "wants"—lacks—horns indicates Astrophil's own lack of success.
[227] Write.

The friendly fray, where blows both wound and heal,
The pretty death, while each in other live,
Poor Hope's first wealth, hostage of promised weal,[229]
Breakfast of Love. But lo, lo, where she is,
Cease we to praise, now pray we for a kiss.

80.

Sweet swelling lip, well may'st thou swell in pride,
Since best wits think it wit thee to admire.
Nature's praise, Virtue's stall, Cupid's cold fire,
Whence words, not words but heav'nly graces, slide,
The new Parnassus, where the Muses bide,
Sweet'ner of music, wisdom's beautifier,
Breather of life, and fast'ner of desire,
Where Beauty's blush in honor's grain is dyed.
Thus much my heart compelled my mouth to say,[230]
But now, 'spite of my heart, my mouth will stay,
Loathing all lies, doubting this flattery is,
And no spur can his resty[231] race renew
Without how far this praise is short of you.
Sweet lip, you teach my mouth with one sweet kiss.

81.

O kiss, which dost those ruddy gems impart,
Or gems, or fruits of newfound paradise,
Breathing all bliss and sweet'ning to the heart,
Teaching dumb lips a nobler exercise.
O kiss, which souls, even souls together ties
By links of love, [232]and only Nature's art.

[228] A group of musical instruments or voices.
[229] Wealth, but also success, well-being.
[230] Compare the last line of *AS* 1.
[231] Restive, resisting control.
[232] Sidney/Astrophil travesties the neoplatonic idea of the beloved's kiss drawing the lover to a higher realm. See Cardinal Bembo's speech in praise of this kind of love, which he says is appropriate for old men, in Book 4 of Baldesare Castiglione's *The Book of the Courtier.*

How fain would I paint thee to all men's eyes,
Or of thy gifts at least shade out some part.
But she forbids. With blushing words, she says
She builds her fame on higher-seated praise,
But my hearts burns. I cannot silent be.
Then since, dear life, you fain would have me peace,
And I, mad with delight, want wit to cease,
Stop you my mouth with still kissing me.

82.
Nymph of the garden,[233] where all beauties be,
Beauties which do in excellency pass
His, who 'til death looked in a wat'ry glass,[234]
Or hers, whom naked the Trojan boy did see.[235]
Sweet garden nymph, which keeps the cherry tree,[236]
Whose fruit doth far th'Hesperian taste surpass.[237]
Most sweet-fair, most fair-sweet, do not, alas,
From coming near those cherries banish me.
For though full of desire, empty of wit,
Admitted late by your best-gracèd grace,
I caught at one of them a hungry bit.[238]
Pardon that fault, once more grant me the place,
And I do swear even by the same delight
I will but kiss, I never more will bite.[239]

---

[233] Stella's body is the garden.
[234] Narcissus, who fell in love with his reflection in the water, fell in, and drowned.
[235] Venus appeared naked before Paris, whose abduction of Helen would start the Trojan War.
[236] Stella's lips, which are cherry-red.
[237] The daughters of Hesperus, the evening star, tended a garden where golden apples grew. In the *Aeneid* (4.483-8), after Dido discovers that Aeneas is about to leave her, in desperation she announces to her sister Anna that she will call upon a priestess of the Hesperides to use magic on Aeneas.
[238] Bite.
[239] Compare the implications of rape in Song 2 and the extreme anger of Song 5.

83.[240]

Good brother Philip,[241] I have born you long,
I was content you should in favor creep
While craftily you seemed your cut to keep,
As though that fair soft hand did you great wrong.
I bear, with envy, yet I bear your song,
When in her neck you did love ditties peep.
Nay, more fool I, oft suffered you to sleep
In lily's nest, where Love's self lies along.
What, doth high place ambitious thoughts augment?
Is sauciness reward of courtesy?
Cannot such grace your silly self content,
But you must needs with those lips billing[242] be,
And through those lips drink nectar from that tongue?
Leave that, sir Phip, lest off your neck be wrung.

Song 3.
If Orpheus' voice had force to breath such music's love
Through pores of senseless trees as it could make them move,
If stones good measure danced, the Theban walls to build,
To cadence of the tunes which Amphion's lyre did yield, [243]
More cause a like effect at leastwise bringeth,
O stones, O trees, learn hearing: Stella singeth.

If love might sweeten so a boy of shepherd brood
To make a lizard[244] dull to taste of love's dainty food,
If eagle fierce could so in Grecian maid delight,
As his light was her eyes, her death his endless night,[245]   10

---

[240] Compare with *AS* 59, in which Astrophil/Sidney complains that Stella pays more attention to her dog than to him.
[241] A sparrow. Sidney is drawing on the early Henrician poet John Skelton's mock elegy, *Philip Sparrow*, as well as Catullus' elegy on Lesbia's sparrow.
[242] Kissing.
[243] On Orpheus and Amphion, see the *Apology*, notes 10 and 11.
[244] Dragon.
[245] These anecdotes come from Pliny, *Natural History*, 8.61 and 10.18.

Earth gave that love, heav'n I trow[246] love refineth,
O birds, O beasts, look Love, lo: Stella shineth.

The birds, beasts, stones and trees feel this, and feeling, love,
And if the trees, nor stones, stir not the same to prove,
Nor beasts, nor birds do come unto this blessèd gaze,
Know that small Love is quick, and great Love doth amaze.[247]
They are amazed, but you with reason armed,
O eyes, O ears of men, how you are charmed.

84.

Highway, since you my chief Parnassus be,[248]
And that my Muse, to some ears not unsweet,
Tempers her words to trampling horses' feet
More oft than to a chamber melody,
Now, blessèd you, bear onward blessèd me
To her, where I my heart safeliest[249] shall meet.
My Muse and I must you of duty greet
With thanks and wishes, wishing thankfully
Be you still fair, honored by public heed,
By no encroachment wronged, nor time forgot,
Nor blamed for blood, nor shamed for sinful deed.
And that you know I envy you no lot
Of highest wish, I wish you so much bliss,
Hundreds of years you Stella's feet may kiss.

85.

I see the house. My heart, thyself contain,
Beware full sails drown not thy tott'ring barge
Lest joy, by Nature, apt sprites to enlarge,

---

[246] Trust.
[247] "Small Love" refers to Cupid; "great Love" might mean Nature's love, or possibly Christ's, since the latter is "greater" than the former.
[248] The road to Stella/Penelope Devereux's estate.
[249] Safest.

Thee to thy wrack beyond thy limits strain.
Nor do like lords, whose weak, confusèd brain,
Not pointing to fit folks each undercharge[250]
While ev'ry office themselves will discharge
With doing all, leave nothing done but pain.
But give apt servants their due place, let eyes
See Beauty's total sum summed in her face;
Let ears hear speech, which wit to wonder ties;
Let breath suck up those sweets, let arms embrace
The globe of weal,[251] lips Love's indentures[252] make,
Thou[253] but of all the kingly tribute take.

Song 4.
Only joy, now here you are,
Fit to hear and ease my care.
Let my whispering voice obtain
Sweet reward for sharpest pain.
Take me to thee, and thee to me.
"No, no, no, no, my dear, let be."[254]

Night hath closed all in her cloak,
Twinkling stars love-thoughts provoke.
Danger hence good care doth keep,

---

[250] Not delegating tasks to appropriate underlings or servants.

[251] The whole ("glove") of good.

[252] Contracts.

[253] Astrophil/Sidney's heart, the addressee of this poem.

[254] The response is by Stella. It is unusual for the beloved to speak in her own voice in a Petrarchan sequence. See also Song 8 and Song 11 for extended speeches by Stella. On the other hand, women also wrote a significant body of Petrarchan verse in the early modern period, for example, Victoria Stampa, Louise Labé, Mary Stuart (best known as Mary, Queen of Scots), and Mary Wroth. See Anne R. Jones, *The Currency of Eros: Women's Love Lyric in Europe, 1540-1620* (Bloomington: Indiana University Press, 1990). On Mary Stuart, see Peter C. Herman, "'mes subjectz, mon ame assubjectie': The Problematic (of) Subjectivity in Mary Stuart's Sonnets," in *Reading Monarchs Writing: The Poetry of Henry VIII, Mary, Queen of Scots, Elizabeth I, and James VI/I* (Tempe, AZ: Medieval and Renaissance Texts and Studies, 2001).

Jealousy itself doth sleep.   10
Take me to thee, and thee to me.
"No, no, no, no, my dear, let be."

Better place no wit can find
Cupid's yoke to loose or bind.
These sweet flowers on fine bed too,
Us in their best language woo.
Take me to thee, and thee to me.
"No, no, no, no, my dear, let be."

This small light the moon bestows
Serves thy beams but to disclose,   20
So to raise my hap more high,
Fear not else, none can us spy.
Take me to thee, and thee to me.
"No, no, no, no, my dear, let be."

That you heard was but a mouse,
Dumb sleep holdeth all the house.
Yet asleep, methinks they say,
Young folks, take time while you may.
Take me to thee, and thee to me.
"No, no, no, no, my dear, let be."   30

Niggard Time threats, if we miss
This large offer of our bliss,
Long stay ere he grant the same.
Sweet, then, while each thing doth frame,
Take me to thee, and thee to me.
"No, no, no, no, my dear, let be."

Your fair mother is abed,
Candles out, and curtains spread.
She thinks you do letters write.
Write, but first let me endite: 40

Take me to thee, and thee to me.
"No, no, no, no, my dear, let be."

Sweet, alas, why strive you thus?
Concord better fitteth us.
Leave to Mars the force of hands,
Your power in your beauty stands.
Take me to thee, and thee to me.
"No, no, no, no, my dear, let be."

Woe to me, and do you swear
Me to hate? But I forbear,   50
Cursed be destines[255] all
That brought me so high to fall.
Soon with my death I will please thee.
"No, no, no, no, my dear, let be."

86.
Alas, whence came this change of looks? If I
Have changed desert, let mine own conscience be
A still-felt plague to self-condemning me,
Let woe grip on my heart, shame load mine eye.
But if all faith, like spotless ermine, lie
Safe in my soul, which only doth to thee,
As his sole object of felicity,
With wings of love in air of wonder fly.
O ease your hand, treat not so hard your slave.[256]
In justice pains come not 'til faults do call.[257]
Or if I needs, sweet judge, must torments have,
Use something else to chasten me withal

---

[255] Destinies, possibly also a reference to the Fates.
[256] Compare *AS* 2.
[257] Meaning, punishment ("pains") should not come until faults are determined and judgment duly rendered.

Than those bless'd eyes, where all my hopes do dwell.
No doom[258] should make one's heaven become his hell.

Song 5.
While favor fed my hope, delight with hope was brought.
Thought waited on delight, and speech did follow thought,
Then grew my tongue and pen records unto thy glory.
I thought all words were lost that were not spent of thee,
I thought each place was dark but where thy lights would be,
And all ears worse than deaf that heard not out thy story.

I said thou wert most fair, and so indeed thou art.
I said thou wert most sweet, sweet poison to my heart.
I said my soul was thine, O that I then had lied.
I said thine eyes were stars, thy breasts the milken way.[259]   10
Thy fingers Cupid's shafts, thy voice the angels' lay,[260]
And all I said so well, as no man it denied.[261]

But now that hope is lost, unkindness kills delight,
Yet thought and speech do live though metamorphosed quite,
For Rage now rules the reins, which guided were by Pleasure.[262]
I think now of thy faults who late thought of thy praise,
That speech falls now to blame, which did thy honor raise.
The same key op'n[263] can which can lock up a treasure.

Thou then whom partial heavens[264] conspired in one to frame,
The proof of Beauty's worth, th'inheritrix of fame,   20
The mansion seat of bliss, and just excuse of lovers.

[258] Judgment, sentence.
[259] Milky Way.
[260] Song, story.
[261] This line can be construed two ways: that no man could deny Astrophil/Sidney's claims about Stella, and that no man could deny the excellence of Astrophil/Sidney's art.
[262] See also *AS* 49. According to tradition, reason, not anger or pleasure, should hold ("rule") the reins.
[263] Open.
[264] Partial to Stella.

See now those feathers plucked wherewith thou flew'st most high.
See what clouds of reproach shall dark thy honor's sky
Whose own fault casts him down, hardly high seat recovers.[265]

And O, my Muse, though oft you lulled her in your lap,
And then, a heav'nly child, gave her ambrosian pap,[266]
And to that brain of hers your hidd'nest gifts infused,
Since she, disdaining me, doth you in me disdain,
Suffer not her to laugh while both we suffer pain.
Princes in subjects wronged must deem themselves abused.[267]   30

Your client, poor myself, shall Stella handle so?
Revenge, revenge, my Muse, Defiance's trumpet blow.
Threaten what may be done, yet do more than you threat'n.
Ah, my suit granted is: I feel my breast doth swell.
Now, child, a lesson new you shall begin to spell:
Sweet babes must babies have, but shrewd girls must be beaten.[268]

Think now no more to hear of warm fine-odored snow,
Nor blushing lilies, nor pearls' ruby-hidden row,[269]
Nor of that golden sea, whose waves in curls are brok'n.
But of thy soul, so fraught with such ungratefulness[270]   40
As where thou soon mightst help, most faith dost most oppress,
Ungrateful who is called, the worst of evils is spoken.

Yet worse than worst, I say thou art a thief. A thief?
Now God forbid. A thief, and of worst thieves the chief:
Thieves steal for need, and steal but goods, which pain recovers.[271]

---

[265] To maintain the meter, "recovers" should be have two syllables ("rec'vers").

[266] The breast milk of the gods.

[267] It is the *subjects* who deem themselves abused by the prince's wrongs (see also below, line 60—"A rightful prince by unright deeds a tyrant groweth").

[268] Good children must have dolls ('babies'), but shrewish girls must be beaten.

[269] Teeth ("pearls") hidden by ruby-red lips.

[270] Compare *AS* 31.

[271] To maintain the rhythm, this word should have two, not syllables ("rec'vers").

But thou, rich in all joys, dost rob my joys from me,
Which cannot be restored by time nor industry.
Of foes the spoil is evil, far worse of constant lovers.

Yet gentle English thieves do rob, but will not slay.
Thou, English murd'ring thief, wilt have hearts for thy prey.   50
The name of murd'rer now on thy fair forehead sitteth,
And even while I do speak, my death wounds bleeding be,
Which, I protest, proceed from only cruel thee,
Who may and will not save, murder in truth committeth.[272]

But murder, private fault, seems but a toy to thee:
I lay then to thy charge unjustest tyranny,
If rule by force without all claim a tyrant showeth,
For thou dost lord my heart, who am not born thy slave,
And, which is worse, makes me most guiltless torments have,
A rightful prince by unright deeds a tyrant groweth.[273]   60

Lo, you grow proud with this, for tyrants make folk bow.
Of foul rebellion then I do appeach[274] thee now,
Rebel by[275] Nature's law, rebel by law of Reason.
Thou, sweetest subject,[276] wert born in the realm of Love,
And yet against thy prince thy force dost daily prove.
No virtue merits praise once touched with blot of treason.

But valiant rebels oft in fools' mouths purchase fame.
I now then stain thy white with vagabonding shame,

---

[272] Perhaps in truth, but not in law, since English criminal law recognizes acts of commission, not omission.

[273] Sidney is playing with political fire in this stanza, inasmuch as the right of the subject to disobey and even overthrow a tyrant was among the most hotly debated topics of 16th century political thought. Elizabeth, needless to say, did not agree with this position. See Blair Worden, *The Sound of Virtue*, for Sidney's adherence to resistance theory and his exploration of this topic in *The Old Arcadia*.

[274] Impeach, to accuse of a crime.

[275] To.

[276] Perhaps because the previous stanza seems to call for rebellion, Sidney changes direction. Now Stella is a subject of Love, not a monarch.

Both rebel to the son, and vagrant from the mother,
For wearing Venus's badge in every part of thee   70
Unto Diana's[277] train thou, runaway, didst flee.
Who faileth one is false, though trusty to another.

What, is not this enough? Nay, far worse cometh here.
A witch I say thou art, though thou so fair appear,
For I protest, my sight never thy face enjoyeth
But I in me am changed. I am alive and dead,
My feet are turned to roots,[278] my heart becometh lead.
No witchcraft is so evil as which man's mind destroyeth.

Yet witches may repent, thou art far worse than they.
Alas, that I am forced such evil of thee to say.   80
I say thou art a devil, though clothed in angel's shining,
For thy face tempts my soul to leave the heav'n for thee,
And thy words of refuse[279] do pour even hell on me.
Who tempt, and tempted plague, are devils in true defining.

You then, ungrateful thief, you murd'ring tyrant you,
You rebel runaway, to lord and lady untrue,
You witch, you devil. Alas, you still of me beloved.
You see what I can say: mend yet your froward mind,
And such skill in my Muse you reconciled shall find,[280]
That all these cruel words your praises shall be proved.   90

Song 6
O you that hear this voice,
O you that see this face,
Say whether of the choice

---

[277] The chaste goddess of the hunt.
[278] Sidney inverts Daphne's fate, who, to escape Apollo, was transformed into a tree (Ovid, *Metamorphoses*, 1.452-567).
[279] Refusal.
[280] If you return to loving me, I will write marvelous verse in praise of you.

Deserves the former place.
Fear not to judge this bate,[281]
For it is void of hate.

This side doth Beauty take,
For that doth Music speak.
Fit orators to make
The strongest judgments weak.   10
The bar to plead their right
Is only true Delight.

Thus doth the voice and face,[282]
These gentle lawyers wage,
Like loving brothers' case
For father's heritage,
That each, while each contends,
Itself to other lends.

For Beauty beautifies
With heavenly hue and grace   20
The heavenly harmonies,
And in this faultless face
The perfect beauties be
A perfect harmony.

Music more loft'ly[283] swells
In speeches nobly placed.
Beauty as far excels
In action aptly graced.
A friend each party draws
To countenance his cause.   30

[281] Debate.
[282] Stella's voice and face have hired Music and Beauty as their "lawyers."
[283] Loftily.

Love more affected seems
To Beauty's lovely light,
And Wonder more esteems
Of Music's wondrous might,
But both to both so bent
As both in both are spent.[284]

Music doth witness call
The ear, his truth to try.
Beauty brings to the hall
The judgment of the eye,   40
Both in their objects such
As no exceptions touch.

The Common Sense,[285] which might
Be arbiter of this,
To be forsooth upright
To both sides partial is.
He lays on this chief praise,
Chief praise on that he lays.

Then Reason, princess high,
Whose throne is in the mind,   50
Which Music can in sky
And hidden beauties find,
Say, whether thou wilt crown
With limitless renown.

Song 7
Whose senses in so evil consort their stepdame Nature lays,
That ravishing delight in them most sweet tunes do not raise,

---

[284] Both are equally matched and so cancel each other out.
[285] According to Renaissance models of cognition, the "common sense" receives impressions from the five senses and then forwards them to the imagination, which turns these impressions into images for processing by reason.

Or if they do delight therein, yet are so cloyed with wit
As with sententious lips to set a title vain on it.
O let them hear these sacred tunes and learn in Wonder's schools
To be, in things past bounds of wit, fools, if they be not fools.

Who have so leaden eyes, as not to see sweet Beauty's show,
Or seeing, have so wooden wits[286] as not that worth to know,
Or knowing, have so muddy minds as not to be in love,
Or loving, have so frothy thoughts as easily thence to move.   10
O let them see these heavenly beams, and in fair letters read
A lesson fit, both sight and skill, love and firm love, to breed.

Hear then, but then with wonder hear. See, but adoring see,
No mortal gifts, no earthly fruits, now here descended be.
See, do you see this face? A face? Nay, image of the skies,
Of which the two life-giving lights are figured in her eyes.
Hear you this soul-invading voice, and count it but a voice?
The very essence of their tunes, when angels do rejoice.

Song 8
In a grove most rich of shade
Where birds wanton music made,
May, then young, his pied weeds showing,[287]
New perfumed with flowers fresh growing,

Astrophil with Stella sweet
Did for mutual comfort meet,
Both within themselves oppressed,
But each in the other blessed.

---

[286] Thick, possibly also mad.
[287] May is the personification of the month; "pied weeds" literally means "multicolored clothes"—in this case, bright and multicolored flowers.

Him great harms had taught much care,
Her fair neck a foul yoke bear,[288]   10
But her sight his cares did banish,
In his sight her yoke did vanish.

Wept they had, alas the while,
But now tears themselves did smile
While their eyes by love directed,
Interchangeably reflected.[289]

Sigh they did, but now betwixt
Sighs of woe were glad sighs mixed,
With arms crossed, yet testifying
Restless rest, and living dying.   20

Their ears hungry of each word
Which the dear tongue would afford,
But their tongues restrained from walking
'Til their hearts had ended talking.

But when their tongues could not speak,
Love itself did silence break.
Love did set his lips asunder,
Thus to speak in love and wonder.

"Stella, sov'reign of my joy,
Fair triumpher of annoy,[290]   30
Stella, star of heavenly fire,
Stella, lodestar[291] of desire.

---

[288] Astrophil/Sidney's "harms" refers to his amorous and political disappointments; Stella/
Penelope's "yoke" is her marriage to Lord Rich.
[289] Compare John Donne's "The Good Morrow: "My face in thine eye, thine in mine
appears, / And true plain hearts do in the faces rest" (15-16).
[290] See n. 51.
[291] The Polestar (Polaris), the star that leads or guides; used for navigation.

Stella, in whose shining eyes
Are the lights of Cupid's skies,
Whose beams, where they once are darted,
Love therewith is straight imparted.

Stella, whose voice when it speaks
Senses all asunder breaks.
Stella, whose voice when it singeth
Angels to acquaintance bringeth.   40

Stella, in whose body is
Writ each character of bliss,
Whose face all, all beauty passeth,
Save thy mind, which yet surpasseth.

Grant, O grant, but speech alas
Fails me, fearing on to pass,
Grant, O me, what am I saying?
But no fault there is in praying.

Grant, O dear, on knees I pray,"
(Knees on ground he then did stay)   50
"That not I, but since I love you,
Time and place for me may move you.

Never season was more fit,
Never room more apt for it,
Smiling air allows my reason,
These birds sing: 'Now use the season.'[292]

This small wind, which so sweet is,
See how it the leaves doth kiss,
Each tree in his best attiring
Sense of love to love inspiring.   60

---

[292] Seize the opportunity.

Love makes earth the water drink;
Love to earth makes water sink;
And if dumb things be so witty,
Shall a heavenly grace want pity?"

There his hands in their speech fain
Would have made tongue's language plain.
But her hands, his hands repelling
Gave repulse, all grace excelling.

Then she spake. Her speech was such
As not ears but heart did touch,   70
While such wise she love denied,
As yet love she signified.

"Astrophil," said she, "my love,
Cease in these effects to prove.
Now be still, yet still believe me,
Thy grief more than death would grieve me.

If that any thought in me
Can taste comfort but of thee,
Let me, fed with hellish anguish,
Joyless, hopeless, endless languish.   80

If those eyes you praised be
Half so dear as you to me,
Let me home return, stark blinded
Of those eyes, and blinder minded.

If to secret of my heart
I do any wish impart,
Where thou art not foremost placed,
Be both wish and I defaced.

If more may be said, I say,
All my bliss in thee I lay, 90
If thou love, my love content thee,
For all love, all faith is meant thee.

Trust me, while I thee deny,
In myself the smart I try,[293]
Tyrant honor doth thus use thee,
Stella's self might not refuse thee.

Therefore, dear, this no more move,
Lest though I leave not thy love,
Which too deep in me is framed
I should blush when thou art named." 100

Therewithal away she went,
Leaving him so passion-rent
With what she had done and spoken
That therewith my song is broken.

Song 9
Go my flock, go get you hence,
Seek a better place of feeding
Where you may have some defense
From the storms in my breast breeding
And showers from mine eyes proceeding.

Leave a wretch in whom all woe
Can abide to keep no measure.
Merry flock, such one forego
Unto whom mirth is displeasure,
Only rich in mischief's treasure. 10

---

[293] The primary meaning of the line is, "When I deny you, I also hurt myself,"; but "try" also means "to feel" or "to experience."

Yet alas, before you go,
Hear your woeful master's story,
Which to stones I else would show.
Sorrow only then hath glory
When 'tis excellently sorry.

Stella, fiercest shepherdess,
Fiercest but yet fairest ever.
Stella, whom O heavens do bless,
Though against me she persevere,[294]
Though I bliss inherit never.   20

Stella hath refusèd me.
Stella, who more love hath proved
In this caitiff[295] heart to be
Than in good ewes to be movèd
Toward lambkins best belovèd.

Stella hath refusèd me,
Astrophil, that so well served,
In this pleasant spring must see
While in pride flowers be preserved
Himself only winter-starved.   30

Why, alas, doth she then swear
That she loveth me so dearly,[296]
Seeing me so long to bear
Coals of hot love that burn so clearly
And yet leave me helpless merely?

Is that love? Forsooth, I trow,
If I saw my good dog grieved

---

[294] The accent should be on the second syllable, and the word pronounced so that it rhymes with "never."
[295] Captive, also vile, base cowardly.
[296] See Song 8.

And a help for him did know,
My love should not be believed
But he were by me relieved.   40

No, she hates me, wellaway,
Feigning love somewhat to please me,
For she knows if she display
All her hate, death soon would seize me
And of hideous torments ease me.

Then adieu, dear flock, adieu,
But alas, if, in your straying,
Heavenly Stella meet with you,
Tell her in your piteous blaying[297]
Her poor slave's unjust decaying.   50

87.
When I was forced from Stella ever dear,
Stella, food of my thoughts, heart of my heart,
Stella, whose eyes make all my tempests clear,
By iron laws of duty to depart,
Alas, I found that she with me did smart.
I saw that tears did in her eyes appear.
I saw that sighs her sweetest lips did part
And her sad words my sadded[298] sense did hear.
For me, I wept to see pearls scattered so.
I sighed her sighs, and wailed for her woe,
Yet swam in joy, such love in her was seen.
Thus while the effect most bitter was to me,
And nothing than the cause more sweet could be,
I had been vexed, if vexed I had not been.

[297] Bleating.
[298] Saddened.

88.

Out, traitor Absence, dar'st[299] thou counsel me
From my dear captainess to run away?
Because in brave array here marcheth she
That to win me, oft shows a present pay?[300]
Is faith so weak? Or is such force in thee?
When sun is hid, can stars such beams display?
Cannot heav'n's food, once felt, keep stomachs free
From base desire on earthly cates[301] to prey?
Tush, Absence, while thy mists eclipse that light,
My orphan sense flies to the inward sight
Where memory sets forth the beams of love.
That where before heart loved and eyes did see,
In heart both sight and love now coupled be:
United powers make each the stronger prove.

89.

Now that of absence the most irksome night
With darkest shade doth overcome my day,
Since Stella's eyes, wont to give me my day,
Leaving my hemisphere, leave me in night,
Each day seems long, and longs for long-stayed[302] night.
The night is tedious, woos th'approach of day.
Tired with the dusty toils of busy day,
Languished with horrors of the silent night,
Suff'ring the evils both of the day and night,
While no night is more dark than is my day,
Nor no day hath less quiet than my night,
With such bad mixture of my night and day
That living thus in blackest winter night
I feel the flames of hottest summer day.

[299] Darest.
[300] Offers immediate satisfaction ("present pay").
[301] Fine food. (The catery was the office charged with feeding the royal household.)
[302] Long-delayed.

90.

Stella, think not that I by verse seek fame,
Who seek, who hope, who love, who live but thee.
Thine eyes my pride, thy lips my history.[303]
If thou praise not, all other praise is shame,
Nor so ambitious am I as to frame
A nest for my young praise in laurel tree.[304]
In truth, I swear, I wish not there should be
'Graved[305] in mine epitaph a poet's name, [306]
Ne[307] if I would, could I just title make
That any laud [308] thereof to me should grow
Without my plumes from others' wings I take.
For nothing from my wit or will doth flow
Since all my words thy beauty doth endite
And Love doth hold my hand and makes me write.

91.

Stella, while now by honor's cruel might[309]
I am from you, light of my life, misled,
And that fair you, my sun, thus overspread
With absence' veil,[310] I live in sorrow's night.
If this dark place yet show, like candlelight,
Some beauty's piece, as amber-colored head,
Milk hands, rose cheeks, or lips more sweet, more red,
Or seeing jets,[311] black, but in blackness bright.
They please, I do confess, they please mine eyes,

---

[303] History.
[304] Starting with Daphne's transformation into a laurel Ovid's *Metamorphoses* (1.452-567) and then given powerfully reiterated in Petrarch's *Rime Sparse*, the laurel wreath is a symbol for poetic glory.
[305] Engraved.
[306] Compare Sidney's assertion in the *Apology* that poetry is his "unelected vocation" (p. 57).
[307] Nor.
[308] Praise.
[309] Presumably, some courtly duty that keeps Astrophil from Stella.

But why? Because of you they models be,
Models such be wood-globes of glist'ring skies.
Dear, therefore be not jealous over me.
If you hear that they seem my heart to move,
Not them, O no, but you in them I love.

92.
Be your words made, good sir, of Indian ware[312]
That you allow me them by so small rate?
Or do you cutted Spartans imitate?[313]
Or do you mean my tender ears to spare
That to my questions you so total[314] are?
When I demand of Phoenix-Stella's state,
You say, forsooth, you left her well of late.
O God, think you that satisfies my care?
I would know whether she did sit or walk,
How clothed, how waited on, sighed she, or smiled,
Whereof, with whom, how often did she talk,
With what pastime time's journey she beguiled,
If her lips deigned to sweeten my poor name.
Say all, and all well said, still say the same.

Song 10
O dear life, when shall it be
That mine eyes thine eyes may see?
And in them thy mind discover
Whether absence have had force
Thy remembrance to divorce
From the image of thy lover?

---

[310] Absence's veil; the possessive "s" is dropped to keep the meter.

[311] Stella's black eyes; compare *AS* 7.

[312] Luxury goods—in particular spices—from India were extremely expensive. See *AS* 32, l. 1.

[313] The Spartans were proverbially terse ("cutted") in their speech.

[314] Brief.

O if I myself find not
After parting aught forgot,
Nor debarred from beauty's treasure,
Let no tongue aspire to tell   10
In what high joys I shall dwell,
Only thought aims at the pleasure.[315]

Thought, therefore, I will send thee
To take up the place for me,
Long I will not after tarry.
There unseen thou may'st be bold,
Those fair wonders to behold
Which in them my hopes do carry.

Thought, see thou no place forbear.
Enter bravely everywhere,   20
Seize on all to her belonging.
But if thou wouldst guarded[316] be,
Fearing her beams, take with thee
Strength of liking, rage of longing.

Think of that most grateful time
When my leaping heart will climb
In my lips to have his bidding,
There those roses for to kiss
Which do breathe a sugared bliss,
Opening rubies, pearls dividing.[317]   30

Think of my most princely power
When I bless'd shall devour
With my greedy licorous senses[318]

---

[315] In *AS* 70, Astrophil concludes that "Wise silence is best music unto bliss."
[316] Careful.
[317] The rubies are her lips, the pearls her teeth.
[318] Lecherous senses. Astrophil praises the "lecherous" Edward IV in *AS* 75.

Beauty, music, sweetness, love,
While she doth against me prove
Her strong darts, but weak defenses.

Think, think of those dallyings,
When with dovelike murmurings,
With glad moaning passed anguish,
We change eyes, and heart for heart,   40
Each to other do impart,
Joying 'til joy makes us languish.

O my thought, my thoughts surcease,
Thy delights my woes increase,
My life melts with too much thinking.
Think no more, but die in me
'Til thou shalt revivèd be
At her lips my nectar drinking.

93.
O fate, O fault, O curse, child of my bliss,
What sobs can give words grace my grief to show?
What ink is black enough to paint my woe?
Through me, wretch me, even Stella vexèd is.
Yet truth, if caitiff's[319] breath might call thee, this
Witness with me that my foul stumbling so
From carelessness did in no manner grow,
But wit confused with too much care did miss.
And do I then myself this vain 'scuse[320] give?
I have (live I and know this) harmèd thee,
Though worlds quit[321] me, shall I myself forgive?
Only with pains my pains thus easèd be,
That all thy hurts in my heart's wrack I read,
I cry thy sighs, my dear, thy tears I bleed.

---

[319] A wretch.
[320] Excuse.
[321] Acquit.

94.

Grief, find the words, for thou hast made my brain
So dark with misty vapors, which arise
From out thy heavy mold, that in-bent eyes[322]
Can scarce discern the shape of mine own pain.
Do thou then, for thou canst, do thou complain
For my poor soul, which now that sickness tries,
Which even to sense, sense of itself denies,
Though harbingers of death lodge there his train.
Or if thy love of plaint[323] yet mine forbears,
As of a caitiff worthy so to die,
Yet wail thy self, and wail with causeful tears
That though in wretchedness thy life doth lie,
Yet grow'st more wretched than thy nature bears
By being placed in such a wretch as I.

95.[324]

Yet sighs, dear sighs, indeed true friends you are,
That do not leave your least friend at the worst,
But as you with my breast I oft have nursed,[325]
So grateful now you wait upon my care.
Faint coward Joy, no longer tarry dare,
Seeing Hope yield when this woe strake[326] him first.
Delight protests he is not for the accursed,
Though oft himself my mate-in-arms he sware.[327]
Nay, Sorrow comes with such main rage that he
Kills his own children, tears, finding that they
By love were made apt to consort with me.
Only, true sighs, you do not go away,

---

[322] Compare the poetics of *AS* 1.

[323] Complaint.

[324] *AS* 95 answers the previous poem.

[325] *AS* 1 also uses childbirth metaphors to describe the poetic process.

[326] Struck.

[327] Swore.

Thank may you have for such a thankful part,
Thank-worth'est[328] yet when you shall break my heart.

96.

Thought, with good cause thou lik'st so well the night
Since Kind[329] or Chance gives both one livery,
Both sadly black, both blackly darkened be,
Night barred from sun, thou from thy own sun's light.
Silence in both displays his sullen might,
Slow heaviness in both holds one degree,
That full of doubts, thou of perplexity.
Thy tears express night's native moisture right,
In both a mazeful[330] solitariness.
In night of sprites, the ghastly powers stir,
In thee, or sprites, or sprited ghastliness,
But, but, alas, night's side the odds hath fur,[331]
For that at length yet doth invite some rest,
Thou though still tired, yet still dost it detest.

97.

Dian,[332] that fain would cheer her friend, the Night,
Shows her oft at the full her fairest face,
Bringing with her those starry nymphs whose chase
From heav'nly standing hits each mortal wight.[333]
But ah, poor Night, in love with Phoebus' light,[334]
And endlessly despairing of his grace,
Herself, to show no other joy hath place,

---

[328] Thank-worthiest.

[329] Nature.

[330] Bewildering, labyrinthine, but also with a sense of being lost in a maze, which further emphasizes Astrophil/Sidney's solipsism.

[331] Far.

[332] Diana, goddess of the moon—in this case, a personification of it.

[333] Diana's nymphs, the stars, strike each mortal from their positions in the sky.

[334] The sun. In order to maintain the proper meter, "Phoebus's light" should have two syllables; the possessive "s" is not pronounced.

Silent and sad, in mourning weeds doth dight.[335]
Even so, alas, a lady, Dian's peer,
With choice delights and rarest company,
Would fain drive clouds from out my heavy cheer,
But woe is me, though joy itself were she,
She could not show my blind brain ways of joy
While I despair my sun's sight to enjoy.

98.[336]

Ah bed, the field where joy's peace some do see,
The field where all my thoughts to war be trained,
How is thy grace by my strange fortune stained!
How thy lee shores by my sighs stormèd be!
With sweet soft shades thou oft invitest me
To steal some rest, but, wretch, I am constrained
(Spurred with Love's spur, though galled[337] and shortly reined
With Care's hard hand) to turn and toss in thee.
While the black horrors of the silent night
Paint woe's black face so lively to my sight
That ted'ous[338] leisure marks each wrinkled line.
But when Aurora leads out Phoebus' dance,[339]
Mine eyes then only wink,[340] for spite perchance,
That worms should have their sun, and I want[341] mine.

99.

When far-spent night persuades each mortal eye,
To whom nor art nor nature granteth light,
To lay his then mark-wanting[342] shafts of sight,

---

[335] Puts on mourning clothes ("weeds"), thus hiding the stars from sight.
[336] For both this poem and *AS* 99, compare *AS* 32, 38, and 39.
[337] Sore produced by rubbing or chafing.
[338] Tedious.
[339] When dawn comes; as in *AS* 97, line 5, the possessive "s" is not pronounced.
[340] Close, shut.
[341] Meaning both "desire" and "lack."
[342] Without a target.

Closed with their quivers in sleep's armory,
With windows ope[343] then most my mind doth lie,
Viewing the shape of darkness and delight,
Takes in that sad hue, which with th'inward night
Of his mazed[344] powers keeps in perfect harmony.
But when birds charm, and that sweet air, which is
Morn's messenger, with rose-enameled skies
Calls each wight to salute the flower of bliss,
In tomb of lids then buried are mine eyes,
Forced by their lord, who is ashamed to find
Such light in sense with such a darkened mind.

100.
O tears, no tears but rain from Beauty's skies,
Making those lilies and those roses grow,
Which aye most fair, now more than most fair show,
While graceful Pity Beauty beautifies.
O honeyed sighs, which from that breast do rise
Whose pants do make unspilling cream to flow,[345]
Winged with whose breath so pleasing zephyrs blow
As can refresh the hell where my soul fries.
O plaints, conserved in such a sugared phrase[346]
That eloquence itself envies your praise
While sobb'd-out words a perfect music give.
Such tears, sighs, plaints, no sorrow is, but joy.
Or if such heav'nly signs must prove annoy,[347]
All mirth farewell, let me in sorrow live.

101.
Stella is sick, and in that sick-bed lies
Sweetness that breathes and pants as oft as she;

---

[343] Open eyes.
[344] See *AS* 96, n. 270.
[345] The rising of Stella's breasts.
[346] Poetry.
[347] See *AS* 18, n. 51.

And Grace, sick too, such fine conclusions[348] tries
That sickness brags itself best graced to be.
Beauty is sick, but sick in so fair guise
That in that paleness beauty's white[349] we see.
And joy, which is inseparate from those eyes,
Stella now learns—strange case—to weep in thee.
Love moves thy pain, and like a faithful page,
As thy looks stir, runs up and down to make
All folks pressed at thy will thy pain to 'suage.[350]
Nature with care sweats for her darling's sake,
Knowing worlds pass ere she enough can find
Of such heav'n stuff[351] to clothe so heav'nly mind.

102.
Where be those roses gone, which sweetened so our eyes?
Where those red cheeks, which oft with fair increase did frame
The height of honor in the kindly badge of shame?
Who hath the crimson weeds stol'n from my morning skies?
How doth the color fade of those vermilion dyes,
Which Nature's self did make, and self-ingrained the same?
I would know by what right this paleness overcame
That hue, whose force my heart still unto thralldom ties?
Galen's adoptive sons,[352] who by a beaten way
Their judgments hackney on,[353] the fault on sickness lay.
But feeling proof makes me say they mistake it fur:[354]
It is but love which makes his paper perfect white
To write therein more fresh the story of delight
While beauty's reddest ink Venus for him doth stir.

---

[348] Delicate experiments.

[349] Purity.

[350] Assuage.

[351] Heavenly stuff, divine matter.

[352] Followers of the ancient Greek physician, Galen—in other words, doctors.

[353] Stumble on, as though they were riding a worn-out, tired horse (a "hackney") on a beaten ("conventional") path.

[354] Far. As in *AS* 1, 3, and 9, others once more "misdeem" Astrophil/Sidney.

103.

O happy Thames, that didst my Stella bear,
I saw thyself with many a smiling line
Upon thy cheerful face, joy's liv'ry[355] wear,
While those fair planets on thy streams did shine.
The boat for joy could not to dance forbear
While wanton winds with beauties so divine
Ravished, stayed not, 'til in her golden hair
They did themselves (o sweetest prison!) twine.
And fain those Aeol's youths[356] there would their stay
Have made, but first by Nature still to fly,
First did with puffing kiss those locks display.
She, so disheveled, blushed, from window I
With sight thereof cried out, "O fair disgrace,
Let Honor's self to thee grant highest place."

104.[357]

Envious wits, what hath been mine offense
That with such pois'nous care my looks you mark,
That to each word, nay, sigh, of mine you hark,
As grudging me my sorrow's eloquence?
Ah, is it not enough that I am thence,
Thence, so far thence, that scarcely any spark
Of comfort dare come to this dungeon dark,
Where rig'rous[358] exile locks up all my sense?
But if I by a happy window pass,
If I but stars upon mine armor bear,
Sick, thirsty, glad, though but of empty glass,
Your moral notes[359] straight my hid meaning tear
From out my ribs, and puffing prove that I
Do Stella love. Fools, who doth it deny?

---

[355] Livery.
[356] Pronounced "A-ee-ol's"; Sons of Aeolus, the god of wind, i.e., breezes.
[357] Compare *AS* 27, 28, and especially 54.
[358] Rigorous.
[359] Allegorical interpretation.

Song 11
"Who is it that this dark night
Underneath my window plaineth?"[360]
It is one who from thy sight,
Being, ah, exiled, disdaineth
Every other vulgar light.

"Why, alas, and are you he?
Be not yet those fancies changèd?"
Dear, when you find change in me,
Though from me you be estrangèd,
Let my change to ruin be.   10

"Well, in absence this will die,
Leave to see, and leave to wonder.
Absence sure will help, if I
Can learn how myself to sunder
From what in my heart doth lie.

"But time will these thoughts remove.
Time doth work what no man knoweth."
Time doth as the subject prove,[361]
With time still th'affection groweth
In the faithful turtle dove.   20

"What if you new beauties see,
Will not they stir new affection?"
I will think they pictures be,
Image-like of saints' perfection,[362]
Poorly counterfeiting thee.

---

[360] Complains or laments.
[361] Time's actions are dependent on the subject. That is, time will make the true lover more true.
[362] Sidney, however, as a confirmed Protestant, would not approve of post-Biblical saints or idolizing them.

"But your reason's purest light
Bids you leave such minds to nourish."
Dear, do reason no such spite,
Never doth thy beauty flourish
More than in my reason's sight.[363]   30

"But the wrongs love bears will make
Love at length leave undertaking."
No, the more fools it do shake
In a ground of so firm making,
Deeper still they drive the stake.

"Peace, I think that some give ear.
Come, no more, lest I get anger."
Bliss, I will my bliss forebear,
Fearing, sweet, you to endanger,
But my soul shall harbor there.   40

"Well, begone, begone I say,
Lest that Argus'[364] eyes perceive you."
O unjustest fortune's sway,
Which can make me thus to leave you
And from louts to run away.

105.
Unhappy sight, and hath she vanished by
So near, in so good time, so free a place?
Dead glass,[365] dost thou thy object so embrace
As what my heart still sees thou canst not spy?
I swear by her I love and lack that I

---

[363] Compare, however, *AS* 10.
[364] Pronounced as "Argus eyes"; the multi-eyed monster Juno used to watch over Io, her husband Jove's mistress (although Mercury, messenger of the gods and himself the god of rhetoric, sent him to sleep).
[365] Astrophil's eyes.

Was not in fault, who bent thy dazzling race[366]
Only unto the heaven of Stella's face,
Counting but dust what in the way did lie.
But cease, mine eyes, your tears do witness well
That you, guiltless thereof, your nectar missed.
Cursed be the page from whom the bad torch fell;
Cursed be the night which did your strife resist;
Cursed be the coachman which did drive so fast
With no worse curse than absence makes me taste.

106.
O absent presence, Stella is not here.
False, flatt'ring hope, that with so fair a face
Bare me in hand, that in this orphan place
Stella, I say, my Stella should appear.
What say'st thou now, where is that dainty cheer
Thou told'st mine eyes should help their famished case?
But thou art gone now that self-felt disgrace
Doth make me most to wish thy comfort near.
But here I do store of fair ladies meet
Who may with charm of conversation sweet
Make in my heavy mould[367] new thoughts to grow.
Sure they prevail as much with me as he
That bade his friend, but then new-maimed, to be
Merry with him, and not think of his woe.

107.
Stella, since thou so right a princess art
Of all the powers which life bestows on me
That ere by them ought undertaken be,
They first resort unto that sov'reign part.

---

[366] "The flickering course of the beams of light" (Ringler, 490).
[367] Ringler glosses "heavy mould" as referring to "earth, the heaviest of the four elements that compose the body" (490). The phrase may also refer to the mind, specifically the imagination, which "molds" new thoughts and is sad ("heavy") due to Stella's absence.

Sweet, for awhile give respite to my heart
Which pants as though it still should leap to thee,
And on my thoughts give thy lieutenancy[368]
To this great cause, which needs both use and art. [369]
And as a queen, who from her presence sends
Whom she employs, dismiss from thee my wit
'Til it have wrought what thy own will attends.
On servants' shame oft master's blame doth sit:
O let not fools in me thy works reprove
And scorning say, "See what it is to love."

108.
When Sorrow, using mine own fire's might,
Melts down his lead into my boiling breast,
Through that dark furnace to my heart oppressed,
There shines a joy from thee, my only light.
But soon as thought of thee breeds my delight,
And my young soul flutters to thee, his nest,
Most rude Despair, my daily unbidden guest,
Clips straight my wings, straight wraps me in his night,
And makes me then bow down my head and say,
"Ah, what doth Phoebus' gold that wretch avail
Whom iron doors do keep from use of day?"
So strangely, alas, thy works in me prevail,
That in my woes for thee art my joy,
And in my joys for thee my only annoy.[370]

[368] Delegated authority. See also *AS* 36.
[369]"Use," meaning experience or skill. The precise referent of the "great cause" remains unclear, perhaps deliberately so. Ringler posits that the phrase refers to public service in general (490); Duncan-Jones suggests either public duty or a translation of Du Bartas's verse (*Sir Philip Sidney: A Critical Edition of the Major Works*, 371). Given the self-referentiality of the sequence, the phrase could also refer to the entirety of *AS*, which requires both skill and "art." Anne Lake Prescott suggests that the phrase might refer to the Dutch revolt or Sidney's translation of the psalms (private correspondence).
[370] See n. 51.

From Sidney's Letters

From Sidney's Letter to Edward Denny (May 22, 1580)
My Ned:

[. . .] You will me to tell you my mind of the directing your studies. I will do it as well as the haste of your boy, and my little judgment, will able me. But first let me rejoice with you, that since the unnoble constitution of our time doth keep us from fit employments, you do yet keep yourself awake with the delight of knowledge, one of the notablest effects of that which makes us differ from beasts. Resolve therefore upon that still, and resolve thus, that whensoever you may justly say to yourself you lose your time, you do indeed lose so much of your life, since of life (though the material description of it be the body and soul) the consideration and marking of it stands only in time. Neither let us leave off because perchance the right price of these things is not had without we should wish ourselves asses because some folks know not what a man means.

But to your purpose I must say this: if I should generally discourse of knowledge, what it is, how many kinds, which worthy, which not, I might build upon a large ground, and yet leave you unsatisfied, and myself wander beyond mine own reach. That no doubt is true, that such is to human minds the infiniteness of them, that to swallow them up is impossible. Well may a man be swallowed in them, and fruitlessly, if he have not the better line to guide him in the labyrinth. The consideration therefore must be particular, and particularly bent to yourself, for one thing is fit to be known by a scholar that will read in the schools, and another by Ned Denny, and even in Ned Denny, one way to have been begun if you were a child, and another of this age you now pass in.

If you were young, surely the tongues of Latin and Greek (which be, as it were, the treasure houses of learning) and the art of logic (which indeed helps much to try the value of each thing) were exactly to be desired, and such like, which now, without a miraculous wit and blessing of God, would bring forth as vain a labor as if a man that must fight tomorrow, would only study how to send for a good sword into Spain. To my Ned Denny, therefore, and even so to myself (for I do in this with you, as we do to one another in horsemanship— teach before we have well learned), this I think may be the course, to know what it is we desire to know. And that I think to be double, the one as concerning ourselves, the other an outward application of ourselves.

The knowledge of ourselves no doubt ought to be most precious unto us, and therein the Holy Scriptures, if not the only, are certainly the incomparable lantern in this fleshly darkness of ours. For, alas, what is all knowledge if in the end of this little and wearisome pilgrimage Hell become our schoolmaster? They, therefore, are diligently to be read. To them, if you will, add as to the help of the second table (I mean that which contains the love of thy neighbor and dealing betwixt man and man) some parts of moral philosophy, I think you shall do very wisely. For in truth oftentimes we err, thinking we do well as long as we mean well, where indeed want of knowledge may make us do as much wickedness, though not so wickedly, as they which even pretencedly commit all naughtiness[1]. Thereout, therefore, may we seek what it is to be truly just, truly valiant, rightly temperate, and rightly friendly, with their annexed qualities and contraries. And thereof are many books written, but to my pleasing Aristotle's *Ethics* pass, but he is sometimes dark and hath need of a logical examination.[2] Tully's *Offices*, next, if not equal, and truly for you and

---

[1] With pretense, meaning, to do evil while pretending to do good.
[2] Sidney gives to Languet a different evaluation of Aristotle's most valuable work and of moral philosophy generally: "Of the works of Aristotle, I consider the politics to be the most worth reading; and I mention this in reference to your advice that I should apply myself to moral philosophy" (February 4, 1574 [*Correspondence*, 28]).

myself, beyond any. With him you may join some of Plutarch's discourses, as of *Refraining Anger, Of Curiosity, Of the Tranquility of the Mind, Of the Flatterer and the Friend, Of Moral Virtue*, and so by pieces, as your leisure serves.[3] But let Tully be for that matter your foundation, next to the foundation of scripture. And when you have read these, we will confer further. [4]

The second part consists, as it were, in the trade of our lives. For a physician must study one thing, and a lawyer another, but to you that with good reason bend yourself to soldiery, what books can deliver stands in the books that profess the art, and in histories. The first shows what should be done, the other what hath been done.[5] Of the first sort is Languet in French and Machiavel in Italian,[6] and many other whereof I will not take upon me to judge, but this, I think, if you will study them, it shall be necessary for you to exercise your hand in setting down what you read, as in the descriptions of battalions, camps, and marches, with some practice of arithmetic, which sportingly you may exercise. Of them I will say no further, for I am witness of mine own ignorance. For historical matter, I would wish you before you began to read a little of Sacro Bosco's *Sphere*,[7] and the geography of some modern writer, whereof there are many, and is a very easy and delightful study. You have already very good judgment of the sea maps, which will make the other much the easier, and provide

---

[3] Plutarch is among Sidney's favorite authors, and Sidney frequently cites him in the *Apology*. In a letter to Languet, Sidney writes, "I wish you would send me Plutarch's works in French, if they are to be bought in Vienna; I would gladly give five times their value for them . . . ." (December 19, 1573[*Correspondence*, 9]).

[4] Compare Sidney's dismissal of moral philosophy in the *Apology*, pp. 71-77.

[5] Although Sidney's definition of history remains the same as in the *Apology*, books on soldiery replace poetry as the source of "what should be done."

[6] Hubert Languet, *Harangue au Faits du Roi Charles IX* (1578); Sidney probably has mind Machiavelli's commentary on Livy, *The Discourses*, not *The Prince*.

[7] Originally produced in the 13th century by Johannes de Sacro Bosco, this work went through many editions in the Renaissance and is available in a modern edition. On December 19, 1573, Sidney informed Languet that "At present I am learning the sphere," which is probably a reference to this work (*Correspondence*, 8).

yourself of an Ortelius,[8] that when you read of any place, you may find it out, and have it, as it were, set before your eyes, for it doth exceedingly confirm both the judgment and memory. So much of this as I account necessary for you is to be done in a month space, or little more, for I do not wish an artificer's wading into it.

Then, for the histories themselves, gladly I would wish you should read the Greek and Roman writers, for they were the wisest and fullest of excellent examples, both of disciplines and strategems, and then would I tell you, you should begin with Philip Melanchthon's *Chronology*,[9] so to Justin, then to Herodotus, Thucydides, Xenophon, Diodorus Siculus, Quintus Curtius, Polybius, Livy, Dionysius, Sallust, Caesar, Dion, Tacitus, and then the Emperor's lives, gathered together in a volume by Henricus Stephanus. Then to take Zonaras and Nicetas, for the Greek parts, and Procopius,[10] and from thence, to fall lower, to the particular chronicles of each country, as Paulus Aemilius for France,[11] Polydore for England,[12] and so of the rest. But because this might seem too long, though indeed not so long as a man would think, my counsel to you is even to begin with our English *Chronicle*, set out by Holinshed,[13] which you should read through until you came to Edward the Third's life, then to take Froissart, after him Anguerard of Monstrelet,[14] written in old French, after him

---

[8] *Theatrum Orbis Terrarum* (1570), an atlas.

[9] Philip Melancthon, a major architect of the German Reformation and a major influence on Sidney's religious thinking. The *Chronicle* to which Sidney refers was probably written by Melanchthon's students and ascribed to their teacher.

[10] All are Latin and Greek historians from antiquity. Henricus Stephanus is the great scholar and printer, Henri Estienne (1531-1598), who was based in Geneva and published editions of the classics. He also wrote satires and polemics. The work Sidney refers to is unknown.

[11] Paulus Aemilius Veronensis wrote on the antiquities of Gaul.

[12] Poydore Vergil, *Anglica Historia*, published in three versions: 1534, 1546, and 1555 (the third brings the history up to 1537).

[13] Raphael Holinshed, instigator and first editor of *Holinshed's "Chronicles"* (1587).

[14] Jean Froissart worked on the *Chronicles* from about 1371 to his death in 1404. They were continued by Anguellard de Monstrelet until 1444, but only Froissart's portion was published in English, translated by Lord Berners, in 1523.

Philippe de Commines,[15] and then Guicciardin,[16] who reacheth almost to our time. And these will serve your turn for historical matters.

But now you may ask me: "What shall I do first?" Truly, in my opinion, an hour to your Testament, and a piece of one to Tully's *Offices*, and that with study. Plutarch's discourses you may read with more ease. For the other matters, allot yourself another hour for Sacroboscus [sic] and Valerius,[17] or any other of geography, and when you have satisfied yourself in that, take your history of England and your Ortelius to know the places you read of, and so, in my conceit, you shall pass both pleasantly and profitably. Your books of the art of soldiery must have another hour, but before you go to them you shall do well to use your hand in drawing of a plot and practice of arithmetic. Whether now you will do these by piecemeal, all in a day, or first go through with one, you must be your own judge, as you find your memory best serve. To me, the variety rather delights me than confounds me.

Thus, not as a general doctrine, but as I think it best for thee, my own Ned, have I spent more lines than I thought to have done words, but good will carries me on to this imprudence, to write my counsel to him that, to say nothing of yourself, hath my Lord Grey's company, which now I will end with these two remembrances:

1. that you forget not to note what you conceive of that you read, and

2. that you remember with your good voice to sing my songs, for they will one well become another.

My Lord of Pembroke, my sister, and your charge thank you with many thanks, and your cakes are reserved against all the

---

[15] Philippe de Commines, *Memoirs* (1524).

[16] Francesco Guicciardini, probably *The History of Italy* (1537), but Sidney may have also had in mind *The History of Florence* (1508).

[17] Cornelius Valerius (1512-1578), *De Sphaera*, and often reprinted book on astronomy.

parish come to dinner. Remember your last promise, and farewell from my heart. At Wilton, this Whit Sunday. 1580.

Your master in name but true friend indeed,

Philip Sidney

From Sidney's Letter to Robert Sidney (October 18, 1580)

For the method of writing history, Bodin hath written at large, you may read him, and gather out of many words some matter.[18] This I think in haste: a story is either to be considered as a story, or as a treatise, which besides that addeth many things for profit and ornament. As a story, he is nothing but a narration of things done, with the beginnings, causes, and appendences thereof. In that kind, your method must be to have *seriem temporum*[19] very exactly, which the chronologies of Melanchthon,[20] Tarchagnota,[21] Languet and such others will help you to. Then to consider by that [. . . .][22] as you not yourself, Xenophon to follow Thucydides, so doth Thucydides follow Herodotus, and Diodorus Siculus follow Xenophon. So generally do the Roman stories follow the Greek, and the particular stories of present monarchies follow the Roman. In that kind you have principally to note the examples of virtue or vice, with their good or evil successes, the establishment or ruins of great states, with their causes, the time and circumstances of the laws they write of, the enterings and endings of wars, and therein the stratagems against the enemy, and the discipline upon the soldier, and thus much as a very historiographer.

---

[18] Jean Bodin, the French scholar and philosopher, author of the *Method for the Easy Comprehension of History* (1566).

[19] Literally, "series of times," that is, a linear chronology.

[20] See the Letter to Denny, n. 8.

[21] Giovanni Tarchagnota, *L'Historia del Mundo* (1562). In a letter to Hubert Languet, Sidney asks his mentor, "if you have got *L'Historia del mondo di Tarchagnota*," which he calls an "interesting" book (December 19, 1573 [*Correspondence*, 9-10]).

[22] The manuscript is unclear at this point.

Besides this, the historian makes himself a discourser, for profit, and an orator, yea, a poet sometimes, for ornament, an orator, in making excellent orations *e re nata*,[23] which are to be marked, but marked with the note of rhetorical remembrances; a poet, in painting forth the effects, the motions, the whisperings of the people, which though in disputation one might say were true, yet who will mark them well shall find them taste of a poetical vein, and in that kind are gallantly to be marked, for though perchance they were not so, yet it is enough they might be so.

---

[23] From the matter in hand.

The Quarrel over Poetry: Selected Attacks and Defenses

From Plato, *Republic*, Book 2

[Socrates begins his discussion of the ideal state by establishing the importance of education and of forming children by presenting them with morally appropriate stories.]

[Socrates:] We must begin, then, it seems, by a censorship over our story-makers, and what they do well we must pass and what not, reject. And the stories on the accepted list we will induce nurses and mothers to tell to the children and so shape their souls by these stories far rather than their bodies by their hands. But most of the stories they now tell we must reject.

What sort of stories? he [Adimantus] said.

The example of the greater stories, I [Socrates] said, will show us the lesser also. For surely the pattern must be the same, and the greater and the less must have a like tendency. Don't you think so?

I do, he said, but I don't apprehend which you mean by the greater, either.

Those, I said, that Hesiod and Homer and the other poets related to us. These, methinks, composed false stories which they told and still tell to mankind.

Of what sort? he said. And with what in them do you find fault?

With that, I said, which one ought first and chiefly to blame, especially if the lie is not a pretty one.

What is that?

When anyone images badly in his speech the true nature of gods and heroes, like a painter whose portraits bear no resemblance to his models.

It is certainly right to condemn things like that, he said, but just what do we mean and what particular things?

There is, first of all, I said, the greatest lie about the things of greatest concernment, which was no pretty invention of him who told how Uranus did what Hesiod says he did to Cronus, and how Cronus in turn took his revenge, and then there are the doings and sufferings of Cronus at the hands of his son. Even if they were true I should not think that they ought to be thus lightly told to thoughtless young persons. But the best way would be to bury them in silence, and if there were some necessity for relating them, only a very small audience should be admitted under pledge of secrecy and after sacrificing, not a pig, but some huge and unprocurable victim, to the end that as few as possible should have heard these tales.

Why yes, said he, such stories are hard sayings.

Yes, and they are not to be told, Adimantus, in our city, nor is it to be said in the hearing of a young man that in doing the utmost wrong he would do nothing to surprise anybody, nor again in punishing his father's wrongdoings to the limit, but would only be following the example of the first and greatest of the gods.

No, by heaven, said he, I do not myself think that they are fit to be told.

Neither must we admit at all, said I, that gods war with gods and plot against one another and contend—for it is not true either—if we wish our future guardians to deem nothing more shameful than lightly to fall out with one another. Still less must we make battles of gods and giants the subject for them of stories and embroideries, and other enmities many and manifold of gods and heroes toward their kith and kin. But if there is any likelihood of our persuading them that no citizen ever quarreled with his fellow citizen and that the very idea of it is an impiety, that is the sort of thing that ought rather to be said by their elders, men and women, to children from the beginning as they grow older, and we must compel the poets to keep close to this in their compositions. But Hera's fetterings by her son and the hurling out of heaven of Hephaestus by his father when he was trying to save his mother from a beating, and the battles of the gods in Homer's verse are things that we must not admit into our city either wrought in allegory or without allegory. For the young are not able to distinguish what is and what is not allegory, but whatever opinions are taken into the mind at that age are wont to prove indelible and unalterable. For which reason, maybe, we should do our utmost that the first stories that they hear should be so composed as to bring the fairest lessons of virtue to their ears.

(377c-378e)

* * *

[In Book 10, after establishing the nature of the ideal state, Glaucon and Socrates return to the matter of poetry.]

And truly, I [Socrates] said, many other considerations assure me that we were entirely right in our organization of the state, and especially, I think, in the matter of poetry.

What about it? he [Glaucon] said.

In refusing to admit at all so much of it as is imitative, for that it is certainly not to be received is, I think, still more plainly apparent now that we have distinguished the several parts of the soul.

What do you mean?

Why, between ourselves—for you will not betray me to the tragic poets and all other imitators—that kind of art seems to be a corruption of the mind of all listeners who do not possess as an antidote a knowledge of its real nature.

What is your idea in saying this? He said.

I must speak out, I said, though a certain love and reverence for Homer that has possessed me from a boy would stay me from speaking. For he appears to have been the first teacher and beginner of all these beauties of tragedy. Yet all the same we must not honor a man above truth, but, as I say, speak our minds.

(595a-c)

* * *

[Next ensues a discussion of the nature of imitation, which, Socrates establishes, is three times removed from nature, therefore, Socrates concludes, "the mimetic art is far removed from truth" (598b).]

[Socrates] And is it not obvious that the nature of the mimetic poet is not related to this better part of the soul and his cunning is not framed to please it, if he is to win favor with the multitude, but is devoted to the fretful and complicated type of character because it is easy to imitate?

It is obvious.

This consideration, then, makes it right for us to proceed to lay hold of him and set him down as the counterpart of the painter, for he resembles him in that his creations are inferior in respect of reality, and the fact that his appeal is to the inferior part of the soul and not to the best part is another point of resemblance. And so we may at least say that we should be justified in not admitting him into a well-ordered state, because he stimulates and fosters this element in the soul, and by strengthening it tends to destroy the rational part, just as when in a state one puts bad men in power and turns the city over to them and ruins the better sort. Precisely in the same manner we shall say that the mimetic poet sets up in each individual soul a vicious constitution by fashioning phantoms far removed from reality, and by currying favor with the senseless element that cannot distinguish the greater from the less, but calls the same thing now one, now the other.

By all means.

But we have not yet brought our chief accusation against it. Its power to corrupt, with rare exceptions, even the better sort is surely the chief cause for alarm.

(605a-605c)

* * *

Then, Glaucon, said I, when you meet encomiasts of Homer who tell us that this poet has been the educator of Hellas, and that for the conduct and refinement of human life he is worthy of our study and devotion, and that we should order our entire lives by the guidance of this poet, we must love and salute them as doing the best they can, and concede to them that Homer is the most poetic of poets and the first of tragedians, but we must know the truth, that we can admit no poetry into our city save only hymns to the gods and the praises of good men. For if you grant admission to the honeyed Muse in lyric or epic, pleasure and pain will be lords of your city instead of law and that which shall from time to time have approved itself to the general reason as the best.

Most true, he said.

Let us, then conclude our return to the topic of poetry and our apology, and affirm that we really had good grounds then for dismissing her [poetry] from our city, since such was her character. For reason constrained us. And let us further say to her, lest she condemn us for harshness and rusticity, that there is from of old a quarrel between philosophy and poetry. For such expressions as "the yelping hound barking at her master and mighty in the idle babble of fools," and "the mob that masters those who are too wise for their own good," and the subtle thinkers who reason that after all they are poor, and countless others are tokens of this ancient enmity. But nevertheless let it be declared that, if the mimetic and dulcet poetry can show any reason for her existence in a well-governed state, we would gladly admit her, since we ourselves are very conscious of her spell. But all the same it would be impious to betray what we believe to be the truth. Is not that so, friend? Do not you yourself feel her magic and especially when Homer is her interpreter?

Greatly.

Then may she not justly return from this exile after she has pleaded her defense, whether in lyric or other measure?

By all means.

And we would allow her advocates who are not poets but lovers of poetry to plead her cause in prose without meter, and show that she is not only delightful but beneficial to orderly government and all the life of man. And we shall listen benevolently, for it will be clear gain for us if it can be shown that she bestows not only pleasure but benefit.

How could we help being the gainers? said he.

But if not, my friend, even as men who have fallen in love, if they think that the love is not good for them, hard though it be, nevertheless refrain, so we, owing to the love of this kind of poetry inbred in us by our education in these fine polities of ours, will gladly have the best possible case made out for her goodness and truth, but so long as she is unable to make good her defense we shall chant over to ourselves as we listen the reasons that we given as a countercharm to her spell, to preserve us from slipping back into the childish loves of the multitude, for we have come to see that we must not take such poetry seriously as serious thing that lays hold on truth, but that he who lends an ear to it must be on his guard fearing for the polity in his soul and must believe what we have said about poetry.

(606e-608b).

From the *Laws*

[The Athenian and Clinias have just finished discussing appropriate and inappropriate forms of dancing.]

[Athenian:] For our tragic poets and their so-called serious compositions, we may conceive some of them to approach us with a question couched in these words or the like. May we pay your city and its territory a visit, sirs, or may we not? And may we bring our poetry with us, or what decision have you reached on the point?

[Clinias:] What would be the right answer to give to such men of genius?

[Athenian:] Why this, I believe. Respected visitors, we are ourselves authors of a tragedy, and that the finest and best we know how to make. In fact, our whole polity has been construed as a dramatization of a noble and perfect life; that is what *we* hold to be in truth the most real of tragedies. Thus you are poets, and we also are poets in the same style, rival artists and rival actors, and that in the finest of all dramas, one which indeed can be produced only by a code of true law—or at least that is our faith. So you must not expect that we shall lightheartedly permit you to pitch your booths in our market square with a troupe of actors whose melodious voices will drown our own, and let you deliver your public tirades before our boys and women and the populace at large—let you address them on the issues as ourselves, not to the same effect, but commonly and for the most part to the very contrary. Why, we should be stark mad to do so, and so would the whole community, if you could find one which would let you do as you are now proposing, until its magistrates had decided whether your compositions are fit to be uttered and edifying to be heard by the public or not. Go to, then, ye scions of the softer Muses, first exhibit your minstrelsy to the magistrates for comparison with your own. Then, if your sentiments prove to be the same as ours, or even better, we will grant you a chorus, but if not, I fear, my friends, we never can.

(Book 7, 817a–817d)

Boccaccio, from *Genealogy of the Gentile Gods*[1]

Chapter 5: Other Cavilers at the Poets and Their Imputations

There is also, O most serene of rulers,[2] as you know far bet-

---

[1] Pagan gods. The *Genealogy of the Gentile [Pagan] Gods* is a compendium of classical mythology and allegorical interpretations of these myths. The last two books are a defense of poetry, and they have been separately translated under the title *Boccaccio on Poetry*, trans. Charles B. Osgood (New York: Liberal Arts Press, 1956). The notes are my own.

[2] Boccaccio dedicated this work to Hugo IV, King of Cyprus and Jerusalem (1324–1358).

ter than I, a kind of house established in this world by God's gift, in the image of a celestial council, and devoted only to sacred studies. Within, on a lofty throne, sits Philosophy, messenger from the very bosom of God, mistress of all knowledge. Noble is her mien and radiant with godlike splendor. There she sits arrayed in royal robes and adorned with a golden crown, like the Empress of all the world. In her left hand she holds several books, with her right hand she wields a royal scepter, and in clear and fluent discourse she shows forth to such as will listen the truly praiseworthy ideals of human character, the forces of our Mother Nature, the true good, and the secrets of heaven. If you enter you do not doubt that it is a sanctuary full worthy of all reverence; and if you look about, you will clearly see there every opportunity for the higher pursuits of the human mind, both speculation and knowledge, and will gaze with wonder till you regard it not merely as one all-inclusive household, but almost the very image of the divine mind. Among other objects of great veneration there, behind the mistress of the household, are certain men seated in high places, few in number, of gentle aspect and utterance, who are so distinguished by their seriousness, honesty, and true humility, that you take them for gods, not mortals. These men abound in the faith and doctrine of their mistress, and give freely to others of the fullness of their knowledge.

But there is also another group—a noisy crowd—of all sorts and conditions. Some of these have resigned all pride, and live in watchful obedience to the injunctions of their superiors, in hopes that their obsequious zeal may gain them promotion. But others there are who grow so elated with what is virtually elementary knowledge, that they fall upon their great mistress's robes as it were with their talons, and in violent haste tear away a few shreds as samples; then don various titles which they often pick up for a price; and, as puffed up as if they knew the whole subject of divinity, they rush forth from the sacred house, setting such mischief afoot among ignorant people as only the wise can calculate.

Yet these rascals are sworn conspirators against all high arts. First they try to counterfeit a good man; they exchange their natural expression for an anxious, careful one. They go about with downcast eye to appear inseparable from their thoughts. Their pace is slow to make the uneducated think that they stagger under an excessive weight of high speculation. They dress unpretentiously, not because they are really modest, but only to mask themselves with sanctity. Their talk is little and serious. If you ask them a question they heave a sigh, pause a moment, raise their eyes to heaven, and at length deign to answer. They hope the bystanders will infer from this that their words rise slowly to their lips, not from any lack of eloquence, but because they are fetched from the remote sanctuary of heavenly secrets. They profess piety, sanctity, and justice, and often, forsooth, titter the words of the prophet, "The zeal of God's house hath eaten me up."[3]

Then they proceed to display their wonderful knowledge, and whatever they don't know they damn—to good effect too. This they do to avoid inquiry about subjects of which they are ignorant, or else to affect scorn and indifference in such matters as cheap, trivial, and obvious, while they have devoted themselves to things of greater importance. When they have caught inexperienced minds in traps of this sort, they proceed boldly to range about town, dabble in business, give advice, arrange marriages, appear at big dinners, dictate wills, act as executors of estates, and otherwise display arrogance unbecoming to a philosopher. Thus they blow up a huge cloud of popular reputation, and thereby so strut with vanity that, when they walk abroad, they want to have everybody's finger pointing them out, to overhear people saying that they are great masters of their subjects, and see how the grand folk rise to meet them in the squares of the city and call them "Rabbi,"[4] speak to them, invite them, give

---

[3] Psalm 69.9. The prophet is David, who was supposed to have authored many of the psalms.
[4] A learned man generally, not a Jewish cleric.

place and defer to them. Straightway they throw off all restraint and become bold enough for anything; they are not afraid to lay their own sickles to the harvest of another; and haply, while they are basely defiling other people's business, the talk may fall upon poetry and poets. At the sound of the word they blaze up in such a sudden fury that you would say their eyes were afire. They cannot stop; they go raging on by the very momentum of their wrath. Finally, like conspirators against a deadly enemy, in the schools, in public squares, in pulpits, with a lazy crowd, as a rule, for an audience, they break out into such mad denunciation of poets that the bystanders are afraid of the speakers themselves, let alone the harmless objects of attack.

They say poetry is absolutely of no account, and the making of poetry a useless and absurd craft; that poets are tale-mongers, or, in lower terms, liars: that they live in the country among the woods and mountains because they lack manners and polish. They say, besides, that their poems are false, obscure, lewd, and replete with absurd and silly tales of pagan gods, and that they make Jove, who was, in point of fact, an obscene and adulterous man, now the father of gods, now king of heaven, now fire, or air, or man, or bull, or eagle, or similar irrelevant things; in like manner poets exalt to fame Juno and infinite others under various names. Again and again they cry out that poets are seducers of the mind, prompters of crime, and, to make their foul charge, fouler, if possible, they say they are philosophers' apes, that it is a heinous crime to read or possess the books of poets; and then, without making any distinction, they prop themselves up, as they say, with Plato's authority to the effect that poets ought to be turned out-of-doors-nay, out of town,[5] and that the muses, their mumming mistresses, as Boethius says, being sweet with deadly sweetness, are detestable, and should be driven out with them

---

[5] See the excerpts from Books 2 and 10 of Plato's *Republic* and the excerpt from the *Laws* in this volume.
[6] Boethius (c. 480-524), *The Consolation of Philosophy*, bk. 1; prose 1, ll. 28-35.

and utterly rejected.[6] But it would take too long to cite everything that their irritable spite and deadly hatred prompt these madmen to say. It is also before judges like these—so eminent, forsooth, so fair, so merciful, so well-inclined—that my work will appear, O glorious Prince; and I know full well they will gather about it like famished lions, to seek what they may devour. Since my book has entirely to do with poetic material, I cannot look for a milder sentence from them than in their rage they thunder down upon poets. I am well aware that I offer my breast to the same missiles that their hatred has already employed; but I shall endeavor to ward them off.

O merciful God, meet now this foolish and ill-considered clamor of mad men, and oppose their rage. And thou, O best of kings, as I advance upon their line, support me with the strength of thy noble soul, and help me in my fight for thee; for courage and a stout heart must now be mine. Sharp and poisonous are their weapons; but weak withal. Foolish judges though they be, they are strong in other ways, and I tremble with fear before them, unless God, who deserteth not them that trust in Him, and thou, also, favor me. Slender is my strength and my mind weak, but great is my expectation of help, borne up by such hope, I shall rush upon them with justice at my right hand.

Chapter 6: Poetry is a Useful Art

I am about to enter the arena, a manikin against these giant hulks—who have armed themselves with authority to say that poetry is either no art at all or a useless one. In the circumstances, for me first to discuss the definition and function of poetry would be hunting a mare's nest. But since the fight must be fought I wish these past masters of all the arts would declare upon what particular point they desire the contest to bear. Yet I know full well that with a sneer and a brazen front they will unblushingly utter the same ineptitudes as before. Come, O merciful God, give ear to their foolish objections and guide their steps into a better way.

They say, then, in condemnation of poetry, that it is naught.[7] If such is the case, I should like to know why, through generation after generation, so many great men have sought the name of poet. Whence come so many volumes of poems? If poetry is naught, whence came this word "poetry"? Whatever answer they make, they are going out of their way, I think, since they can give no rational answer that is not directly against their present vain contention. It is absolutely certain, as I shall show later, that poetry, like other studies, is derived from God, Author of all wisdom; like the rest it got its name from its effect. From this name "poetry" at length comes the glorious name of "poet" and from "poet," "poem." In that case poetry apparently is not wholly naught, as they said.

If then it prove a science, what more will those noisy sophists have to say? They will either retract a little, or rather, I think, flit lightly over the gap thus opening in their argument to the second point of their objection, and say that if poetry *is* a mere art, it is a useless one. How rank!

How silly! Better to have kept quiet than hurl themselves with their frivolous words into deeper error. Why, do not the fools see that the very meaning of this word "art" or "faculty" always implies a certain plenitude? But of this elsewhere. Just now I wish that these accomplished gentlemen would show how poetry can reasonably be called futile when it has, by God's grace, given birth to so many famous books, so many memorable poems, clearly conceived, and dealing with strange marvels. They will keep quiet at this, I think, if their vain itch for display will let them.

Keep quiet, did I say? Why they would rather die than confess the truth in silence, not to say with the tip of their tongues. They

---

[7] Nothing. The charge is that poetry is not a science or domain of knowledge (like medicine or law).

will dart off on another tack, and by their own arbitrary interpretation, will say, with slight addition, that poetry must be regarded a futile and empty thing, nay, damnable, detestable, because the poems which come of it sing the adulteries of the gods they celebrate, and beguile the reader into unspeakable practices.[8] Though this interpretation is easy to refute—since nothing can be empty that is filled with adulteries—in any case it may be borne with a calm mind; nay their contention based upon it may be granted in all reason, since I readily acknowledge that there are poems of the kind they describe, and if the bad kind were to corrupt the good., then the victory would be theirs. But, I protest; if Praxiteles or Phidias,[9] both experts in their art, should choose for a statue the immodest subject of Priapus on his way to Iole[10] by night, instead of Diana glorified in her chastity; or if Apelles,[11] or our own Giotto[12]—whom Apelles in his time did not excel—should represent Venus in the embrace of Mars instead of the enthroned Jove dispensing laws unto the gods, shall we therefore condemn these arts? Downright stupidity, I should call it!

The fault for such corruption lies in the licentious mind of the artist. Thus for a long time there have been "poets," if such deserve the name, who, either to get money or popularity, study contemporary fashions, pander to licentious taste, and at the cost of all self-respect, the loss of all honor, abandon themselves to these literary fooleries. Their works certainly should be condemned, hated, and spurned, as I shall show later. Yet if a few

---

[8] Stephen Gosson will repeat exactly these charges in *The School of Abuse*. See the excerpt in this volume.

[9] Praxiteles (c. 375-330 B. C.) and Phideas (c. 465-25 B. C.), master sculptors of Greek antiquity.

[10] Ironically, there is no such story. It is likely that Boccaccio means the story of Priapus, a fertility god represented with an enormous, erect phallus, and his unsuccessful attempt to have sex with the nympth Lotis in Ovid's *Fasti* 1.415-40.

[11] Apelles (c. 332 B. C.), the most famous painter of antiquity.

[12] Giotto (1266-1337), Florentine artist, widely considered the father of Renaissance painting.

writers of fiction erred thus, poetry does not therefore deserve universal condemnation, since it offers us so many inducements to virtue, in the monitions and teaching of poets whose care it has been to set forth with lofty intelligence and utmost candor, in exquisite style and diction, men's thoughts on things of heaven.

But enough! Not only is poetry more than naught, it is a science worthy of veneration; and, as often in the foregoing as well as in succeeding pages, it is an art or skill, not empty, but full of the sap of natural vigor for those who would through fiction subdue the senses with the mind. So, not to be tedious, it would seem that at the first onset of this conflict these leaders have turned tail, and, with slight effort on my part, have abandoned the arena. But it is my present duty to define that they may see for themselves how stupid they are in their opinion that poetry is an empty art.

Chapter 7: The Definition of Poetry, Its Origin, and Function

This poetry, which ignorant triflers cast aside, is a sort of fervid and exquisite invention, with fervid expression, in speech or writing, of that which the mind has invented. It proceeds from the bosom of God, and few, I find, the souls in whom this gift is born; indeed so wonderful a gift it is that true poets have always been the rarest of men. This fervor of poesy is sublime in its effects: it impels the soul to a longing for utterance; it brings forth strange and unheard-of creations of the mind;[13] it arranges these meditations in a fixed order, adorns the whole composition with unusual interweaving of words and thus it veils truth in a fair and fitting garment of fiction. Further, if in any case the invention so requires, it can arm kings, marshal them for war, launch whole fleets from their docks, nay, counterfeit sky, land, sea, adorn young maidens with flowery garlands, portray human

---

[13] In the *Apology*, Sidney will also claim that the poet "doth grow in effect another nature in making things either better than nature bringeth forth, or quite anew, forms such as never were in nature, as the heroes, demigods, Cyclops, Chimeras, Furies, and such like" (p. 64).

character in its various phases, awake the idle, stimulate the dull, restrain the rash, subdue the criminal, and distinguish excellent men with their proper meed of praise: these, and many other such, are the effects of poetry. Yet if any man who has received the gift of poetic fervor shall imperfectly fulfil its function here described, he is not, in my opinion, a laudable poet. For, however deeply the poetic impulse stirs the mind to which it is granted, it very rarely accomplishes anything commendable if the instruments by which its concepts are to be wrought out are wanting—I mean, for example, the precepts of grammar and rhetoric, an abundant knowledge of which is opportune. I grant that many a man already writes his mother tongue admirably, and indeed has performed each of the various duties of poetry as such; yet over and above this, it is necessary to know at least the principles of the other Liberal Arts, both moral and natural, to possess a strong and abundant vocabulary, to behold the monuments and relics of the ancients, to have in one's memory the histories of the nations, and to be familiar with the geography of various lands, of seas, rivers and mountains.

Furthermore, places of retirement, the lovely handiwork of Nature herself, are favorable to poetry, as well as peace of mind and desire for worldly glory; the ardent period of life also has very oft been of great advantage. If these conditions fail, the power of creative genius frequently grows dull and sluggish.

Now since nothing proceeds from this poetic fervor, which sharpens and illumines the powers of the mind, except what is wrought out by art, poetry is generally called an art. Indeed the word poetry has not the origin that many carelessly suppose, namely *poio, pois,* which is but Latin *fingo, fingis;*[14] rather it is derived from a very ancient Greek word *poetes,* which means in

---

[14] Greek and Latin for "to form or shape, to create." A 16th century Latin-English dictionary would define "Fingo" as "To make . . . to feign, to counterfeit: to image: to devise" (Thomas Cooper, *Thesaurus Linguae Romanae & Brittanicae* [1565], sig. Ddd 6v). Compare the *Apology,* pp. 63-64.

Latin exquisite discourse. For the first men who, thus inspired, began to employ an exquisite style of speech, such, for example, as song in an age hitherto unpolished, to render this unheard-of discourse sonorous to their hearers, let it fall in measured periods; and lest by its brevity, it fail to please, or, on the other hand, become prolix and tedious, they applied to it the standard of fixed rules, and restrained it within a definite number of feet and syllables. Now the product of this studied method of speech they no longer called by the more general term poesy, but poem. Thus as I said above, the name of the art, as well as its artificial product, is derived from its effect.

Now, though I allege that this science of poetry has ever streamed forth from the bosom of God upon souls even yet in their tenderest years, these enlightened cavillers perhaps say that they cannot trust my words. To any fair-minded man the fact is valid enough from its constant recurrence. But for these dullards I must cite witnesses to it. If, then, they will read what Cicero, a philosopher rather than a poet, says in his oration delivered before the senate in behalf of Aulus Licinius Archias, perhaps they will come more easily to believe me. He says: "And yet we have it on the highest and most learned authority, that while other arts are matters of science and formula and technique, poetry depends solely upon an inborn faculty, is evoked by a purely mental activity. and is infused with a strange supernal inspiration."[15]

But not to protract this argument, it is now clear to reverent men, that poetry is a practical art, springing from God's bosom and deriving its name from its effect, and that it has to do with many high and noble matters that constantly occupy even those who deny existence. If my opponents ask when and in what circumstances, the answer is plain: the poets would declare with their own lips under whose help and guidance they compose their inventions when, for example, they raise flights of symbolic steps

---

[15] *On Behalf of Archias the Poet*, 8:18.

to heaven, or make thick-branching trees spring aloft to the very stars, or go winding about mountains to their summits. Haply, to disparage this art of poetry now unrecognized by them, these men will say that it is rhetoric which the poets employ. Indeed, I will not deny it in part, for rhetoric has also its own inventions. Yet, in truth, among the disguises of fiction rhetoric has no part, for whatever is composed as under a veil, and thus exquisitely wrought, is poetry and poetry alone.

From Juan Luis Vives, *Truth Dressed Up, or of Poetic License: To What Extent Poets May be Permitted to Vary from the Truth* (1522)[16]

[This dialogue between Vives and his friend Vergara describes a dispute between "Truth" and "False"—meaning poetic license—which concludes with False and her adherents acknowledging that Truth ought to rule human minds. Consequently, a committee consisting of Homer, Hesiod, Lucian and Apuleius hammer out the following treaty with Truth]:[17]

1. Those who are called "poets" in Greek may relate whatever distortions and embellishments of Truth that Public Fame (that monster of many heads) has concocted. But he who makes up the whole of what he tells is thought a fool, or rather a liar, than a poet.

2. The historically confused period before the institution of the Olympian games (that is, four hundred years after the destruction of Troy and thirty years before the foundation of Rome) is a field free for embellishment, as long as a nucleus of truth is retained. Later writers, however, may not alter what was written by great poets of ancient times and accepted by public opinion.

3. To Truth is reserved whatever occurred after the first Olympiad, save that some embellishment may be permitted to

---

[16] Juan Luis Vives (1492-1540), Spanish humanist, tutor to Mary Tudor, and author of many important works of social philosophy, education and science.

[17] The translation of the contract is by William Nelson, *Fact or Fiction: The Dilemma of the Renaissance Storyteller.*

give the story beauty, pleasure, or public utility. Such poetic practices, however, should not impair the truth of the work.

4.   A mixture of truth and invention may be permitted in the relation of things that happened before the Olympic games which are known to be fabulous and are presented as such.

5.   Since latitude should be given to efforts to cultivate morality, writers may invent apologues out of whole cloth. "New" comedies portraying human passions and dialogues which tend to the improvement of manners may also be permitted.

6.   Free license is given to the use of many varieties of rhetorical figure for the embellishment of Truth.

7.   In the exposition of arts and learning, whether in verse or in prose, no deviation from Truth is permitted save for the use of metaphor.

8.   Whatever dressing up may be given to Truth must be characterized by verisimilitude, consistency, and decorum.

9.   Any of the train of False who takes no account of morality or utility may be tolerated if he openly professes his nature.
. . . .

10.   Anyone acting contrary to these provisions is to be expelled from the schools and academies without honor, name, money, class, land or citizenship.

[At the conclusion of the dialogue, however, "Vergara" assumes that Truth's eminence will ensure compliance, but "Vives" tartly asks his companion, "How long do you think the poets, a band of wandering and free men, will suffer with a calm soul these limits?"[18]]

[18] My translation.

From Sir Thomas Elyot, *The Defense of Good Women* (1545)[19]

[Candidus rebuts Caninius' tales of the perfidy of women by undermining the credibility of the persons who created these tales.]

Candidius: Nay, ye now do but rail. I promise you truly, indeed both by reading and hearsay, I have found women much blamed for their inconstancy, but for mine own knowledge I never perceived any such lack to be in them, but rather, the contrary.

Caninius: Sir, by the consent of all authors, my words be confirmed, and your experience in comparison thereof is to be little esteemed.

Candidius: I perceive ye be of the company, which disappointed sometime of your purpose, are fallen in a frenzy, and for the displeasure of one do spring on all women the poison of infamy. But now, Caninius, since ye be wise and well-learned, subdue your passion, for unpatient hearing, with words hastily and unadvisedly spoken, is a sign of folly and little discretion, wherefore now hear me speak, though it shall not favor your opinion. The authors whom ye so much do set by, for the more part were poets, which sort of persons among the Latins and Greeks were never had but in small reputation. For I could never read that in any weal public[20] of notable memory poets were called to any honorable place, office, or dignity. Plato, out of the public weal which he had devised, would have all poets utterly excluded. Tully,[21] who next unto Plato excelled all other in virtue

---

[19] Sir Thomas Elyot (c. 1490-1446), English humanist, diplomat for Henry VIII, and author of (among other works) *The Book Named the Governor* (1531), a manual for educating the sons of the gentry for careers in serving the commonwealth. Elyot intended *The Defense of Good Women*, which is among the first Platonic dialogues written in English, as a conduct guide for women, and in the preface to *The Image of Governance* (1540), he asserts that the *Defense* "not only confoundeth villainous report, but also teacheth good wives to know well their duties." It is a strong indicator of antipoetic sentiment's respectability and cultural force that Elyot has his defender of women employ it as part of his rebuttal of the misogynist Candidius's attack.

[20] Commonwealth.

[21] Cicero.

and eloquence,[22] would not have in his public weal any poets admitted. The cause why they were so little esteemed was, for as much as the more part of their inventions consisted in leasings,[23] or in stirring up of wanton appetites, or in pouring out in railing their poison and malice. For with their own gods and goddesses were they so malapert that with their adulteries they filled great volumes. . . Other poets there be which in their most lamentable and woeful ditties so do humble themselves to their mistresses, as they would lick the dust from their slippers, and as soon as either by age, or with haunting of brothels, the flame of carnality is thoroughly quenched, or else if women do constantly refuse their unhonest desires, anon arm they their pens and tongues with serpentine malice, objecting against all women most beastly conditions. Whereby they more detect their proper inconstancy than women's unfaithfulness.

Caninius: Now, in good faith, ye have well circumscribed your master's properties.

Candidus: Whom call ye my masters?

Caninius: Mary, poets, for in their works is the only study of you that be lovers, for that book, which lacketh complaints with weepings and sighings, is to you men that be amorous wonderful tedious.

Candidus: Truly, Caninius, ye are much abused, taking me to be of that sort of wanton. Nay, truly, true lovers, of which company I confess myself to be one, are in no part of their conditions, for only delighting in the honest behavior, wisdom and gentleness of ladies, or other matrons or damsels, we therefore delight to be in their companies and by mutual devising to use honest solace. But show me, Caninius, what other authority have ye to prove that in women lacketh fidelity.

Caninius: Why set ye so little by poets and poetry?

---

[22] Sidney equally praises Cicero in the letter to Edward Denny. See pp. 212-13.
[23] Lies.

Candidus: Ye, when they exceed the terms of honesty. But if they make verse containing quick sentence, void of ribaldry, or in the commendation of virtue some pretty allegory, or do set forth any notable story, that do I set by them as they be well worthy.

Caninius: If ye will give no credence to poets, what say ye to philosophers and writers of stories,[24] with whom ye may find such abundance of examples and sentences of the falsehood of women and their unhappiness, that if they should be rehearsed, I trow[25] ye would not abide it, I know so your shamfastness.[26]

From Julius Caesar Scaliger, *Poetics* (1561)[27]
1.2: The Name Poet, The Origin of Poetry, Its Causes, Effects, Form, and Material

The word poet is not, as popularly supposed, derived from the fact that the poet employs the fictitious, but from the fact that he makes verse. Indeed, the propensity for rhythm, the medium of poetry, is an instinct with man. There is in fact a degree of quality and quantity in every vocal movement. Quality is determined by the pitch, whether high or low; quantity by the length of time that the sound is audible; time, in turn, by the extent to which the air is moved; and the air in movement is the sound proper. Again the child cries before it can speak, and many children cannot go to sleep without crying.

After certain more inspired composers were successful in providing the old forms of poetry with new themes, they were called poets, and they arrogated to themselves, as guardians, the protection of the muses, the muses by the inspiration of whom

---

[24] Historians.
[25] Believe.
[26] Modesty.
[27] Julius Caesar Scaliger (1484-1558). The *Poetics* is one of the first systematic treatments of poetry, and Sidney was highly influenced by it. This excerpt is take from *Select Translations from Scaliger's Poetics*, trans. F. M. Padelford, *Yale Studies in English* 26 (1905). The annotations are my own.

they had discovered what was concealed from others. Those, on the other hand, who lacked this inspiration, and simply composed metrical narratives, were called versifiers.

Plato deduced the name Muses, to whom of course invention is attributed, from a form of the verb *maiomai* (to *seek after*). Other derived the word from the passive of *mueô* (*to be initiated*), whence *mysta* (*a priest of the mysteries*) , and *mysterium* (*secret rites*). This last word implies discernment, and of course discerning judgment was used in the choosing of the sacred mysteries, and in election, to the secret order.

Clearly, everything that enter into an intellectual product is the result either of intellection, or of invention, or of judgment, a classification which is better than that made by Cicero in his *Topics*, where it is said that invention has to do with topics only, and judgment only with dialectics, or logical questions.[28] This is clearly wrong, for, on the one hand, one must be as careful to observe the limits of necessity in demonstration as of probability in topics, and these limits are determined by invention; and, on the other, logic is common to all kinds of argumentation, since arguments present themselves as either good or bad, necessary or contingent, and judgment must determine what of these are to be used.

You can now see why the early theologians, the self-styled disciples of the muses, recognized only two muses, one *Meleta*,[29] who invented through meditating, the other *Poiêta*,[30] who arranged the inventions according to an established or logical method. Next, because they unearthed records relating to the creation, and unknown to the common herd, some poets added a third muse, whom the appropriately named *Mnêma*, Memory, and these same men chose to call the muse which they had previ-

---

[28] *Topics*, 1.6.
[29] Meaning "To practice." These are not the actual Muses, but witty inventions.
[30] "The maker."

ously named *Poiêta, Aoida,* the Singer, rather than the Maker. But the earlier name is the better, for song is not essential to poetry. Later, those who approved this change, and regarded themselves as even more precise, made a threefold classification of *aoida,* in accordance with their notion of early music. They recognized harmony as one element, which they said was dependent upon sound alone; brass, as another element, suggested of course by the instruments; and water as a third, an element which Vitruvius says was first used in the instrument which Ctesibius invented, and called the hydraulic organ.[31] But, if we must analyze, this analysis is far from complete, for sound is produced by striking the air, and the vibration of the air either results from a vibration external to itself, or is air in process of vibration. Then it is clear, is it not, that the flute and pipe and the voice alike employ breathing as an agency. Further, water does not give forth any sound without air; and finally, harmony, which is the blending of properly related sounds, is clearly generic to all the others.

According to my way of thinking, it seems more reasonable to suppose that in the early times the number of the muses was determined by the number of those engaged in rendering a piece of music. So when four performers came to take part, many were disposed to recognize a fourth muse, and when three more instruments were added, the number of muses was raised to seven. Finally, the number became fixed at nine, and quite properly so, for nine is the perfect number.[32]

[In this section, Scaliger discusses music and the origin of the muses.]

---

[31] Vitruvius (c. 1st century B. C.), Roman architect; *On Architecture*, 9.8.

[32] 9 results from 3 times 3.

[33] Plato, *Phaedrus*, 244a-245b; Aristotle, *Poetics*, 1455a. Unlike Plato, Aristotle does not say that poetry necessarily results from inspiration: "Hence it is that poetry demands a man with a special gift for it, or else one with a touch of madness in him; the former can easily assume the required mood, and the latter may be actually beside himself with emotion."

We may make a threefold classification of poets, according to poetical inspiration, age, and subjects. Plato first, and then Aristotle, said that there are diversities of inspiration, for some men are born inspired, while others, born ignorant and rude, and even averse to the art, are seized on by the divine madness, and wrested from their lowliness.[33] It is the work of the gods, who, though divine, use even these as their servants. Thus Plato himself, in the *Ion*, calls such men the interpreters and expounders of the gods.[34] Wherefore the dictum expressed in the *Republic*, which some crude and insensible men would construe to the exclusion of poets from the republic, should be taken less seriously, for though he condemns certain scurrilous passages in the poets,[35] we are not on that account to ignore those other passages which Plato cites time out of mind in support of his own theories. Plato should remark how many impertinent and low stories he himself employs, what filthy thoughts this Greek rogue often forces upon us. Surely the *Symposium*, the *Phaedrus*, and other such monstrous productions, are not worth reading.[36] The poets invoke the muses, that the divine madness may imbue them to do their work. Of these divinely possessed ones, two classes are to be recognized. The one class are those to whom the divine power comes from above, with no mental effort on their part except the simple invocation. Hesiod classed himself in this category,[37] and Homer is placed there by universal consent. The other class is aroused by the fumes of unmixed wine, which draws out the instruments of the mind, the spirits themselves, from the material parts of the body. Horace said that Ennius was such a poet, and such we consider Horace himself.[38] Tradition says the same of Alcaeus and

[34] *Ion*, 534d.
[35] Compare the excerpts from the *Republic* and the *Laws*.
[36] Both works concern male-male love. Compare, however, Scaliger's reliance on Plato's theory of inspiration above.
[37] Hesiod, *Theogony*, l. 22.
[38] *Epistles*, 1.19.7-8.

Aristophanes.[39] Alcman did not escape such censure, and Sophocles applied it to Aeschylus: "Wine," he said, "not Aeschylus, was the author of his tragedies."[40]

Again, poets may be divided into three classes, according to the age in which they wrote. First, there was that pristine, crude, and uncultivated age, of which only a vague impression remains. No name survives, unless it be that of Apollo, the originator of poetry. Then there is the second and venerable period, when religion and the mysteries are first sung. Among the poets of this period are numbered Orpheus, Musaeus, and Linus;[41] Plato includes Olympus also.[42] Of the third period Homer is the founder and parent, and it includes Hesiod and other such writers. If it were not for historical records, one could fancy that Musaeus was later than Homer, for he is more polished and refined. Aelian states that Orobantius of Troezan and Dares the Phrygian flourished before Homer, and that in Homer's time the *Iliad* of Dares was held in esteem. The same author has it that Syager the poet even antedated Musaeus and Orpheus, and that he was the first to write of the Trojan war. [43] The third classification is according to subject-matter. This the Greeks call *hupokeimenon*;[44] our uncultivated philosophers, most correctly, subject; and the Latin philosophers, somewhat inappositely, argument. Of this class of poets there are as many kinds as there are styles of subjects treated. Yet for the sake of treatment, the poets may be classed under three principal heads. The first is that of the religious poets.

---

[39] Alcaeus (c. 625-20 B. C.), lyric poet; Aristophanes (5th century B. C.), , comic playwright, author of the *Lysistrata* (in which women stop a war by refusing all sexual activity), *Clouds*, and *Frogs*.

[40] Plutarch, from a fragment called *A Woman Too Should be Educated*, *Moralia* 15, fragment 130.

[41] On Orpheus and Linus, see the *Apology*, n. 10; on Musaeus, see the *Apology*, n. 9.

[42] Along with Marsyas, credited with inventing music, in particular the art of playing the flute. See Plato, *Laws*, 677d.

[43] Aelian (c.170-c.235 A. D.), *Historical Miscellany*, 11.2, 14.21.

[44] "That which lies under."

Such are Orpheus and Amphion, whose art was so divine that they are believed to have given a soul to inanimate things. The second is that of the philosophical poets, and these again are of two sorts—natural, as Empedocles, Nicander, Aratus, and Lucretius;[45] and moral, including the political, as Solon and Tyrtaeus;[46] the economical, as Hesiod;[47] and the general, as Phocylides, Theognis, and Pythagoras.[48]

Now all that we have been saying may be equally well applied to women authors. They too merit praise. Such authors are Sappho; Corinna, the mistress of Pindar; Hedyle, the mother of the Samian or Athenian poet Hedylus, who excelled in iambic poetry; Megalostrata, whom Alcman loved, and others.[49] I leave it to the judgment of each one to determine whether or no the poetry of Martius and of the Sibyls should be referred to such categories as the above. My preference is not to do so, for they do not narrate past events, but predict future ones. This part of theology is not simply learning about the gods, but actual utterance of the things disclosed by the gods. As for our poetry, Gellius is authority for the statement that it was born during the Second

---

[45] Empedocles (c. 492-32 B. C.); Nicander (c. 130 B. C.), author of a scientific poem on poisonous insects; Aratus (c. 315-240 B. C.), author of the *Phaemomena*, an astronomical poem); Lucretius (c. 1st century B. C.), author of *On the Nature of Things*.

[46] See the *Apology*, n. 18.

[47] Hesiod also wrote the *Works and Days*; "economical" refers to the home, not its present sense.

[48] For Phocylides and Pythagoras, see the *Apology*, n. 17. Theognis (late 6th-early 5th century B. C.), a Greek elegiac poet.

[49] Sappho (fl. c. 610-c.580 B. C.), celebrated Greek lyric poetess, whose work survived primarily in fragments quoted by other writes. Only one complete poem survives; Corinna (c. 500 B. C.), anecdotes preserved by later writers, such as Plutarch, suggest that she may have been a contemporary, a competitor, or even a teacher of Pindar. Nothing, however, in her verse proves what kind of connection, if any, she had with Pindar, nor do these sources suggest that the she was Pindar's mistress. Athanaeus (c. 200 A. D.) records that Hedylus's mother, Hedyle, and his grandmother, Moschine, were both poets (*The Learned Banquet* 297a). The same source records that Alcman (fl. c. 631 B. C.) fell in love with Megalostrata, "a poetess" (*Greek Lyric*, vol. 2, 437). Scaliger's explicit approbation of women poets significantly contrasts with Sidney's elision of them from his canon and his construction of the Right Poet as overgoing and correcting a feminine nature.

Punic War. Let me give his choice words: "In the Second Punic War, with winged step, the Muse bore herself to the warlike, rugged race of Romulus."[50] On the other hand, it is commonly received that Livius Andronicus wrote his dramas before Naevius, who gave his to the public in the year 519 [BC].[51]

Now that the poets are enumerated and classified, certain questions may receive attention. Why does Horace question whether or not comedy is poetry? Forsooth, because it is humble, must it be denied the title of poetry? Surely an unfortunate ruling! So far from comedy not being poetry, I would almost consider it the first and truest of all poetry, for comedy employs every kind of invention, and seeks for all kinds of material.

Another question: Was Lucan a poet?[52] Surely he was. As usual, the grammarians deny this, and object that he wrote history. Well now! Produce a pure history. Lucan must differ from Livy, and the difference is verse. Verse is the property of the poet.[53] Then who will deny that all epic poets go to history for their subjects. History, sometimes delineated only in semblance, sometimes idealized, and always with changed aspect, is made the basis of poetry. Is not this the practice of Homer? Do we not do this in the tragedies themselves? Such is the practice of Lucan. Instance the image of the country offering itself to Caesar, the spirit called forth from Hades,[54] and other such episodes. Wherefore, indeed, it seems to me that it would be better give the title of poet to Livy than to deny it to Lucan. For as the tragic poets base their plays upon true events, but adapt the actions and

---

[50] Aulus Gellius (2nd century A. D.), *Attic Nights*, 17.21.45. Gellius is actually quoting Porcius Licinus, who wrote a now-lost verse history of literature.

[51] Livius Andronicus (c. 284-04 B. C.) and Gnaeus Naevius (c. 270-201 B. C.) are early Latin epic poets and dramatists. Scaliger's chronology is wildly mistaken.

[52] Author of the *Pharsalia*. See the *Apology*, n. 45.

[53] Sidney, on the other hand, argues that verse is "but an ornament and no cause to poetry" (p. 69).

[54] *Pharsalia*, 1 .466-520 and 3.1-135.

speeches to the characters, so Livy and Thucydides insert ora-
tions which were never recognized by those to whom they were
attributed. Moreover, although Aristotle exercised this censure
so severely that he would refuse the name of poet to versifiers, yet
in practice he speaks differently, and says, "As Empedocles poeti-
cally wrote (*epoiêsen*)"; so he even calls Emedocles, who feigned
not at all, a poet.[55]

Some writers, among whom is Plutarch,[56] make a distinc-
tion between *poesis* and *poema*, calling the former a legitimate
work, and the latter an insignificant one, and citing the *Iliad* as
poesis, and the *Margites*[57] as *poema*. Surely this is mischievous.
For *poema* is the very work itself, the material, I might say, which
is used in the making. *Poesis*, on the other hand, is the plan and
form of the poem. From the three persons of a verb[58] we get the
three words, *poema, poesis,* and *poeta*: thus *poema: pepoiêmai* (I
have made myself, or I have been made); *poesis: pepoiêsai* (you,
etc.); *poeta: pepoiêtai* (he, etc.). You will find an exact analogy in
heurêma (an invention), *heuresis*, (a discovery), and *heuretês* (an
inventor). So *poema* may be applied to the *Iliad, poeta,* to Homer,
and *poesis* to the form and plan of the *Margites*.

The poetical art is a science, that is, it is a habit of produc-
tion in accordance with those laws which underlie that symmetri-
cal fashioning known as poetry. So it has three elements—the
material, the form, and the execution. In the higher criticism, a
fourth element is recognized, the end, that is imitation, or the
ulterior end, instruction—for if Cicero uses the word guidance
(*rectio*), may I not be allowed the same privilege? Poems differ in

[55] *Rhetoric*, 3.5.4 (1407a).
[56] There is no such reference in Plutarch.
[57] The *Margites* is a fragment of a mock epic, attributed to Homer. In the *Poetics*, Aristotle
says that this poem constitutes the origin of comedy just as the *Iliad* and the *Odyssey*
constitute the roots of tragedy (1449a). It is included, along with other examples of
Homerica and the Homeric Hymns, in the Loeb edition of Hesiod.
[58] I, you, and we.

the objects of imitation, the means, and the manner. Ovid imitates the same Medea in the *Metamorphoses*[59] that Seneca does in his tragedy, but the verses whereby they are imitated are different, and since one is dramatic presentation, and the other receives an epic setting, the mode or manner is different. The *Aeneid* and the *Eclogues* use the same medium, but differ in the objects of imitations and the manner. The *Eclogues* and comedies, again, agree in the manner of imitation, but differ in objects and media.

Richard Willes, from *A Disputation Concerning Poetry (De Re Poetica*, 1573)[60]

I am sure, Wykehamists,[61] that there are none among you strangers to the study of poetry insofar as you have come to that most renowned emporium of noble arts for this very reason, that you may carry back home with you—besides other paint-boxes of humane letters—a good supply of the pigments and "colors" of rhetoricians and poets. To that same end, indeed, our most noble founder Wykeham (add whatever praise you like) established the very beautiful buildings which you have, bestowed the estates you enjoy, and gave a Warden, Fellows, and Master, so that, learned "In studies of the Muses, Rhetoric's tropes" (as that great benefactor of your College says), you might some day at length have thoughts of Oxford. Nevertheless, because in our age certain men who are evidently barbarous and enemies of the muses despise and hold in contempt not only philosophy, that is, the

---

[59] *Metamorphoses*, 1.1-58.

[60] Richard Willes (1546-1578). Originally a Catholic who emigrated to the Continent and entered the Jesuit order around 1568, Willes converted to Protestantism by the time of the St. Bartholomew Massacre in August 1572, which he witnessed on his way back to England. The *Disputation* is of double interest because, in addition to this text being the first extended discussion of poetry published in England, Willes and Sidney may have met while in Paris. Willes wrote his defense of poetry in the form of a forensic oration, which may have given Sidney the idea, and the two works have roughly the same organization. Willes begins with a chapter "on the Nature and Evolution of Poetry, the Meaning of *Poet*, and the Various Kinds of Poets," and proceeds to defend three

study of wisdom, but even those most noble sciences, rhetoric and poetry, reject the humanities completely, in fact, and try to drive them out of doors, I was intensely annoyed that the noblest and most beautiful arts should be ignominiously and unfairly condemned, even by completely ignorant enemies, without, as it were, the case being heard. A time will come, will certainly come, when I shall not desert the defense of philosophy, perhaps I am already preparing myself; and rhetoric, too, will have to be defended in its own place. But this book of poems, which has now for the first time gone forth out of my hands, if it did not demand the profoundest defense of poetry, at least required some explanation of it, by which all might comprehend the very honorable nature of poetry, might thoroughly understand the most ancient origin of the art, and its excellence, usefulness, and delightfulness, and, finally, might know this part of humane letters to be defended by the strongest arguments against the petty abuse of these obscure men. There will be three parts, therefore, to our disputation. Firstly, I shall gather out of various authors a note on the nature and origin of poetry, the meaning of "poet," and the different kinds of poets. [I will then write] on the origin of metrical form and on the practice of poetry. Next, I shall set out in three propositions, as briefly as I can, the dignity, profitableness and pleasure of poetry. Others will think out, I know, countless other arguments to this effect. Finally, I shall bring to your notice the churlish arguments of the calumniators of the art of

theses: "That Poetry is Superior to Other Arts"; "That the Art of Poetry is Profitable"; and "That Poetry is Most Delightful." Willes concludes with his refutation of the "Objections That Are Usually Made Against Poetry." Willes included his defense in his *Poematum Liber* (*Book of Poems*) in between the poems and his explanations of the poems. On Willes and Sidney, see Roger Kuin, "Querre-Muhau: Sir Philip Sidney and the New World.." The translation is by A. D. S. Fowler, *De Re Poetica*, Luttrell Reprints no. 17 (1958). I have occasionally modified the translation and altered some of the punctuation. The notes are my own.

[61] William of Wykeham (1324-1404), founder of Winchester College and of New College, Oxford, which admitted Willes on October 27, 1562.

poetry. Yes, I shall even, perhaps, assemble far more false accusations than they themselves are sometimes able to make, so that they may see quite clearly by the obliteration of these what an injustice they do in disparaging poetry, and how shamefully they are deceived. Surely they must either have overlooked the rise and fullness of poetry, and been ignorant of it, or else they have not been able to maintain their case strongly enough. After they have seen poetry brought forth from the heart of philosophy, opened at large, and established with the most veracious arguments, I am confident that it will come about that they will not only love and embrace poetry, but defend it stoutly.

The Objections That Are Usually Made Against Poetry May Be Refuted In The Following Manner.

Every reason for praising a thing is drawn either from its nobility or from its usefulness. But the art of poetry is neither noble nor useful. I speak too mildly: it is my contention that poetry is most base and pernicious. Its baseness I shall show by the following arguments. Firstly: What is the purpose of poetry? You will, I know, reply that it is pleasure, of the mind and of the senses. Now this is something that we have in common with animals if, that is, the poets themselves teach that beasts were charmed and captivated by the song of Orpheus. An illustrious art indeed, when its end does not distinguish man from animal!

Next, what does this art teach or expound? What is its content? Read the poets themselves, Greek, Latin, or barbarian, you will learn in the first place the genealogies and deeds of damned men, especially those to whom ignorant antiquity erected altars and temples because they had invented the sickle or the wheel, and paid honors owed to the one God Immortal. So the poets relate the wandering, mating, hunting, feasting, and debauchery of these men. As long as they write about all this, what do they retain of nobility? Or what greatness and dignity do they show us? Furthermore, when they describe the deeds of those the people regarded as gods, when they describe their wars, parricides, adulteries, defilements, deceptions, impieties, and other abominable sins and shameful acts, they say such things about the providence of the gods, and about rewards for the good and punishment for the evil, as any old woman, any grandmother, must despise and ridicule as silly.

Let us descend now from gods to men. What are the poets going to say about men, other than what they have said already about the gods? To represent men as better than the gods is monstrous. They sang the loves of the gods, their wars and luxury and cruelty and crimes, and considered those men worthy of the greatest honor who by imitation approached the iniquity of the gods as nearly as possible. This was certainly keen reasoning; for what fuller praise could be found, than that a man most closely resembled the immortal gods?

The image of the noblest prince was expressed by Homer in Achilles, yet no-one was more angry and savage. The idea of a wise man was expressed in Ulysses, yet no one was his match for deceit, wiles, and lies. Lastly, poets admire the power and riches of kings, and it is their custom to fawn on them.

I come now to the second part, in which I must show that poetry is a corrupting influence. And firstly, what a plague do poets bring on the young, by representing either their own amorous passions or those of other people? For they corrupt good character by their evil influence. Nor, indeed, do they write these poems of lust, cruelty, vain-glory, and deceit roughly and without polish; on the contrary, they are so embellished with every beauty of words and thought, that they captivate and caress men's ears and minds by the allurement even of style itself. What harm must this certainly do, in the representation of things which our depraved and corrupt nature already by its own inclination desires greatly, which it loves to see, which it follows closely with every sense, to which indeed it is carried by its whole impulse? But if the subject-matter attracts us by its nature without words, and if words without matter are so alluring, what do we think happens where the sweet spice of words is added to the sweet poison of the subject matter?[62] Were not poetical measures devised for the content in this way so that evil might the better be commended to the minds of men? Did the poets reach so high in their singing that they are named divine seers, pious, even holy?

So says Ovid: [63]

There is a god within us. It is when he stirs that our bosom warms.

It is his impulse that sows the seeds of inspiration.

Tell me then, Publius Naso,[64] since you teach how a girl should be taken, or sing a triumph song as victor over her ruin, would it not be more appropriate to ask:[65]

Is Pluto in you? Stirred by him do you burn?

This passion, has it seeds of savage Dis?

Nor do Tibullus' poems, Catullus' elegiacs, Propertius' elegies, Martial's epigrams, or Horace's odes offer anything better. I wonder whether it was because he feigned as he did, and carried over to the gods the folly, vanity, wantonness, and sings of men, that Horace, or Homer, was called the Father of Genius? How much more apt and exact to call them Fathers of Lies! Neither poets nor their art can possibly be of any help to us, because it is almost all taken up with extolling cruelty, deceit, ambition, lust, and shamefulness.

Eratosthenes was there quite right to call poetry trash.[66] If indeed Plato says in *Phaedrus* that it is fitting for a poet to feign,[67]

---

[62] In *Plays Confuted in Five Actions* (1582), Stephen Gosson will reiterate this fear of artistic success: "the better they [poems] are penned, or cunninglier handled, [the] more to be fled; because that by their pleasant action of body, & sweet numbers flowing in verse, we are most enchanted" (*The Dramatic Criticism of Stephen Gosson*, ed. Arthur F. Kinney, 130).

[63] *Fasti*, 6.5-6

[64] Ovid.

[65] Willes is rewriting Ovid, *Fasti*, bk 6: 5-6 (quoted above) to make inspiration appear sinister.

[66] Eratosthenes (c.276-194 B. C.), astronomer who measured the circumference of the earth.

[67] Plato never says precisely this in the *Phaedrus*, but throughout this dialogue Socrates consistently denigrates poetry, asserting that "of that place beyond the heavens none of

and if Aristotle says, "Poets tell many lies,"[68] how much then is their art worth, when it turns entirely on feigning and lying. The weightiest authors, in fact, consider no-one worthy of the name of poet if he sings what is true. For this reason Lucan, who describes in heroic verse civil wars not invented by himself but waged by the Romans, will not retain the name of poet.[69] Nor does Virgil, when he transmits true precepts about husbandry,[70] because poetry, whose prerogative is fiction, rests in lying and not in the truth.

What shall I say about the licentiousness and baseness of comedy? For poetry came on to the stage, to be gazed at by the public, so that the poet might abuse anyone he hated with insolence of language and style. This effrontery and impudence was opposed first by the wealthiest and most influential people, and later by laws, which guarded against anyone writing a scurrilous poem about another, or naming an individual on stage for slanderous purposes. But it was without doubt at this point that satiric comedy began to be muffled and disguised, and gradually the whole matter of dramatic poetry was changed to trifling subjects— to love, the intrigues of prostitutes, the swearing of panders, and the fierceness and insolence of soldiers. And when such things are treated in plays, in theatres crammed full of patrons, girls, women, artisans, and uneducated people, morals are corrupted to an alarming degree, and the minds of those listening and watching are tempted to shamefulness.

I pass by in silence the fact that lovers, that is, slaves of most damnable passions, find this device exceedingly useful for their intrigues, so that poetry is the bawd of shamelessness and lust. It is a commonplace that to enjoy his lusts the lover has to be musician and poet as well. An illustrious art this, which parents propose

---

our earthly poets has yet sung, and none shall sing worthily . . . [because] it is there that true being dwells . . . ; reason alone, the soul's pilot, can behold it, and all true knowledge is knowledge thereof" (247c).

[68] *Metaphysics*, 983a.

should be taught to their children, so that they may be trained and educated to-shamefulness! Can anything be imagined with a worse influence on the young?

Plato accordingly expelled the poets from the commonwealth he conceived as ideal; for he understood that their art is harmful to the state.[71]

If the art of poetry were good, it would make poets themselves good. But consult the stories of the ancient writers, and you will discover that all poets were either sodden drunkards or shameless rascals, or else completely wild and even quite insane. For this reason most of them savor of drink, or talk about adultery and fornication. But if by any chance they did write anything pure, their lives were completely inconsistent with their works, so that the poet is laughable when he writes: "Our page is wanton, but our life upright." [72]

Finally, Democritus and others deny that those who are not possessed are poets.[73] Then long live the art which is not consistent with a sane mind! Let us shun and detest poets by the example of Augustus, who had the poet Ovid, founder of the *Art of Love*, thrown out of the city, and took care that he was banished to the ends of the earth, there to bewail the hardships of his exile among savage and barbarous nations, with the help of the same poetic art on account of which he had been condemned and banished.

These and similar objections which are urged by the persistent calumniators of the art of poetry seem to the uneducated absolutely true, to those with insufficient education, plausible, but to the truly wise and learned, false and ridiculous. For all these arguments are taken from the abuse of the art, in a way that no wise man has ever argued. They make no attack on the art

[69] Lucan, author of the *Pharsalia*. See the *Apology*, n. 45, and Scaliger's comments above.
[70] *Georgics*.
[71] See the excerpts from the *Republic* and the *Laws*.
[72] *Tristia*, 2.354.
[73] Horace, *Ars Poetica* (*Art of Poetry*), 296-7

itself.[74] If they convince us of anything, it is of course that poets who are vicious should be avoided. But if we concede this—as we do concede it—we shall be in agreement with our opponents, and poetry will enjoy its honor and dignity as before. Let us reply, however, to each objection separately. All their arguments are divided into two sections. The first of these describes the baseness and vileness of poetry in four ways; the second recounts the harms and injuries that result from seven causes. The first misrepresentation is easily refuted by considering the purpose of poetry, which is certainly not merely a kind of sensual pleasure, as we have said, but the moral education of the minds of the citizens to virtue through poetical harmony.

The second argument does not so much condemn poetry as the religion of the heathen. Thus all the states, countries, and peoples, all the princes and emperors, all the philosophers, all the sages, all who did not know the religion of the one true God, are confuted, no less than the poets, who, like divine heralds of the pagan gods, tried to extol with the highest praises those whom the whole world judged worthy of honor. And from this blindness of poets we gain an enlightenment, so that spurred on by their example, steeped in their erudition, equipped with their rules, harmony, rhythms, and measures, and replenished with their choicest words, we may more fitly sing the praises of the High and Eternal God—unless, that is, we wish to give place to the heathen in piety.

And yet, poets celebrate the crimes and shamefulness of men. But add, not only the shameful acts, but also the penalties which shameless and impious men incur. This can be seen in Prometheus, in Sisyphus, in Ixion, and in the children of Belus.[75] Besides, poets have celebrated good men, and their virtues, and the rewards of their virtues. Nor have all poets praised evil men:

---

[74] See the *Apology*, p.100.
[75] For all four, see Ovid, *Metamorphoses*, 4.456-63

Virgil sang, not vices, but arms and the man,[76] while he places before our eyes the piety of Aeneas, and nothing could be more chaste, more elegant, and more exalted, than his poem. But if he ever descends to lighter matters, such as the loves of Aeneas and Dido,[77] these are related with such skill and modesty and dignity, that nothing could be bettered. In a play of Aristophanes', Euripides passes the same judgement on Aeschylus.[78]

If Achilles was angry, if Ulysses was deceitful, in this Homer should please all the more, because when he praised their virtues he did not remain silent about their vices, a thing, however, which many rhetoricians have done, and not uncommonly historians too, when they praise the great deeds of princes in their narrations, but do not mention their crimes. What of the fact that the poets obviously inveigh against and condemn men's vices in their poetry? What servants of wickedness are not censured by the satirists, Horace, Juvenal, and Persius? Did Catallus in his elegiacs not brand Julius Caesar with a stigma of lasting infamy, because he shamelessly dallied with Mamurra?[79] Within the memory of our fathers princes, kings, Caesars, emperors, and Popes were all afraid of a certain Aretino.[80] So we can see that poets do not spare the vices of princes and emperors, far less refrain from hard words or wink at their faults. It is common with poets, however, as also with orators and other artists, to exalt someone to the sky with praise.

There follows the other section, in which the attackers try to show that poetry is to be avoided like the plague. But if this is so, why did Aristotle judge that no precepts could educate the

---

[76] The opening words of the *Aeneid* are "Arma virumque cano [Of arms and the man I sing]."

[77] *Aeneid*, Bk. 4.

[78] Willes is clearly misremembering Aristophanes' *Frogs*, because in this play, Euripides does not have a good word to say about Aeschylus.

[79] Poem 57.

[80] Pietro Aretino (1492-1556), Italian poet and satirist, best known for his pornographic verses. It is undoubtedly an exaggeration to say that rulers feared Aretino, but he was certainly hated by those he ridiculed.

still tender mind of King Alexander to virtue, better than reading the poet Homer?[81] From that poet he could derive an abundant store of whatever pertained to living well and blessedly and in the manner of princes. Why did Ptolemy the King of Egypt employ Menander at such an expense?[82] Why did Archelaus of Macedonia bestow on Euripides, Maecenas on Horace, so many rewards of praise? [83] Why were Catullus and Archias and Caelius so dear to Cicero? [84] With the highest commendation Virgil recited his own poetry to Augustus, as Sophocles did to the Athenians, and Aeschylus to Hiero of Syracuse. More, even Lucullus, too, watched a comedy by Caecillus.[85] But let us see whatever the cause can be of such a great hostility towards poets. They sing their loves. Away with lewd poets. What then? Must we say that all poets are lewd? By no means: Virgil is pure, Aeschylus is pure, and others too. But the poems of most are full of lust. Yet not all poems. Certainly let any books that are lewd be thrown out. This, reason commands, Moral integrity requires, the Christian religion entreats.

Let us therefore read Virgil in safety; let us read Horace-but purged of vices; and let us read Martial, but cut by Augerius.[86]

---

[81] See the *Apology*, n. 178.

[82] Menander (c. 342-292 B. C.), Athenian dramatist reputed among ancient critics as the best exponent of the New Comedy.

[83] Archelaus, King of Macedonia from 413 to 399 B. C. A great admirer of Greek civilization, invited many renowned artists, among them the tragedian Euripides, to his new capital at Pella. Gaius Maecenas (c. 78-8 B. C.), Roman diplomat, counselor to the Emperor Augustus, and patron of Virgil and Horace.

[84] See *On Behalf of the Poet Archias*.

[85] Lucius Licinius Lucullus (117 B. C.- 58/56 B. C.), Roman general who retired to a life of such extravagance that the adjective *lucullan*, which means "luxurious," derives from his name. Statius Caecillus (d. 168 B. C.), Roman comic playwright who was highly regarded in antiquity.

[86] Emond Auger (Augerius; no dates available), editor of an expurgated edition of Martial's epigrams, marvelously entitled *The Epigrams of Marcus Valerius Martial Vindicated From Every Kind of Obscenity and Base Language, With Only a Very Few Words Either Rejected or Altered with No Harm to Latinity* (*M. Valerii Martialis Epigrammata paucis admodum vel reiectis, vel immutatis nullo Latinitatis damno, ab omni rerum obscoenitate, verboru[m]u´que turpitudine vindicata*). The Society of Jesus (the Jesuits) published Auger's edition in

Let us keep the *Fasti* of Ovid, the *Tristia* and the *Pontine Epistles*, but let us omit those verses which he himself condemned:[87]

> Even that work which was once his ill-starred amusement in
> the green of youth,
>
> Too late, alas, he condemns and hates.

I would not venture to advise anyone to read the poems of Catullus or the comedies of Terence to the young. On the other hand, I do advise and urge schoolmasters to draw from their writings the quality of Latin style, the diction, and the elegances which they diligently set forth to their students. Let the boys learn clarity from Tibullus,[88] for he writes more pleasantly, delicately, simply, sweetly, and, most of all, relies on nature. Let them take from Propertius a certain exotic strangeness.[89] The imitator of Callimachus,[90] he was more. sinewy, more accurate, and more careful than Tibullus.[91] They should be taught from a tender age to avoid lust. As Catullus himself says, "the sacred poet ought be chaste."[92] The rest of the poets, certainly, I don't value highly. For however illustrious Lucan and Seneca appear superficially, being Spanish they have introduced an inflation and tumidity of style more adapted to their own national character; and rather turn away from the right, simple imitation of nature (as we read that those living away from Athens did), than offer the native elegance of Roman speech.

Again (as the poets' writings I have enumerated were not altogether free from wantonness), if we wish to throw out all

---

1585. I am grateful to Anne Lake Prescott for providing this reference, and to Professor E. N. Genovese for the translation.

[87] *Tristia*, 3.1.7.

[88] Aulus Tibullus (55-19 B. C.), the rhetorician Quintilian considered him the finest Roman poet.

[89] Sextus Propertius (1st century B. C.), the most important Roman elegiac poet.

[90] Not to be confused with the sculptor of the same name. Callimachus (c. 305-240 B. C.) was known for his poetic craftsmanship.

[91] In the marginal note, Willes inserts this caveat: "Yet I do not advise that the boys themselves should read the works of either of those two [Tibullus and Propertius]."

[92] 16.5. The full passage, however, is "For [while] the sacred poet ought to be chaste himself, his verses need not be so."

those books in which any wantonness is related, then goodbye to the chronicles of the historians, and the philosophers' disputations about nature, and medical dissertations, and the distinctions of canon law. I might even mention certain chapters of sacred law, and many Scriptural genealogies, and the Song of Solomon itself.

But poets feign everything, so that Lucan cannot be called a poet.[93] I shall reply in a Homeric manner, taking the second point first: it is not only the function of the poet to feign what does not exist, but also to imitate what does. Besides, the poets' feigning of things should not be turned into a fault; just as it is not considered shameful for mathematicians to imagine in the sky so many circles which do not exist. And how often do mathematicians consider shapes as abstracted from all matter? When in fact everything which has magnitude is united with matter. And whatever poets feign, at least they do so in such a way that they teach what is profitable and what is not. For example, trees were stirred by the song of Orpheus: that is, rustics and ignorant men are delighted by poetry. So with Actaeon changed into a stag and devoured by dogs:[94] that is, a spendthrift wastes his riches most if he supports many favorites. It would be tedious to go through each one.

The boldness of drama, satires, and other poems of that kind was invented not to excite wickedness, but to deter men from vice. For this reason, anything lewd or reprehensible is called "*scaenica.*"[95] Nor should the wantonness of one poet be blamed on all, besides, we often find satirical and slanderous passages elsewhere, even in the orators themselves.

In the same way, clearly, we reply that poetry is not the servant of vice, although bad poets may possibly have abused the art, in just the same way as perverse philosophers have abused

---

[93] See Scaliger's rebuttal of this charge, pp. 244-45.
[94] *Metamorphoses*, 3.155-206.
[95] Theatrical.

dialectic (as often happens), or dishonest rhetoricians eloquence. If we hand over all the opportunities of speaking to these men, says Cicero, we shall certainly not make them orators, but we shall just as certainly have given arms to madmen.[96] Otherwise, even music would have to be rejected too, because a great many have used it for vicious purposes. Plato himself explains his meaning in the very same passage. In it he does not reject poets simply, but bad poets. [97]

What is remarkable in the fact that there were some lewd and drunken poets? These were the vices not so much of poets as of almost the whole human race. And for this reason certain lighter poets have recounted vice in their poetry, so that the stories they told would please the corrupt taste of the public. As Catullus says in his hendecasyllabics:[98]

> Verses only have wit and grace
> When voluptuous and wanton.

But to say that all poets are either lechers or drunks is sheer impudence.

I have it on good authority that there are four kinds of "frenzy" or enthusiasm. Of these, two have some blame attached; but the others must be counted among the virtues themselves. Plato gives them the following names:[99] mystical frenzy, amorous, ecstatic, and poetical. The first kind is seen in those who are drunk. Not without frenzy do they reveal whatever is hidden. The raging passions of lovers clearly display the second kind. As indeed Plato says: "And love is not as they assert a god, but bitterness and trembling fear."[100] The third kind of frenzy is said to be that of seers, and the last is seen in poets. Democritus says that

---

[96] *On Oratory*, 2.
[97] Both Scaliger (p. 241) and Sidney (pp. 105-7) make the same argument. Compare their responses with the excerpts above from Plato.
[98] *Carmina* 16.7.
[99] *Phaedrus*, 244a-245c.
[100] *Phaedrus*, 245c.

poets are so possessed not because they are out of their mind, but because they apply their mind to subjects, and enter into the passions they describe, to such an extent that they almost seem to be excited into a frenzy, or transported to and fro by a divine inspiration and afflatus. This often happens to us, if we are concentrating on anything seriously: in a sense we do not notice what we are doing. So Aristotle has written that philosophers also are possessed, and Democritus has asserted that no one can become a great poet this side of frenzy.

As for Ovid, he was certainly not banished to Scythia because he was a poet, but because he was lewd,—or rather, as he himself often complained, not so much on account of the *Art of Love* as because he had seen I know not what base deed committed by Caesar:[101]

Why did I look and make my eye guilty?

Why foolishly let the fault be known to me?

This is quite enough about the art of poetry and the writings of poets; now let us set forth into the notes themselves, which may clarify my poems.

Theodore Beza, *"A Sportful Comparison between Poets and Papists,"* translated in *Flowers of Epigrams*, ed. Timothy Kendall (London, 1577).[102]

---

[101] *Tristia*, 2.104.

[102] Theodore Beza (Théodore de Bèze, 1519-1605), French Protestant theologian and heir of John Calvin. As a young man, Beza studied law and practiced for a short while in Orleans. During this period, he published a small book of poems, *Juvenilia* (1548), which contained some rather tepid erotic verses that were later used by his enemies to embarrass him (and that Beza partly repudiates in the prefatory letter to his biblical drama, *Abraham Sacrafiant* [*The Sacrifice of Abraham*]). After a severe illness, he vowed to devote himself to religion, abandoned the law, and in 1548 joined Calvin in Geneva. In 1569 Beza published another book of verse, the *Poemata*, which drops the erotic poetry. Thomas Heywood would retranslate ten of Beza's poems for his *Pleasant Dialogues and Dramas* (1637), including the comparison between monks and poets. Judging by the large number of editions and translations, Beza's works were extremely popular in England. See Anne Lake Prescott, "English Writers and Beza's Latin Epigrams: The Uses and Abuses of Poetry," *Studies in the Renaissance* 21 (1974): 83-117.

Lo, hear the cause to Francis,[103] why
Homerus I compare:
Lo, hear the cause wherefore I think
That monks like poets are.
Franciscus could not see one whit,[104]
And Homer he was blind,
Homerus he was blind of light,
Franciscus blind of mind.
Franciscus was a beggar bare,
No beggar Homer was,
Bare beggars both, their time they did
In merry singing pass.
Franciscus filled the world with lies,
Lies likewise Homer taught—
Franciscus by his brethren,
Homer by books he wrought.
In secret woods and gloomy groves,
First poets led their lives;
In dampish dens and deserts dead
Monks live without their wives.
Each town with monks was pestered,
When woods at last they left;
With poets every city swarmed,
They could not thence be reft.
Still poets sing, and moping monks
Sing likewise day and night;
And none so much as they themselves
Do in their songs delight.
Each poet hath his wanton wench
To dandle all the day;
For fear of failing every monk

---

[103] St. Francis of Assisi (1181-1226), founder of the order of Franciscan monks.
[104] St. Francis was blind for the last two years of his life.

Hath four to keep him play.
The poet lauds (and likes of life)
Full cups which flow and swim;
The monk if he his liquor lack
All goes not well with him.
The poet with his louring lute,[105]
His sonnets singeth shrill.
The monk with pot fast by his side,
His carols chanteth still.
With divers furies both are vexed:
The poet bears a spear
With ivy decked; the masking monk
A golden cross doth bear.
The poet's crown is dressed with bays
And myrtle branches brave;
White shining shitten shaven crowns
The Popish prelates have.
For fine,[106] to monk give poetry,
To poet give the wood,
And so thou shalt make both of them
Right monks and poets good.

From Theodore Beza, *Abraham's Sacrifice*, trans. Arthur Golding (London, 1577)

Theodore de Beza to the Readers, greeting in the Lord.

It is now two years since God granted me the grace to forsake the country where he is persecuted, to serve him according to his holy will. During which time, because that in my adversity many fancies fan in my head, I resorted to God's word, where I found two things that comforted me marvelously. The one is the infinite number of promises uttered by the mouth of him which

---

[105] Gloomy, sad.
[106] In fine; in conclusion.

is the truth itself, whose sayings are always matched with effect. The other is the multitude of examples whereof even the least are able enough, not only to encourage and hearten the weakest and faintest-hearted in the world, but also to make them invincible. Which thing we must needs see to have come to pass, if we consider by what means God's truth hath been maintained to this present time. Howbeit among all them that are set afore us, for example, in the old Testament. I find three persons, in whom (to my seeming) the Lord meant to set forth his greatest wonders, namely, Abraham, Moses, and David. In the lives of whom, if men would nowadays look upon themselves, they should know themselves better than they do.

Therefore, as I read those holy stories with wonderful pleasure and singular profit, there came a desire upon me to exercise myself in writing such matters in verse, not only of intent to consider and remember them the better, but also to praise God by all the means I could devise. For I confess, that even of nature I have delighted in poetry, and I cannot yet repent me of it. Nevertheless, it grieveth me right sore that the little grace which God gave me in that behalf was employed by me in such things as the very remembrance of them irketh me now at the heart. Therefore, I gave myself as then to more holy matters, hoping to go forward in them afterward, especially in the translating of the Psalms, which I am now in hand with. And would God that the great number of good wits which I know in France would in stead of busying themselves about unhappy inventions or imitations of vain and unhonest fancies (for so they be, if a man judge them according to truth), rather than set their minds to the magnifying of the great God, of whom they have received those so great gifts than to the flattering of their idols, that is to say, of their Lords and Ladies, whom they uphold in their vices by their feignings and flatterings.[107] Of a truth it would become them better to sing a

---

[107] Beza has in mind the poets of the Pléiade (see the introduction, n. 70).

song of God than to counterfeit a ballet of Petrarch's, and to make amorous ditties worthy to have the garland of sonnets, or to counterfeit the furies of the ancient poets, to blaze abroad the glory of this world, or to consecrate this man or that woman to immortality, things which bear the readers on hand that the authors of them not only are mounted up to the top of their Parnassus, but also are come to the very circle of the moon.

Othersome, of which number I myself have been, to my great grief as now, write two-edged epigrams, cutting on both sides or sharp-pointed and pricking at both ends. Others busy themselves rather in overturning than in turning of things, and othersome intending to enrich our tongue, do powder it with Greek and Latin terms. But how now, will some man say, I looked for a tragedy, and thou givest us a satire. I confess that in thinking upon such madness I was carried away and overshot myself. Nevertheless, I meant not to rail upon good wits, but only to discover them so plainly the open wrongs which they do both to God and to themselves as they might through a certain envy take upon them to pass me in the description of such matters as I have taken taste of to their hands, according as I know that it shall be very easy for them, if the meanest of them will give himself thereto.

From Stephen Gosson, *The School of Abuse* (1579)[108]

Dedication: To the right noble Gentleman, Master Philip Sidney, Esquire, Stephen Gosson wisheth health of body, wealth of mind, reward of virtue, advancement of honor, and good success in Godly affairs.

---

[108] Stephen Gosson (1554-1624), author of the most famous attack on poetry and drama, *The School of Abuse* (1579), which was commissioned by London's civic authorities, who were alarmed at the success of the new phenomenon of the commercial stage. Gosson was in turn a playwright, a controversial pamphleteer, and a successful clergyman and preacher. In addition to the *School*, he wrote two other attacks on fictions, *An Apology of the "School of Abuse," against Poets, pipers, Players, and their Excusers* (1579), and *Plays Confuted in Five Actions* (1582).

The Syracusans used such variety of dishes in their banquets that when they were set, and their boards furnished, they were many times in doubt which they should touch first or taste last. And in my opinion the world giveth every writer so large a field to walk in that before he set pen to the book, he shall find himself feasted at Syracuse, uncertain where to begin or where to end. This caused Pindarus to question with his Muse whether he were better with his art to decipher the life of the nymph Melia, or Cadmus's encounter with the dragon, or the wars of Hercules at the walls of Thebes, or Bacchus' cups, or Venus's juggling.[109] He saw so many turnings laid open to his feet that he knew not which way to bend his pace.

Therefore, as I cannot be commend his wisdom, which in banqueting feeds most upon that that doth nourish best, so must I dispraise his method in writing, which, following the course of amorous poets, dwelleth longest in those points that profit least; and like a wanton whelp, leaveth the game to run riot. The scarab flies over many a sweet flower and lights in a cowshard.[110] It is the custom of the fly to leave the sound places of the horse and suck at the botch. The nature of colloquintida to draw the worst humors to itself.[111] The manner of swine to forsake the fair fields and wallow in the mire. And who whole practice of poets, either with fables to show their abuses, or with plain terms to unfold their mischief, discover their shames, discredit themselves, and disperse their poison through all the world. Virgil sweats in describing his gnat; Ovid bestirreth him to pain out his flea; the one shows his art in the lust of Dido, the other his cunning in the incest of Myrrha, and that trumpet of bawdry, *The Craft of Love*.[112]

---

[109] Plutarch, *Moralia*, "On the Fame of the Athenians," 348a.
[110] A pile of cow manure.
[111] An extremely bitter herb.
[112] The *Ars Amatoria*.

I must confess that poets are the whetstones of wit, notwithstanding that wit is dearly bought. Where honey and gall are mixed, it will be hard to sever the one from the other. The deceitful physician giveth sweet syrups to make his poison go down the smoother; the juggler casteth a mist to work the close; the Siren's song is the sailor's wreck; the fowler's whistle, the bird's death; the wholesome bait, the fish's bane; the Harpies have virgins' faces and vultures' talons; Hyena speaks like a friend, and devours like a foe; the calmest seas hide dangerous rocks; the wolf jets in weathers fells. Many good sentences are spoken by Davus to shadow his knavery,[113] and written by poets as ornaments to beautify their works and set their trumpery to sale without suspect.

But if you look well to Epeus' horse, you find in his bowels the destruction of Troy; [114] open the sepulchre of Semiramis, whose title promiseth such wealth to the kings of Persia, you shall see nothing but dead bones;[115] rip up the golden ball that Nero consecrated to Jupiter Capitolinus, you shall have it stuffed with the shavings of his beard;[116] pull off the visard that poets mask in, you shall disclose their reproach, bewray[117] their vanity, loath their wantonness, lament their folly, and perceive their sharp sayings to be placed as pearls in dunghills, fresh pictures on rotten walls, chaste matrons' apparel on common courtesans. These are the cups of Circe that turn reasonable creatures into brute beasts,[118] the balls of Hippomenes,[119] that hinder the course of Atalanta, and the blocks of the Devil that are cast in our ways to cut off the race of

---

[113] Servant in Terence's comedy, *Andria*.

[114] The son of Panopeus, who built the Trojan horse. *Aeneid*, 2.264.

[115] The queen of Assyria. Plutarch, *Moralia*, "Sayings of Kings and Commanders,"173a.

[116] Cassius Dio Cocceainus (Dio Cassio), 150-235, Roman administrator and author of an 80 book history of Rome written in Greek and called *Romoika*. Its title in the Loeb edition is *Dio's Roman History*. Nero created a festival called the "Juvenalia" or "Games of Youth" to celebrate his shaving for the first time (62.19.2). See below, n. 135.

[117] Discover.

[118] Homer, *Odyssey*, 10.135-574.

[119] Ovid, *Metamorphoses* 10.557-682.

toward wits. No marvel though[120] Plato shut them out of his school and banished them quite from his commonwealth as effeminate writers, unprofitable members, and utter enemies to virtue.

The Romans were very desirous to imitate the Greeks, and yet very loath to receive their poets. Insomuch that Cato layeth it in the dish of Marcus the noble[121] as a foul reproach that in the time of his consulship he brought Ennius the poet into his province. Tully, accustomed to read them with great diligence in his youth, but when he waxed graver in study, elder in years, riper in judgement, he accompted them the fathers of lies, the pipes of vanity, and schools of abuse.[122] Maximus Tyrius taketh upon him to defend the discipline of these doctors under the name of Homer, wresting the rashness of Ajax to valor, the cowardice of Ulysses to policy, [123] the dotage of Nestor to grave counsel, and the battle of Troy to the wonderful conflict of the four elements, where Juno, which is counted the air, sets in her foot to take up the strike and steps boldly betwixt them to part the fray.[124] It is a pageant worth the sight, to behold how he labors with mountains to bring forth mice, much like to some of those players that come to the scaffold[125] with drum and trumpet to proffer skirmish, and when they have sounded alarm, off go the pieces to encounter a shadow, or conquer a paper monster. You will smile, I am sure, if you read it, to see how this moral philosopher toils to draw the lion's skin upon Aesop's ass, Hercules' shoes on a child's feet, amplifying that which the more it is stirred, the more it stinks, the less it is talked of, the better it is liked, and as wayward children, the more they be flattered, the worse they are, or

---

[120] That.

[121] The consul Marcus Fulvius. See the *Apology*, n. 181.

[122] Seneca, *Moral Letters* (*Epistulae Morales*), Letter 49, "On the Shortness of Life," 5.

[123] "Policy" means political cunning. See the *Apology*, p. 75, n. 70.

[124] Maximus of Tyre (2nd century A. D. neoplatontist), *Philosophical Orations*, trans. M. B. Trapp (Oxford: Clarendon Press, 1997), Oration 26, p. 219.

[125] Stage.

as cursed sores with often touching wax angry, and run the longer without healing. He attributeth the beginning of virtue to Minerva, if friendship to Venus, and the root of all handicrafts to Vulcan, but if he had broke his arm as well as his leg when he fell out of heaven into Lemnos, either Apollo must have played the bonesetter, or every occupation been laid a water.

Plato, when he saw the doctrine of these teachers, neither for profit necessary, nor to be wished for pleasure, gave them all drum's entertainment, not suffering them once to show their faces in a reformed commonwealth. [126]And the same Tyrius that lays such a foundation for poets in the name of Homer overthrows his whole building in the person of Mithecus, which was an excellent cook among the Greeks, and as much honored for his confections as Phidias for his carving. But when he came to Sparta, thinking there for his cunning to be accounted a god, the good laws of Lycurgus and custom of the country were too hot for his diet. The governors banished him and his art, and all the inhabitant, following the steps of their predecessors, used not with dainties to provoke appetite, but with labor and travail to whet their stomachs to their meat.[127]

I may well like Homer to Mithecus, and poets to cooks,[128] the pleasures of the one wins the body from labor and conquereth the sense; the allurement of the other draws the mind from virtue and confoundeth wit. As in every perfect commonwealth there ought to be good laws established, right maintained, wrong repressed, virtue rewarded, vice punished, and all manner of abuses thoroughly purged, so ought there such schools for the furtherance of the same to be advanced, that young men may be taught that in green years that becomes to practice in gray hairs.

---

[126] See the excerpts from Plato in this edition.
[127] Maximus of Tyre, Oration 17, p. 151.
[128] Plato, *Gorgias*, 462a-465c. Plato compares rhetoric with cookery because neither, according to Socrates, can produce knowledge or explain its own nature (465a).

Anacharsis, being demanded of a Greek whether they had not instruments of music, whether they had not instruments of music, or schools of poetry, in Scythia, answered yes, and without vice, as though it were either impossible or incredible that no abuse should be learned where such lessons are taught and such schools maintained.[129]

Sallust, in describing the nurture of Sempronia, commendeth her wit in that she could frame herself to all companies, to talk discretely with wise men, and vainly with wantons, taking a quip ere it came to ground, and returning it back without a fault. She was taught (saith he) both Greek and Latin, she could versify, sing, and dance better than became an honest woman.[130] Sappho was skilful in poetry and sung well, but she was whorish.[131] I set not this down to condemn the gifts of versifying, dancing, or singing in women, so they be used with mean[132] and exercised in due time. But to show you that as by Anachisis' report the Scythians did it without offense, so one swallow brings not summer, nor one particular example sufficient proof for a general precept. White silver draws a black line; fire is as hurtful as healthy; water as dangerous as it is commodious; and these qualities as hard to be well used when we have them as they are to be learned before we get them. He that goes to sea must smell of the ship, and that sails into poets will savor of pitch.

C. Marius, in the assembly of the whole senate at Rome, in a solemn oration giveth an account of his bringing up. He showeth that he hath been taught to lie on the ground, to suffer all weathers, to lead men, to strike his foe, to fear nothing but an evil name, and challengeth praise unto himself in that he never learned the Greek tongue , neither meant to be instructed in it hereafter,

---

[129] Maximus of Tyre, Oration 17, pp. 154-55.
[130] Sallust, *War with Catliline*, 25.
[131] Maximus of Tyre, Oration 18, p. 165.
[132] With moderation.

either that he thought it too far a journey to fetch learning beyond the field, or because he doubted the abuses of those schools where poets were ever the headmasters.[133] Tiberius, the emperor, saw somewhat when he judged Scaurus to death for writing a tragedy;[134] Augustus, when he banished Ovid, and Nero, when he charged Lucan to put up his pipes, to stay his pen, and write no more. Burrus and Seneca, the schoolmasters of Nero, are flouted and hated of the people for teaching their scholar the song of Attis. For Dion sayeth that the hearing thereof wrung laughter and tears from most of those that were then about him.[135] Whereby I judge that they scorned the folly of the teachers and lamented the frenzy of the scholar, who, being emperor of Rome, and bearing the weight of the whole commonwealth upon his shoulders, was easier to be drawn to vanity by wanton poets than to good government by the fatherly counsel of grave senators. They were condemned to die by the laws of the heathens which[136] enchanted the grain in other men's grounds, and are they not accursed, think you, by the mouth of God, which having the government of young princes with poetical fantasies draw them to the schools of their own abuses, bewitching the grain in the green blade that was

---

[133] Gaius Marius (b. 157 B. C.), Roman general and statesman (the "C." stands for "Consul") who defeated the North African king, Jugurtha, in 105 B. C. Marius is not speaking to the Roman senate, but to "an assembly of the people," and his purpose is "to bait the nobles." Gosson thus alters Marius' anti-aristocratic position to one more in line with his own (Sallust, *War with Jugurtha*, 85.31-36).

[134] Mamercus Aemilius Scaurus died because he composed a tragedy on Atreus which urged "the subjects of that monarch to endure the folly of the reigning prince." Tiberius thought that Scaurus referred obliquely to him, and compelled him to commit suicide (*Dio's Roman History*, 58.24.4).

[135] The crowning moment of the "Juvenalia" arrived when Hero himself took the stage. According to Dio, "this Augustus sang to the lyre some piece alled 'Attis' or 'The Bacchantes,' while many soldiers stood by and all the people that the seats would hold sat watching." But because he was such a miserable singer, "he moved his whole audience to laughter and tears at once. Beside him stood Burrus and Seneca, like teachers, prompting him" (*Dio's Roman History*, 62. 20.1-4). Dio, however, says nothing about Burrus or Seneca being hated for Nero's attempts at poetic greatness.

[136] Who.

sowed for the sustenance of many thousands, and poisoning the spring with their amorous lays, whence the whole commonwealth should fetch water? But to leave the scepter to Jupiter and instructing of princes to Plutarch and Xenophon, I will bear a low sail and row near the shore lest I chance to be carried beyond my reach, or run aground in those coasts which I never knew. My only endeavor shall be to show you that in a rough cast, which I see in a cloud, looking through my fingers.

Because I have been matriculated myself in the school where so many abuses flourish,[137] I will imitate the dogs of Egypt, which coming to the banks of the Nile to quench their thirst, sip and away, drink running, lest they be snapped short for a prey to crocodiles. I should tell tales out of the schools, and be ferruled for my fault, or hissed at for a blab, if I laid all the orders open before your eyes. You are no sooner entered but liberty looseth the reins, and gives you head, placing you with poetry in the lowest form. When his skill is shown to make his scholar as good as ever twanged, he prefers you to piping, from piping to playing, from play to pleasure, from pleasure to sloth, from sloth to sleep, from sleep to sin, from sin to death, from death to the devil, if you take your learning apace, and pass through every form without revolting.

* * *

Poetry and piping have always been so united together that until the time of Melanippides,[138] pipers were poets' hirelings. But mark, I pray you, how they are now both abused.

The right use of ancient poetry[139] was to have the notable exploits of worthy captains, the wholesome counsels of good fa-

---

[137] Gosson was himself a playwright before turning against the theater and poetry. None of his dramatic works are extant.

[138] Melanippides (2nd half of 5th century B. C.), musical innovator. In the fragments of his *Marsyas*, Athena throws away a flute in disgust, which Gosson interprets as signifying a split between poetry and music.

[139] Compare Sidney's discussion of the "right use" of poetry, pp. 67-70, 87-93.

thers, and virtuous lives of predecessors set down in numbers, and sung to the instrument at solemn feasts, that the sound of the one might draw the hearers from kissing the cup too often, the sense of the other put them in mind of things past, and chalk out the way to do the like. After this manner were the Baeotians[140] trained from rudeness to civility. The Lacedaemonians instructed by Tyrtaeus' verse,[141] the Argives by the melody of Telesilla,[142] and the Lesbians by Alcaeus's odes[143]. . . . [But] if you inquire how many such poets and pipers we have in our age, I am persuaded that every one of them may creep through a ring, or dance the wild Morris in a needle's eye. We have infinite poets and pipers and such peevish cattle among us in England that live by merry begging, maintained by alms, and privily encroach upon every man's purse. But if they that are in authority and have the sword in their hands to cut off abuses, should call an accompt to see how many Chirons, Terpandri,[144] and Homers are here, they might cast the sum without pen or counters and sit with Rachel to weep for her children because they were not.[145]

* * *

Consider with thyself, gentle reader, the old discipline of England, mark what we were before, and what we are now. Leave Rome awhile, and cast thine eye back to thy predecessors, and tell me how wonderfully we have changed since we were schooled with these abuses. Dion sayeth that Englishmen could suffer watching and labor, hunger and thirst, and bear of all storms with head and shoulders; they used slender weapons, went naked, and were good soldiers; they fed upon roots and barks of trees, they would stand up to the chin many days in marshes

---

[140] According to legend, the inhabitants of Thebes were civilized by Musaeus.

[141] See the *Apology*, n. 18.

[142] Telesilla (c. 5th century B. C.), Greek lyric poet who wrote for choirs of girls.

[143] See the excerpt from Scaliger, n. 39, above.

[144] For Chiron and Terpandrus, see Plutarch, *Moralia*, "Concerning Music."

[145] Jeremiah 31:15, quoted in Matthew 2:18.

without victuals, and they had a kind of sustenance in time of need of which if they had taken but the quantity of a bean, or the weight of a pea, they did neither gape after meat, nor long for the cup, a great while after.[146] The men in valor not yielding to Scythia, the women in courage passing the Amazons. The exercise of both was shooting and darting, running and wrestling, and trying such masteries as either consisted in swiftness of feet, agility of body, strength of arms, or martial discipline. But the exercise that is now among us, is banqueting, playing, piping, and dancing, and all such delights as may win us to pleasure, or rock us asleep.

* * *

Oh want a wonderful change is this? Our wrestling at arms is turned to wallowing in ladies' laps, our courage to cowardice, our running to riot, our bows into bowls, and our darts to dishes. We have robbed Greece of gluttony, Italy of wantonness, Spain of pride, France of deceit, and Dutchland of quaffing. Compare London. to Rome, and England to Italy, you shall find the theaters of the one, the abuses of the other, to be rife among us.

Edmund Spenser, from Spenser and Gabriel Harvey, from *Two Other Very Commendable Letters of the Same Men's Writing: Both Touching the Foresaid Artificial Versifying* (1580)[147]

As for the two worthy Gentlemen, master Sidney and Master Dyer, they have me, I thank them, in some use of familiarity, of whom, and to whom, what speech passeth for your credit and

---

[146] *Dio's Roman History*, 62.5. Ironically, given Gosson's earlier praise of the women of antiquity, it is not Dio himself who says this about the Britons but Buducia, who is urging her countrymen to regain their native freedom by revolting against the Romans.
[147] Edmund Spenser (1554?-1599), author of *The Shepheardes Calendar* and *The Faerie Queene*. Gabriel Harvey (1550?-1630), English academic and friend of Spenser. Both shared an interest in reforming English versifying and jointly published their letters, partly as a way of attracting attention to themselves and furthering their careers. Spenser's comment about Sidney's reaction to Gosson needs to be taken with a grain of salt because it is unclear whether the two actually knew each other at this time. Furthermore, as Spenser had just published the *Calendar*, in which he announces his intention to become England's epic poet, he had a vested interest in undercutting Gosson's credibil-

estimation I leave yourself to conceive, having always so well conceived of my unfeigned affection and zeal towards you. And now they have proclaimed in their *areopagus* a general surceasing and silence of bald rhymers, and also of the very best to: instead whereof, they have, by authority of their whole senate, prescribed certain laws and rules of quantities of English syllables for English verse, having had thereof already great practice, and drawen me to their faction. New books I hear of none, but only of one, that writing a certain book, called *The School of Abuse*, and dedicating it to Master Sidney, was for his labor scorned, if at least it be in the goodness of that nature to scorn. Such folly is it not to regard aforehand the inclination and quality of him to whom we dedicate our books. Such might I happily incur, entitling my *Slumber* and the other pamphlets unto his honor. I meant them rather to Master Dyer.

From George Puttenham, *The Art of English Poesy* (1589)[148]

From Chapter 8: *In what reputation poesy and poets were in old times with Princes and otherwise generally, and how they be now become contemptible and for what causes.*

For the respects aforesaid in all former ages and in the most civil countries and commonwealths, good poets and poesy were highly esteemed and much favored of the greatest princes. For proof whereof we read how much Amyntas, King of Macedonia, made of the tragical poet Euripides.[149] And the Athenians of Sophocles.[150] In what price the noble poems of Homer were

---

ity. In addition, Spenser never published a poem called *Slumber* or any other pamphlets dedicated to the poet and courtier Sir Edward Dyer (1543-1607).

[148] Sir George Puttenham (1559?-1590), courtier and generally acknowledged as the author of *The Art of English Poesy*, which was published anonymously.

[149] Despite his advanced age, Euripides left Athens in 408 B. C. to live at the court of the Macedonian king, Archelaus (Puttenham mistakes the name), a noted patron of the arts.

[150] Unlike Euripides, Sophocles was very popular in Athens. His dramatic career was an unprecedented success, and he won first prize at the dramatic festival 24, 20, or 18 times, depending on the source. Sophocles also played an important role in the public

holden with Alexander the Great in so much as every night they were laid under his pillow,[151] and by day were carried in the rich jewel coffer of Darius lately before vanquished by him in battle.[152] And not only Homer, the father and prince of the poets, was so honored by him, but for his sake all other meaner poets, in so much as Cherillus, one no very great good poet, had for every verse well made a Phillip's[153] noble of gold, amounting in value to an angel English, and so for every hundreth verses (which a cleanly pen could speedily dispatch) he had a hundred angels.[154] And since Alexander the Great, how Theocritus, the Greek poet, was favored by Ptolemy, king of Egypt, and Queen Berenice, his wife; Ennius, likewise, by Scipio, Prince of the Romans,[155] Virgil also by the Emperor Augustus. And in later times how much were Jean de Meun and Guillaume de Lorris made of by the French kings,[156] and Geoffrey Chaucer, father of our English poets, by Richard II, who as it was supposed gave him the manner of new Holme in Oxfordshire.[157] And Gower to Henry IV, and Hardyng to Edward IV.[158] Also how Francis, the French king,

---

life of Athens. In 440, for example, he was elected one of the ten commanders of the military, and his senior colleague was Pericles.

[151] In the *Apology*, Sidney writes, "This Alexander left his schoolmaster, living Aristotle, behind him, but took dead Homer with him" (pp. 102-3).

[152] Darius III, last king of the Persian Achaemenid dynasty. Alexander defeated him at the battle of Gaugemela in 331 B. C.

[153] Father of Alexander the Great.

[154] See Horace, *Epistles* 2.1, "To Augustus."

[155] See the *Apology*, n. 186.

[156] Authors of the *Romance of the Rose*. Guillaume de Lorris (c. 1212-1237?) started the poem but left it incomplete at line 4058, and Jean de Meun (1237?-1305) continued the poem until ending at line 21,780. Both authors lived in the 13th century.

[157] Chaucer never lived in Oxfordshire, but on May 10, 1374, Chaucer did receive from Richard II a lifelong lease for an apartment over the city gate at Aldgate, and a month later he was appointed controller of the Wool Custom. See Donald Howard, *Chaucer: His Life, His Works, His World* (New York: Dutton, 1987), 207.

[158] John Gower (1330?-1408), English allegorical poet and friend of Chaucer, was granted two casks of wine a year by Henry IV in recompense for a complimentary reference in one of his poems. John Hardyng (1378-165) wrote a metrical chronicle of England that he presented to Edward IV after his marriage to Elizabeth Grey (see *AS* 75, n. 217).

made Saint-Gelais, Salmonius Macrinus, and Clément Marot[159] of his privy chamber for their excellent skill in vulgar and Latin poesy. And King Henry VIII, her Majesty's father, for a few psalms of David turned into English meter by Sternhold made him groom of his privy chamber and gave him many other good gifts.[160] And one Gray, what good estimation did he grow with the same king, Henry, and afterward with the Duke of Somerset, Protector, for making certain merry ballads, whereof one chiefly was "The hunt is up, the hunt is up." [161] And Queen Mary, his daughter, for one Epithalamie[162] or nuptial song made by Vargas, a Spanish poet,[163] at her marriage with King Philip in Winchester, gave him during life two hundred crowns pension. Nor this reputation was given them in ancient times altogether in respect that poesy was a delicate art, and poets themselves cunning prince-pleasers, but for that also they were thought for their universal knowledge to be very sufficient men for the greatest charges in their commonwealths, were it for counsel or for conduct, whereby no man need to doubt but that both skills may very well concur and be most excellent in one person. For we find that Julius Cae-

---

[159] Mellin de Saint-Gelais, (1491-1558), friend of Marot; Jean Salmon (1490-1537), a very influential neo-Latin poet who was called "the new Horace" by his contemporaries. He was given the name "Maigret," or in Latin, "Macrinus" ("the Thin") by King Francis I and was also given patronage by Cardinal Jean du Bellay; Clément Marot (1496?-1544), one of the greatest poets of the French Renaissance. In addition to his other works, Marot translated many of the Psalms.

[160] Thomas Sternhold (d.1546), published, with John Hopkins, a metrical translation of the psalms that had a larger circulation in England than any work other than the Bible and the Book of Common Prayer.

[161] William Gray (d. 1551), early 16th century radical Protestant who wrote antipapal ballads for Thomas Cromwell (1485-1540, who implemented much of the English Reformation, in particular the dissolution of the monasteries. Gray subsequently enjoyed the patronage of Edward Seymour, Duke of Somerset and Lord Protector for King Edward VI (1537-53). Some of his poems were included in *Tottell's Miscellaney* (1557-58), and all his extant verse, including "The Hunt is Up," can be found in Ernest W. Dormer, *Gray of Reading: A Sixteenth-Century Controversialist and Ballad-Writer* (Reading: Bradly & Son, 1923).

[162] Epithalamion, or marriage song.

[163] Unidentified.

sar, the first emperor and a most noble captain, was not only the most eloquent orator of his time, but also a very good poet,[164] though none of his doings therein be now extant . . . . So as are the poets seemed to have skill not only in the subtleties of their art, but also to be meet for all manner of functions civil and martial, even as the found favor of the times they lived in, insomuch as their credit and estimation generally was not small.

But in these days (although some learned princes may take delight in them), yet universally it is not so. For as well poets as poesy are despised, and the name become of honorable infamous, subject to scorn and derision. And rather a reproach than a praise to any that useth it, for commonly who is studious in the art or shows himself excellent in it, they call him in disdain a *phantastical*, and a light-headed or phantastical man, by conversion, they call a poet. And this proceeds through the barbarous ignorance of the time, and pride of many gentlemen, and others, whose gross heads not being brought up or acquainted with any excellent art, nor able to contrive, or in manner conceive, any matter of subtlety in any business or science, they do deride and scorn it in all others as superfluous knowledges and vain sciences, and whatsoever devise be of rare invention, they term it *phantastical*, construing it to the worst side, and among men such as be modest and grave, and of little conversation, nor delighted in the busy life and vain ridiculous actions of the popular, they call him in scorn a philosopher or poet, as much to say, as a phantastical man, very injuriously, God wot,[165] and to the manifestation of their own ignorance, not making difference betwixt the terms. . . .

---

[164] Suetonius, *Lives of the Caesars*, 1. 56.
[165] God knows.

Suggestions for Further Reading

Sidney's Works

The Countesse of Pembrokes Arcadia [*The New Arcadia*]. London: William Ponsonby, 1590.

Syr P. S. His Astrophel and Stella. To the End of Which Are Added, Sundry Other Rare Sonnets of Divers Gentlemen. London: T. Newman, 1591 [contains a preface by Thomas Nashe and poems by Campion, Daniel and Greville]. Revised as *Syr P. S. His Astrophel and Stella. Wherein the Excellence of Sweet Poesie is Concluded*. London: T. Newman, 1591 [Nashe's preface and the additional poems are omitted].

The Countesse of Pembrokes Arcadia. Now Since the First Edition Augmented and Ended. [Composite version of the *New* and *Old Arcadia*]. London: William Ponsonby, 1593.

An Apologie for Poetrie. London: Henry Olney, 1595.

The Defence of Poesie. London: William Ponsonby, 1595.

The Countesse of Pembrokes Arcadia. Now for the Third Time Published, with Sundry New Additions of the Author. London: William Ponsonby, 1598. [Contains the full version of *Astrophil and Stella* as well as *The Lady of May* and *Certain Sonnets*.]

Selected Modern Editions

An Apology for Poetry, ed. Forrest G. Robinson. Indianapolis: Bobbs-Merrill, 1970.

An Apology for Poetry; or, The Defence of Poetry, ed. Geoffrey Shepherd. London: Thomas Nelson, 1965.

The Complete Works of Sir Philip Sidney, ed. Albert Feuilerate. 4 vols. Cambridge: Cambridge University Press, 1912-1926.

The Countess of Pembroke's Arcadia [conflated version], ed. Maurice Hunt. Harmondsworth: Penguin, 1977

The Countess of Pembroke's Arcadia [The New Arcadia], ed. Victor Skretkowicz. Oxford: Clarendon Press, 1987.

The Countess of Pembroke's Arcadia: The Old Arcadia, ed. Jean Robertson. Oxford: Clarendon Press, 1973.

Miscellaneous Prose of Sir Philip Sidney, ed. Katherine Duncan-Jones and Jan van Dorsten. Oxford: Clarendon Press, 1973.

The Poems of Sir Philip Sidney, ed. William A. Ringler. Oxford: Clarendon Press, 1962.

Sir Philip Sidney: A Critical Edition of the Major Works, ed. Katherine Duncan-Jones. Oxford: Oxford University Press, 1989.

Anthologies of Criticism

Essential Articles for the Study of Sir Philip Sidney, ed. Arthur F. Kinney. Hamden, CT: Archon Books, 1986.

Sidney in Retrospect: Selections from "English Literary Renaissance", ed. Arthur F. Kinney and the editors of *ELR*. Amherst: University of Massachusetts Press, 1988.

Sir Philip Sidney: 1586 and the Creation of a Legend, ed. Dominic Baker-Smith and Arthur F. Kinney. Leiden, Netherlands: E. J. Brill; Leiden University Press, 1986.

Sir Philip Sidney: An Anthology of Modern Criticism, ed. Dennis Kay. Oxford: Clarendon Press, 1987.

Sir Philip Sidney and the Interpretation of Renaissance Culture., ed. Gary F. Waller and Michael D. Moore. London: Croon Helm, Totawa, NJ: Barnes and Noble, 1984.

Sidney's Biography

Buxton, John. *Sir Philip Sidney and the English Renaissance*. New York: St. Martin's, 1966.

Camden, William. *The History of the Most Renowned and Victorious Princess,Elizabeth*, 4th ed. London, 1688. Rpt. New York: AMS Press, 1970.

The Correspondence of Sir Philip Sidney and Hubert Languet, ed. Steuart A. Pears. London: William Pickering, 1845.

Duncan-Jones, Katherine. *Sir Philip Sidney: Courtier Poet.* New Haven: Yale University Press, 1991.

Elegies for Sir Philip Sidney (1587), ed. A. J. Colaianne and W. L.

Godshalk. Delmar, NY: Scholars' Facsimiles and Reprints, 1980.

Greville, Sir Fulke. *A Dedication to Sir Philip Sidney*. In *The Prose Works of Fulke Greville, Lord Brooke*, ed. John Gouws. Oxford: Clarendon Press, 1986. 3-135.

Heninger, S. K., "Spenser and Sidney at Leicester House." *Spenser Studies* 8 (1987): 239-249.

Howell, Roger. *Sir Philip Sidney: The Shepherd Knight*. London: Hutchinson, 1968.

Levy, F. W. , "Philip Sidney Reconsidered." *Sidney in Retrospect*, 3-14.

Moffett, Thomas. *Nobilis or A View of the Life and Death of a Sidney*, ed. and trans. Virgil B. Heltzel and Hoyt H. Hudson. San Marino, CA: Huntington Library, 1940.

Osborn, James M. *Young Philip Sidney: 1572-1577*. New Haven: Yale University Press, 1972.

Wallace, Malcom W. *The Life of Sir Philip Sidney*. Cambridge: Cambridge University Press, 1915.

An Apology for Poetry

Barish, Jonas. *The Antitheatrical Prejudice*. Berkeley: University of California Press, 1981.

Barnes, Catherine. "The Hidden Persuader." *PMLA* 86 (1971): 422-427. Rpt. in *Essential Articles for the Study of Sir Philip Sidney*, 155-166.

Berry, Edward. "The Poet as Warrior in Sidney's *Defence of Poetry*." *Studies in English Literature* 29.1 (1989): 21-34.

Colie, Rosalie L. *Paradoxia Epidemica: The Renaissance Tradition of Paradox*. Princeton: Princeton University Press, 1962.

DeNeef, A. Leigh. *Spenser and the Motives of Metaphor*. Durham: Duke University Press, 1982.

Doherty, M. J. *The Mistress-Knowledge: Sir Philip Sidney's "Defence of Poesie" and Literary Architectonics in the English Renaissance*. Nashville: Vanderbilt University Press, 1991.

Donno, Elizabeth Story. "Old Mouse-Eaten Records: History in Sidney's *Apology*." *Studies in Philology* 72 (1975): 275-98.

Rpt. in *Sir Philip Sidney: An Anthology of Modern Criticism*, 147-167.

Eden, Kathy. *Poetic and Legal Fiction in the Aristotelian Tradition*. Princeton: Princeton University Press, 1986.

Evans, Frank B. "The Concept of the Fall in Sidney's *Apology*." *Renaissance Papers 1969* (1970): 9-14.

Ferguson, Margaret W. *Trials of Desire: Renaissance Defenses of Poetry*. New Haven: Yale University Press, 1983.

Fraser, Russell. *The War against Poetry*. Princeton: Princeton University Press, 1970.

Gosson, Stephen. *The School of Abuse, An Apologie of "the Schoole of Abuse", Playes Confuted in Five Actions, The Ephemerides of Phialo*. In *Markets of Bawdrie: The Dramatic Criticism of Stephen Gosson*, ed. Arthur F. Kinney. Salzburg: Salzburg Studies in English Literature, 1974.

Greene, Roland. "Fictions of Immanence, Fictions of Embassy." *The Project of Prose in Early Modern Europe and the New World*, ed. Elizabeth Fowler and Roland Greene. Cambridge: Cambridge University Press, 1997. 176-202.

Hardison, O. B., Jr. "The Two Voices of Sidney's *Apology for Poetry*." *English Literary Renaissance* 2 (1972): 83-99. Rpt. in *Sidney in Retrospect*, 45-61.

Helgerson, Richard. *The Elizabethan Prodigals*. Berkeley: University of California Press, 1976.

—. *Self-Crowned Laureates: Spenser, Jonson, Milton, and the Literary System*. Berkeley: University of California Press, 1983.

Heninger, S. K. Jr. "Sidney and Serranus' *Plato*." In *Sidney in Retrospect*, 27-44.

Herman, Peter C. *Squitter-Wits and Muse-Haters: Sidney, Spenser, Milton and Renaissance Attacks on Poetry*. Detroit: Wayne State University Press, 1996.

Kinney, Arthur F. "Parody and Its Implications in Sydney's Defense of Poesie." *Studies in English Literature* 12 (1972): 1-19.

—. "The Significance of Sidney's *Defence of Poesie* as a Parody." *Studies in English Literature* 7 (1969): 1-20.

Lamb, Mary Ellen. "Apologizing for Pleasure in Sidney's *Apology for Poetry*: The Nurse of Abuse Meets the Tudor Grammar School." *Criticism* 36.4 (1994): 499-519.

Levao, Ronald. *Renaissance Minds and Their Fictions: Cusanus, Sidney, Shakespeare.* Berkeley: University of California Press, 1985.

Matz, Robert. "Sidney's *Defence of Poesie*: The Politics of Pleasure." *English Literary Renaissance* 25.2 (1995): 131-146.

Myrick, Kenneth. *Sir Philip Sidney as a Literary Craftsman.* Lincoln: University of Nebraska Press, 1965.

Nelson, William. *Fact or Fiction: The Dilemma of the Renaissance Storyteller.* Cambridge: Harvard University Press, 1973.

Prescott, Anne Lake. "King David as a 'Right Poet': Sidney and the Psalmist." *ELR* 19 (1989): 131-51.

Raitiere, Martin. "The Unity of Sidney's *Apology for Poetry*." *Studies in English Literature* 21 (1981): 37-57.

Ringler, William A. *Stephen Gossen: A Biographical and Critical Study.* New York: Octagon Books, 1972.

Robinson, Forrest. "Introduction." *An Apology for Poetry*, ed. Forrest G. Robinson. Indianapolis: Bobbs-Merrill, 1977. i-xxviii.

—. *The Shape of Things Known: Sidney's Apology in its Philosophical Tradition.* Cambridge: Harvard University Press, 1972.

Shepherd, Geoffrey. " Introduction." *An Apology for Poetry or The Defence of Poesy*, ed. Geoffrey Shepherd. London: Nelson, 1965. 1-91.

Sinfield, Alan. "Sidney and Du Bartas." *Comparative Literature* 27 (1975): 8-20.

—. "The Cultural Poetics of the *Defence of Poetry*." In *Sir Philip Sidney and the Interpretation of Renaissance Culture.* 124-143.

Smith, G. Gregory. "Critical Introduction." In *Elizabethan Critical Essays*, ed. G. Gregory Smith. Oxford: Oxford University Press, 1904. Vol. 1. xi-xcii.

Spingarn, Joel E. *Literary Criticism in the Renaissance.* Intro. Bernard Weinberg. 2nd ed. New York: Harcourt, Brace, Jovanovitch, 1908. Rpt. 1963.

Trimpi, Wesley. "Sir Philip Sidney's *An Apology for Poetry.*" *The Cambridge History of Literary Criticism, III: The Renaissance,* ed. Glyn P. Norton. Cambridge: Cambridge University Press, 1999. 187-198.

Ulreich, John C., Jr. "'The Poets Only Deliver': Sidney's Conception of *Mimesis.*" *Studies in the Literary Imagination* 15 (1982): 67-84. Rpt. in *Essential Articles for the Study of Sir Philip Sidney,* 135-154.

Waller, Gary F. "'This Matching of Contraries': Bruno, Calvin and the Sidney Circle." *Neophilologus* 56 (1972): 331-43.

—. "'This Matching of Contraries': Calvinsim and Courtly Philosophy in the Sidney Psalms." *English Studies* 55 (1974), 22-31. Rpt. in *Essential Articles for the Study of Sir Philip Sidney,* 411-424.

Petrarch, Petarchism, and Astrophil and Stella

Coldiron, A. E. B. "Sidney, Watson, and the 'Wrong Ways' to Renaissance Lyric Poetics." *Renaissance Papers 1997*: 49-62.

Dolan, Frances E. "Taking the Pencil out of God's Hand: Art, Nature, and the Face-Painting Debate in Early Modern England." *PMLA* 108.2 (1993): 224-240.

Duncan-Jones, Katherine. "Philip Sidney's Toys." In *Sir Philip Sidney: An Anthology of Modern Criticism,* 61-80.

Estrin, Barbara. *Laura: Uncovering Gender and Genre in Wyatt, Donne, and Marvell.* Durham: Duke University Press, 1994.

Hull, Elizabeth M. "All My Deed But Copying Is: The Erotics of Identity in *Astrophil and Stella.*" *Texas Studies in Literature & Language* 38.2 (1997): 175-90.

Hulse, Clark. "Stella's Wit: Penelope Rich as Reader of Sidney's Sonnets." In *Rewriting the Renaissance: The Discourses of Sexual Difference in Early Modern Europe,* ed. Margaret W. Ferguson, Maureen Quilligan, and Nancy J. Vickers. Chicago: University of Chicago Press, 1986. 259-271.

Jones, Ann R. and Peter Stallybrass. "The Politics of *Astrophil and Stella.*" *Studies in English Literature* 24 (1984): 53-68.

Klein, Lisa M. *The Exemplary Sidney and the Elizabethan Sonneteer*. Newark, DE: University of Delaware Press, 1998.

Kuin, Roger, *Chamber Music: Elizabethan Sonnet-Sequences and the Pleasure of Criticism*. Toronto: University of Toronto Press, 1998.

Marotti, Arthur F. "'Love is not Love'": Elizabethan Sonnet Sequences and the Social Order." *ELH* 49 (1982): 396-428.

Mauss, Katherine E. , "A Womb of his Own: Male Renaissance Poets in the Female Body." In *Sexuality and Gender in Early Modern Europe*, ed. James G. Turner. Cambridge University Press, 1993. 266-288

Mazzotta, Giuseppe. *The Worlds of Petrarch*. Durham: Duke University Press, 1993.

Miller, Paul Allen. "Sidney, Petrarch, and Ovid: Or, Imitation as Subversion." *ELH* 58.3 (1991): 499-522.

Minogue, Sally. "A Woman's Touch: Astrophil, Stella and 'Queen Vertue's Court.'" *ELH* 63.3 (1996): 555-570.

Petrarch. *Petrarch's Lyric Poems: The "Rime Sparse" and Other Lyrics*, trans. Robert M. Durling. Cambridge: Harvard University Press, 1976.

Prendergast, Maria. "The Unauthorized Orpheus of *Astrophil and Stella*." *Studies in English Literature* 35.1 (1995): 19-34

Quilligan, Maureen. "Sidney and His Queen." In *The Historical Renaissance: New Essays on Tudor and Stuart Literature and Culture*, ed. Heather Dubrow and Richard Strier. Chicago: University of Chicago Press, 1988, 171-96.

Roche, Thomas, Jr. "*Astrophil and Stella*: A Radical Reading." In *Sir Philip Sidney: An Anthology of Modern Criticism*, 185-226.

Spiller, Michael R. G. *The Development of the Sonnet: An Introduction*. London: Routledge, 1992.

Woudhuysen, H. R. *Sir Philip Sidney and the Circulation of Manuscripts 1558-1640*. Oxford: Clarendon Press, 1996.

General Works on Sidney and His Reputation

Baker-Smith, Dominic. "Great Expectations: Sidney's Death and the Poets." In *Sir Philip Sidney: 1586 and the Creation of a Legend*, 83-103.

Bos, Sander, Marianne Lange-Meyers, Jeanine Six. "Sidney's Funeral Portrayed." In *Sir Philip Sidney: 1586 and the Creation of a Legend*, 38-61.

Connell, Dorothy. *Sir Philip Sidney: The Maker's Mind.* Oxford: Clarendon Press, 1977.

Day, J. F. R. "Death be very Proud: Sidney, Subversion, and Elizabethan Heraldic Funerals." In *Tudor Political Culture*, ed. Dale Hoak. Cambridge: Cambridge University Press, 1995, 179-203.

Hager, Alan. *Dazzling Images: The Masks of Sir Philip Sidney.* Newark, DE: University of Delaware Press, 1991.

—. "The Exemplary Image: Fabrication of Sir Philip Sidney's Biographical Image and the Sidney Reader." *ELH* 48 (1981): 1-16. Rpt. in *Sir Philip Sidney: An Anthology of Modern Criticism*, 45-60.

Herman, Peter C. "'Best of Poets, Best of Kings': King James VI/I and the Scene of Monarchical Verse." In *Royal Subjects: Essays on the Writings of James VI/I*, ed. Daniel Fischlin and Mark Fortier. Detroit: Wayne State University Press, forthcoming.

Kalstone, David. *Sidney's Poetry: Contexts and Interpretations.* Rpt. New York: W. W. Norton, 1970.

Kuin, Roger. "Querre-Muhau: Sir Philip Sidney and the New World," *Renaissance Quarterly* 51.2 (1998): 549-585.

Pask, Kevin. *The Emergence of the English Author: Scripting the Life of the Poet in Early Modern England.* Cambridge: Cambridge University Press, 1996.

Rudenstine, Neil. *Sidney's Poetic Development.* Cambridge: Harvard University Press, 1967.

Sidney: The Critical Heritage, ed. Martin Garrett. London: Routledge, 1996.

van Dorsten, Jan. *Poets, Patrons, and Professors: Sir Philip Sidney and the Leiden Humanists.* Leiden, Netherlands: The Sir Thomas Brown Institute, 1962.

Warkentin, Germaine. "Ins and Outs of the Sidney Family Library." *Times Literary Supplement,* 6 December 1985, 1411.

Weiner, Andrew D. *Sir Philip Sidney and the Poetics of Protestantism.* Minneapolis: University of Minnesota Press, 1978.

Worden, Blair. *The Sound of Virtue: Philip Sidney's "Arcadia" and Elizabethan Politics.* New Haven: Yale University Press, 1996.

Selected Recordings of Sidney's Songs and Sonnets
While we do not know what melodies Sidney might have had in mind for the songs in *Astrophil and Stella,* a number of important Renaissance composers set his lyrics to music, and these CDs feature performances of some of these settings.

"As I Went to Walsingham: ElizabethanMusic." The Musicians of Swan Alley. Lyle Nordstrom and Paul O'Dette, directors. Harmonia Mundi. HMC 905192. 1987.

"O Sweete Woods the Delight of Solitarienesse. Music by Dowland, Morley, Corkine and Others. Lovesongs and Sonnets of Donne and Sidney." Paul Agnew, tenor and Christopher Wilson, lutes. Metronome Recordings. CD 1006. 1995.

"O Sprite Heroeic: The Life, Love and Death of Sir Philip Sidney Explored." The Trinity Consort. Editions Audiovisuel Beulah. 1RF2. 1998.